Remarkable Incidents and Modern Miracles Through Prayer and Faith

by
GC Bevington

Schmul Publishing Co.
Schmul's Wesleyan Book Club   Salem, Ohio

COPYRIGHT © 2001 BY SCHMUL PUBLISHING CO.
All rights reserved. No part of this publication may be reproduced or used in any form or by any means—graphic, electronic, or mechanical, including photocopying, recording, taping, or information storage or retrieval systems—without prior written permission of the publishers.

Published by Schmul Publishing Co.
PO Box 716
Salem, Ohio USA

Printed in the United States of America

Contents

Foreword 5

Introduction 7

1 A Sketch of My Beginnings 8

2 Beginning and Some Work at Sixth Street and Freeman Avenue, Cincinnati, Ohio 20

3 First Light on Divine Healing, Evangelism 28

4 Work at Cleveland and Chattanooga; My Rib Experience 50

5 Important Truths 75

6 Personal Dealings of and from God 94

7 Children's Chapter 136

8 Instances of Healing 155

G. C. Bevington

Foreword

AFTER MUCH PRAYER I have finally concluded to make another effort at setting forth some incidents of my life — incidents that have been of great importance to me, and will be to those directly or indirectly touched by them. I hope that each one reading these incidents will read carefully this foreword, as it contains a very useful key to the book; for as soon as I ventured out from the mission work in Cincinnati, where I had spent several years, I began to realize that mine was not a feather-bed vocation. God had called me to labor among the poorest of people, but few of whom ever entered the church. So, from the start, mine was a life entirely of faith. I never took up an offering for myself, nor asked anyone else to, nor made my wants known, only to God. I never had any objection to those who did take up offerings; but as for me, I never could. Often I thought that I would, but when I reached the platform, I took an inventory of the crowd, and I said to myself, "Well, there is Brother Jones; he has that large family, and is not any too well. His little place is not paid for, so I couldn't expect him to give anything. Next is Brother Smith; he lost a cow just last week, and of course he couldn't spare anything. And next is Sister Bell with those four children to care for; she of course couldn't give anything. And Brother Brown has seven mouths to feed, and backs to clothe; and his horse got hurt last week, and he had to hire a horse, so of course he couldn't give anything."

So I went all over the congregation, and excused everyone. Hence, it was a work of trusting God, all of which has enabled me to ferret out many cases that otherwise would have been turned down, overlooked, or classed as the impossible. So as these incidents occurred, I became impressed with their significance. I got a large book, and when I would come in for a little rest, I would write down the important incidents as a stimulus to my faith. Many a time, after coming in from a very hard pull, without money, and but little visible results, and feeling not the best, I dived into that book, and invariably was greatly encouraged. Several times when I was getting pretty low in faith, the records in that book lifted the clouds, and gave me great victory. Knowing that what God had done once He could do again, if conditions were met, I generally kept a pretty close watch on the conditions, to see that they were up to the standard.

Then, as several people got hold of these records, they insisted that I put them in book form. That was so far from my idea and ability that I paid little attention to it.

Others kept at me until I did manage to bring the matter before God. At first I received great encouragement in the mentioning of it to my Father, until I just had to say "Yes," but I had no money to live on while writing the book, nor any typewriter, and the publishers wanted it typewritten. So I dropped the matter; but the Lord kept at me, and soon the way was opened up for me to get a typewriter through Rev. John Fleming.

Well, one obstacle was removed; but still another, equally as large, confronted me — lack of money to write the book. It was not long until I was invited over from Ironton, Ohio, to Ashland, Ky., and I preached in the Ashland Heights Church, Saturday and Sunday. I was invited to the home of dear Brother and Sister Simpson. On Monday, Sister Simpson said, "Brother Bevington, here we have a houseful of children, and husband is away all day, and I have so much work to do that I am not caring for the children as I ought to. So we believe that God wants you in our home to live before these children." After I had prayed over the matter, it seemed quite clear that I should stay with them.

Then I began writing. But when about half done, I got tired of such confinement, and went out for a few meetings. In the meantime dear Brother Fleming, Rev. John Fleming's brother, wanted me to come to his home, then in Willard, Ky., and finish my book. This I did, but before the book was entirely finished, I was called out in meetings. Thinking that I would have a rest sometime, which would enable me to finish it, I just went along that way, waiting for a more favorable opportunity, until I guess the Lord got tired of my waiting, and the book was burned up, with all else that I had, while I was living at Rush, Ky.

The object in writing this foreword is to give a reason for the absence of names and dates. I drew my manuscript from the book of records which was burned. I had given up all idea of rewriting; but through the past winter and this spring, several told me that I ought to rewrite the story of my life. Others have written me— some who knew nothing of the former book — and of late dear Brother Heins, of Kingswood, Ky., has importuned me to write. So I related to him all that I have said here relative to my first book, and told him that I had no record of names, dates, or places. He said that they are of little importance in such a work as this. So after praying over it, I concluded to rewrite the incidents. Read as impartially as you can, for all that follows is true.

I hope that these incidents will be as great a blessing to you and others as they have been to me. If they are, pass the book on, keep it traveling, and hence spreading the deeper truths of the hidden nuggets contained in God's great gold mine, the Bible. Read, pray, lay hold, take in, and give out. Eat, and get fat.

—G. C. Bevington

Introduction

IT GIVES US VERY great pleasure to commend to the reading public this little volume, which was conceived in prayer, and brought forth from one of the most consecrated lives we have ever known. We have known Brother Bevington for fifteen years, and have always found him the same true, loyal, prayerful, holy and devout Christian, with a burden for a lost and dying world.

Since the days of George Muller we doubt if there has been a man who has prayed more, had more direct answers to prayer, and witnessed more remarkable cases of Divine healing than has the author of this book. We bespeak for it a very wide circulation, and heartily commend it to all lovers of deep spiritual things.

—*John and Bona Fleming.*

1

A Sketch of My Beginnings

Now to my starting point. You see my name is Bevington, and that was my father's and mother's name. I suppose that is why I have carried that long name more than seventy-four years. My father was a Methodist preacher, and they said he was a "rattler" too. I have been told that he made men's hair stand straight on their heads. He was especially led to preach on Hell. He preached to the Indians in Wyandotte County, Ohio, and the adjoining counties; and built log churches and school-houses. This was all before I made my appearance in this arena. When I came on the scene, he was filling the place of a backslider, carrying on blacksmithing, wagon-making and carpentering at Little Sandusky, Ohio. He had backslidden over a barrel of soap; so you see that Satan can use most anything to get a preacher to backslide. But mother held on to her God and had prayer with us children, all of which had much to do in after life, in our finding God and keeping Him. The most beautiful features of her life were never seen until she was gone; then they seemed to stand out on every corner or crossroad as sign boards pointing in the right direction.

Now, you may wonder how father came to backslide over a barrel of soap, for it was over it and not in it. Had he gotten into it, especially headfirst, there might be some logical conclusion as to how he backslid. Father, as I stated, built churches and schoolhouses where the people were too poor to do so, and took pledges from them as payments on the church; such as meat, corn, wheat, potatoes, etc., and one man promised him a barrel of soap. Of course, father expected the soap, but the man never delivered it.

Father, soon after that, settled in Little Sandusky, seven miles from Upper Sandusky, in Wyandotte County, Ohio, and so did this member who had promised him the soap. Well, father preached there, and when this matter had run as long as he thought it ought to, he demanded that this man be put out of the church, as he was a liar, as he called him. He concluded that if the man was not fit for Heaven, he was not fit to be a member of his church. But he was then a good paying member and the class leader, so they voted with quite a majority to let him remain. So father handed in his resignation and never went into the church again; and of course he backslid.

But our home was a preachers' home as long as the preachers did as they agreed. When they came there, I suppose every one said, "Well, he is an old friend of mine, and I will go and get him back into the church." I well remember being in the shop one time when the preacher who was conducting the quarterly meeting Saturday and over Sunday came up there to draw father over to the church. He was using quite tempting bait, as it seemed to me; but finally father got tired of it, and said, "This whole. thing reminds me of an incident which occurred when I was a boy.

We had a neighbor, a farmer, who had three sons and two daughters, all married but one, and he was considered quite foolish. He never went to school. After the father and mother were laid beneath the sod, these children concluded to divide the property and the stock. Jim was so weak-minded that they thought they could easily dupe him, especially on the stock line. They had a lot of sheep, and, as usual, quite a number of poor, bony, scrawny old ones; and they said, 'Now Jim has that pet sheep of his that he has raised, and of course would not part with it; so let us take all the poor sheep and put them in a pen and put his pet with them, and then put the others in pens, and tell Jim to go ahead and take his choice.' They supposed, of course, that he would take the pen his pet sheep was in.

So Jim went out and looked at them all, and the last pen was the one where his pet was. As he looked over the fence, and saw his dear pet in there, he said, 'Mickey, we have been together for three years eating out of the same dish, drinking out of the same pond, and sleeping in the same bed. We have had many good times together; but, Mickey, you have gotten in such bad company that we will have to part.' So Jim selected a pen of the choicest sheep." Father said, "That is the condition here — bad company, and we can't fellowship. We part as Jim and Mickey did." How father would laugh as he told us that, and they never got him back in that church nor in any other, though I hope that he got back to the Lord. So you see Satan has pretty reasonable excuses, viewed from a backslider's angle. The only hope for me is to keep in the middle of the road, and never backslide; then Satan can't get such a hold.

Now, back again. I was born quite unhealthy, and never went to school until I was ten years old. I had a disease that baffled all physicians. Father, having a drug store in connection with his other work, had studied medicine some, and concluded to take me out to an uncle who lived in Indiana, and had a tamarack swamp. The chewing of that tamarack gum would cure me. So mother fixed me up, when I was thirteen years of age, and I went out there, and chewed and chewed that gum, and, sure enough, it cured me in less than a year. Then I got strong and hearty.

Father had a rule that I considered quite unreasonable, as boys often think that they know more than their parents. I got so strong that I said that I would fool him. He will never come that racket on me, that he has come on the older boys, I thought, so I foolishly ran off from my uncle's, and went into Michigan.

Now comes the point that has led me to write this part, as mother's life and her family prayers had made an indelible impression on me, and I could not get away from it. On Sunday morning, Christmas, fifty-nine years ago, I started down the pike at 11:30 p.m., to walk to Kindleville, Indiana, a distance of some fifteen or twenty miles. The snow was nearly knee deep, and I had a pair of overalls and one shirt, wrapped up in an old-fashioned colored handkerchief, which constituted my wardrobe and suitcase. I had washed sheep the spring before, for a neighbor, and received $1.25 for it, and had kept that even over the Fourth of July and all fall and winter.

I arrived at Kindleville about daylight, and found that a train was going to Elkhart shortly. I purchased a ticket for Elkhart, and arrived there about 8:00 a.m., hungry as a bear. I slipped into an alley to see how much money I had, and found that I had forty-five cents. I had to go a little slow, as I had then sixteen miles to go to Edwardsburg, and then twelve miles to Cassopolis; but I must have something to eat. I went into a grocery, and got some bologna and cheese. I will never forget what a picture I presented with a hunk of cheese in one hand and a piece of bologna in the other, and my suit case under my arm. There I was stalking down the principal street of Elkhart, the largest town I had ever been in and oh, the sights in the windows, and the busy folks running here and there, were all so new to me that I would find myself standing, gaping after sights, chewing my cheese and bologna, holding fast to them, a laughable sight to the passerby.

Finally, I was accosted by a "Hello Bub". That was the name someone called me out at my Uncle's. My name Guy was hard to remember, so Bub was the name that I mostly went by; and now I was terribly frightened to hear that name. I never stopped to see who called it, but struck out, up the street, on a run, supposing that some one had gotten on my track and followed me that far, to take me back. I ran like a trooper; but the man holloed, and said, "I won't hurt you," and came after me, and with the help of some others he got me headed off and rounded up, with the cheese and bologna and suit case, and finally got me to go back with him, after convincing me that he never saw nor heard of me before. He saw that I was cold and, no doubt, hungry, and wanted to take me into his home as he saw that I was a stranger to the sights in Elkhart. I went through a hall away back, and into the kitchen where the good wife was eating breakfast. He said, "Oh, Mamma, here is our boy. I just found him." And she came over and took off my cap and brushed my hair and even kissed me. Well, that kiss, as I had not had one since I left home a year before, broke me all up; but I was so bashful and shy that I could not show any appreciation of her motherly affection.

I could not stand it to be in that strange house, though she had relieved me of my cheese and bologna and red suit case, and both had tried to relieve me of the embarrassment under which they saw I was suffering. She had me eat a good breakfast, and then I spied the wood box as being about empty, and asked permission to fill it, anxious to get out from under that terrible strain; so he showed me the wood house.

I sawed and split wood until they came out and asked me to come in for lunch about 9:00 a. m. But I never could go into that nice fine kitchen, and sit down to their nice table, as I was a perfect stranger, so I began to beg off, to present excuses, as people did of old. Pretty soon the man holloed, "Oh, Mary." I wondered who Mary was, and soon I saw bounding and laughing and smiling, a rosy-cheeked, plump girl about my size and age, and she just took hold of me and hugged me and kissed me, and said, "You will come in, for we all love you." She soon got me started, but I was wondering what in the world had made them love me, as no one but mother had ever used that expression, and I knew that she was not my mother. But I stumbled in and ducked in, being finally persuaded by Mary, who said, "Now I am your sister, and you are my brother; now come on and sit down right here by me, and Mamma will give us some fine buckwheat cakes and maple syrup." Well, the cakes and Mary were quite inviting; but, oh, if I only had the cakes and syrup out in the wood house! But, no, here I was, and what could I do? Such fine linen was on the table, and silverware, forks and knives— something we had never seen or heard of. Somehow I managed to eat some as Mary cut it up for me, and was so nice; but I was suffering untold agony, as boys these days are farther advanced at eight years than I was at fifteen. As soon as I could, I got up, but not till I had blundered out what mother had taught me, "Excuse me."

I went out to the wood house and brought up wood until I had piled it away up in the box. Then I saw that the water bucket was empty, and I filled that and the tea kettle. Now, all this mother had drilled into me, and I have always found it to be so helpful, as in a few years that I have been out in the work I have gotten into homes, to hold meetings, that others could not get into, just because I would chop up some wood and carry water and help some. They let me in for the work I would do, and that gave me a chance to preach the Gospel to them, that they had never heard, as they had been brought up on the "meetin' house crumbs" and had never had a square meal given to them. It pays to be prepared for most anything to win the people.

Well, back to this home again, as I want you to see what a praying mother can do, though my mother did not know at this time but what I was at my uncle's, as any boy should have been. Her prayers were not confined to Noble County, Indiana, but to me, and that meant wherever I was. Glory to God! I am sure that they leaped the bounds of that home with my uncle, and followed me closely every step I took, as you will see and be convinced that God hears a mother's prayer. Amen and amen! Oh! how I praise God for a praying mother!

I kept on sawing wood all day, and had many thoughts. I had not told them who I was, nor where I had came from. They had tried every conceivable scheme to find out; but I just would not tell, as I was afraid it was a scheme to get me back to my uncle's. When evening came, I was pretty homesick, and was intending to crawl in back of the large cook stove, and curl down for a nap; but soon in bounded Mary from school, and the first thing she cried, "Oh, where is my brother, my twin brother, where is he?" She soon grabbed me by the shoes and pulled me out of there, and out into the yard to play ball.

When supper was called, I mustered up courage to go in without so much persuasion; but as soon as supper was over, I was in behind the stove again. As soon as the dishes were washed, here came Mary taking me by the feet, and getting me out again; and the first thing I knew I was in the parlor, singing with her some of the good old Sunday School songs that mother had taught me, and soon I was crying. Mary soon discovered that, and changed tactics on me and got me interested in a picture book. Then about the next thing I realized, she had pumped me entirely dry — had gotten my first and last name, and where I had come from, and where my people lived.

That man, then, though not a Christian, wanted me to go back to my uncle; but I refused. First, because I was afraid to go back; secondly, because I had no money to go back. He said, "Maybe you do not have money enough to take you there. I will give you money enough, and you need never pay it back." But I persistently refused, though I wanted to go home, but I was too proud to do so. He then said that he would give me a ticket to Upper Sandusky, within seven miles of my home, but I said, "No."

Well, I stayed all night, and in the morning I saw that the wood box and the water bucket were full. The man came in and said, "Mamma, we need just such a boy. Let us try to get him to stay with us." So they made many propositions. He said, "All you will need to do is to sweep out my room, and clean a few glasses each morning, and build the fire, and look after the wood and water, and go to school and share equally with Mary." He said, "We lost our only boy just a year ago, a twin to Mary; and Mary says that you are to take his place as you are much like him. We have all fallen in love with you; and as Mary is the only child, when Mamma and I are gone, all our property will be yours and Mary's. We have a farm in the country, and just came into town to give our children a better education. When Mary graduates, we expect to return to the farm. But whatever we do, you shall share equally with Mary." Well, that appealed to me wonderfully, as that would give me an education, and prevent me from being under the galling yoke, as I looked at home discipline through my carnal and young eyes.

I split wood that day; and as Mary came out on her way to school, and kissed me, she said, "You will be my brother, won't you, as I need a brother to go to school with me?" I tell you that went farther than my chin. But there was one thing that seemed to bother me, and that was the washing of those glasses. What could that mean? By and by, the man came out and called me in to dinner. Going in I met Mary at the door, and she clasped me by the hand, and said, "Oh, my brother, my brother." She made me feel considerably like I was her brother— but those glasses, what did that mean? After we had eaten our dinner and Mary had gone to school, the whole thing was gone over again, preparatory to the clinching. I said, "You spoke about washing some glasses and sweeping out your room. What is all this?"

There was a silence that could be felt even by an inexperienced boy. Finally, the man raised his head to speak, but seemed to be hesitating. He was going through a struggle that I could not diagnose, and his wife soon spoke up, and said, "Guy, he doesn't like to mention the business he is in. He has a saloon in front, and we are all ashamed of it, even he is; but he is in it, and it seems that he cannot get out of it without losing all that he has put into it." So then he rallied, and said, "Yes, Guy, we wanted to give the children a better chance than they could get out on the farm, and so we moved. As times were dull, I could not get any work. I was idle and hunting work about eight months, and the only thing that I could find was this saloon. The man wanted to sell out, and offered it at a great bargain; and, not fully realizing all that was involved in the business, I finally bought him out. We have been here three years, and neither of my children has ever been in the saloon, though it is right in front of us here. Neither has my wife been in there."

Well, now comes what is involved in a mother that knows and does what is right. When I left home to go to my uncle, she called me to her, and took me between her limbs, raised my chin as I was on my knees, and said, "Now, Guy, you are going away from home, away from your mother's personal care. I want you to promise your mother this one thing. Will you promise it? "What is it, mother? " Tears were falling because of the near departure from my mother. "Well, Guy, do you believe your mother would ask you to do a thing that you could not do or that would hurt you?" That was a stunner. I said, "No, but what is it?"— a child's curiosity. Finally I said, "Yes, I will do what you ask." Then she said, "I want you to promise never to go into a saloon." "Oh, well," I said, "that is nothing. I am glad it is nothing harder than that." I placed but little stress on her request at that time, for I had never been in a saloon, and supposed of course that I never would be. So I thought that I was let off remarkably easy. But as time went on, I soon saw that mother had a broader vision than I had.

Now I told these people what mother had made me promise. He jumped, threw his arms around me, and said, "God bless that mother of yours. You give me her name, and I will write to her and tell her that I have her boy, and will tell her of the proposition I made you, and how you refused as a result of her covenant with you. I will adopt you if your parents will give their consent, and you need never go into the saloon, as we will soon be out anyway. You stay here and do the other chores, and go to school with Mary, and be my boy until we hear from your mother and father.

But don't you know I was afraid of that saloon, as I saw then that there must be some danger in it, or mother would never have singled that out for me at that time. However, I persisted then in going up into Michigan.

Now I am coming to the lesson. The man said, "If you are determined to go, as it is so cold, a friend of mine that is going to Edwardsburg will take you in the morning in his bobsleigh." After breakfast, the precious Mary kissed me good-bye, as tears rolled down her cheeks. I never saw her after that. I got in the sleigh, all covered up. I had no overcoat or overshoes; but an overcoat was handed to me, and a pair of rubbers, and some underclothing, wrapped up, that I did not know was for me, and a basket of provisions also. "When you get to E—, go in and eat at the hotel," they said. We arrived all O. K., and I went into a room that proved to be the office of a hotel; and the man who brought me asked the privilege of my sitting in behind the stove to eat my dinner. So I slipped in out of sight, and took the lid off the basket, and there I saw a five dollar bill. I said, "They got that in there by mistake." When the gent came out from his dinner, I said, "They got this bill in here by mistake, so you please take it back." But he said, "No, that is from Mary; I saw her put it in. That is what she intended to put into a pair of furs this week; but she said that she would and could go without the furs, so this is yours." I just broke down there, and cried behind that stove. He, seeing me crying, said, "Would you like to go back? If so, I will take you back, and charge you nothing." (I learned that he was running a hack, but my fare was paid by the saloon keeper.) But I said, "No, I will go on to—."

Now comes the main thing of my whole life, which prompted me to relate all this, as this book is to be on the results of prayer. I started on a twelve mile walk, and had more to carry. The longing to be with mother, and the meditation on the kindness and the remarkable proposition made at that kind home, and the lovely Mary, as a prospective sister, as I had a sister at home, only two years younger— all of these combined to get me in a mixed up state and had woven a web around my heart, that seemed to about engulf me.

I lifted up my head, and saw a large tree just several rods off from the road. I went up there, and under that tree I thought I would say, "Now I lay me." I thought that would lift me out of the despondency that seemed to settle down on me like a dark heavy cloud. I started in on "Now I lay," as that was the only prayer I had ever undertaken to say; and I being not quite fourteen years old, supposed that was all that was necessary. But I was under that tree nearly two hours. I believe I offered the best prayer there that I ever offered, for I just got to really praying, and got lost in prayer. I don't know what all I prayed; but I well remember that as I progressed in this prayer that the clouds began to break, and it seemed that I was being lifted up on a plane to which I had been an entire stranger. But I remember saying, "O God, just lead me to a religious home where they pray as mother did, where they read the Bible and they pray as mother did." I got very happy, and rose from under that tree most wonderfully blessed. I believe that I was then regenerated; but not knowing what regeneration is, and being so young, I was kept, by Satan, from realizing that this was conversion. I do not remember all that I asked or promised, but have ever since believed that all was included that was required for my regeneration. I just ran down the road, and holloed and laughed and jumped and cried; I had never experienced such inward rapture. I ran for hours under that mighty something that made me feel as I never had felt.

Not supposing it to be regeneration, of course I never testified to it, but it was such a marked experience in my life that it stuck to me for years, and in fact I never did get entirely away from under its influence. I look back to that tree with great reverence. I had said under that tree, "Lord, if you will take me to a religious home, I will serve you the best I know how," supposing I had to be older to get salvation. I ought to have known better than that, as I was sure that mother never left that impression. But Satan is always well on his job, and knows just where to get in his diabolical work. He cheated me out of what God had just given me.

While I was at my uncle's, a niece of his spent several months there. She was from Michigan, and was a friend of my uncle's old schoolmate whom he had not seen or heard of for years. They talked much about Mr. N——, who was a wealthy farmer in Michigan. I was aiming to reach him and tell him of my uncle. I got to S—— about 5:00 p. m., and enquired the way to Mr. N——'s, and was directed. It was about four miles. Off I went, and traveled until I was sure that I had walked about four miles, and yet had seen no sign as I was told would appear.

Finally about 8:30 p. m., I met a man on his bobs, and asked him how far it was to Brush-ridge Schoolhouse. He said, "My dear boy, you are twelve or fourteen miles from there." "No," I said, "they said it was only four miles from S——," He said, "Yes"; but I had gotten on the wrong road back there at the lake. I was now ten miles from the lake; and if I went back to S——, it would be fourteen miles I had walked. He asked me to go with him, and stay all night, as he lived only five miles from where I wanted to go. But, I had some of that same old fear in me, that some trap was being set to take me back to uncle's (guilty). That bell, as Brother Kulp calls it, in our inner being, conscience, would keep ringing.

The man said that it was only about seven miles across. As the moon shone brightly on the snow, he put me on the fence and got his bearings, and sighted me through by some trees that stood so he could make a line straight to the place. That dear old man worked with me over an hour trying to get me to understand the trick of keeping the line by following certain trees. So I got to understand his principle, and started; but, oh, what a time, as the snow was drifted over the fences and I went down three times, away over my head, and had a terrible time digging out. Then I had to go back on my track and get my line. I trudged along, going through those drifts; a crust was formed, but I broke through occasionally.

Finally, I got out just where I was headed for. There was the mansion just in sight, and it was larger, I guess, than any building I had ever seen in the country. It was all lit up, three stories, I wondered what could be going on at that time in the morning. But I ventured up, and saw no signs of anything to indicate that my bashfulness should cause me any fear. Planking my suit case down at the gate, I cautiously ventured up to the porch. I heard unusual noises for that time of the night, and there I stood hungry as a bear, but trembling from head to foot. Oh, how I dreaded to knock at the door; but I must not stand there, as someone might come out, and I might be branded as a sneak. Stepping up to knock, I broke down, and slipped off the porch and started back to C—. But I said, "Well, having gone to all this trouble, I had better return. Maybe someone is sick." With that argument, much in my favor, I slipped upon the porch; and for fear that I would back out, I plunged right to the door, and rapped . Some one said, "Come in," so I opened the door, and saw a great big fat man, who looked so good and fatherly that I felt quite at home. He said, "Good morning, Bub;" and that big bell was ringing again. He said, "Take that chair, Bub." So I was confronted with a great big stove, and it was so nice and hot that I cuddled up to it, and said, "I am from Uncle Dave Voorhees, in Indiana." Well, he brightened up and was so pleased to hear from his old school chum.

His wife came in, and he said, "Mamma, bring this boy something out to eat." I was as hungry as a bear, being too stingy to break the five dollar bill that Mary had slipped into the basket the morning before. I said nothing, but sat there trembling, saying to myself, "If those folks don't come down, I'll eat something;" but I had a terrible fear of that noise which I could hear through all parts of the house. Finally Mrs. N— had a nice steaming meal, and oh, so tempting, all hot — mashed potatoes, rich mince pie, and such tempting cake. This was all put on a little stand, with a nice white cloth; and, oh, the food was so inviting, so appealing to my stomach. I was watching it as well as all the doors. The man said, "Bub" (there it was again, Bub) "come now, and sit up and have something to eat." I buckled up courage, and was just going to eat, when there swung open a large door, and out they marched — a lady and a gentleman. Oh, such fine clothes! The lady's dress had a long silken train, and the man had such long coat tails, and everyone had flowers. I had my head pretty nearly between my knees and was as close to that stove as I dared to get; and they all stared at me when they passed through, until I felt like a whipped dog.

Trembling fearfully when they all got out, I said, "Well, I must be going." "Going!" said Uncle N—, "where are you going?" I answered, "To C—." He told me to sit down and eat something and then go to bed. He said that I looked tired, and needed a good night's rest, and that if I had to go to C—, the boys would take me in the morning. "Whom do you know at C—? " he asked. I answered, "No one." "Well then," he said, "you sit up here." But don't you know that I was so completely scared out at the wonderful beauty and display and style and fixings, that I could not stay and walked out and started down to C—, four miles; and, oh, so hungry and tired! By and by, about 4:00 a. m., I arrived at C—. There I was, but the girl who had been at my uncle's lived nine miles from there. So I started for that place.

God was on my track, and though I had made what seemed terrible blunders, yet I believe all was in accordance with His will, in order that He might answer the prayer that I made under the tree, the day before. While I was trudging down the sidewalk, all covered with snow, I soon heard some sleigh bells. I stopped and listened. What could that mean at that time of the day? Soon the sleigh overtook me, and the man said, " Good morning, Bub." (There was that name again.) He asked where I was going. "Going to D—." "What are you going there for?" "To get work," I answered. "Well, you are a pretty small boy to be out hunting work this time of the year — and morning." "You come here, and get in my bob, and go home with me, and then if you want to go to D—, I will help you." Somehow I felt my fear and timidity leaving under the soft, mellow voice and the entreaties of this man. He drove up to the walk, and I jumped in with my suit case. We had only a mile to drive.

The man took me up to the well lighted and warm kitchen, and there a sweet faced woman was sitting waiting for her husband who had been in South Bend, Indiana, with a load of black walnuts for the Singer Sewing Machine Company. That was why he was getting home at that hour of the morning. He said, "Well, Em, here is our boy." She jumped up and took hold of my hands, and rubbed them, and kissed me. She got some hot water, and washed me, and then set me down to a well-filled table. She hauled out one dish after another from the warm oven, and set them on the table, steaming. Oh, I will never forget her motherly actions toward me that morning, and that fine table so temptingly spread, and how I did wade into those fine delicacies! It seemed that I had lost all of my bashfulness.

But I must not fail to tell you of the blessing that the man asked as we sat down to that table. He thanked God for sparing his life, allowing no accident on the trip; for getting so much money for his load; and, last but not least, for picking a little boy, and, oh, he just talked to Jesus there until he had me crying. As he said "Amen," his wife took her clean apron, and wiped the tears all away, and kissed me again, and said, "There now, have some of this nice fried chicken and some of these warm mashed potatoes and some of this gravy; and she soon had me so hypnotized that I just ate and ate. After breakfast he took down the well-worn Bible, and read the fourteenth chapter of John. I was so wonderfully impressed that I investigated as to where it was, and that chapter has been a great blessing to me, and I have preached holiness as a second work of grace, from that notable chapter, until many have been brought into the sanctifying grace through it.

So you see, here is the answer to my prayer that I offered under that tree, as God had brought me into a religious home, and the home of a staunch Methodist at that — the same as I had been brought up in. Soon I gave God my heart in such a way that I knew I had salvation.

2

Beginning and Some Work at Sixth Street and Freeman Avenue, Cincinnati, Ohio

As this book is to treat of the results of sanctification, the blessed second work, I shall aim to stick close to the incidents that have occurred as a result of the sanctification which I received at St. Louis, thirty-two years ago, up on the fourth floor of a six-story brick, after tarrying nine days in real soul agony, wrestling and dying out. Every sanctified man or woman enters a school, not simply a holiness school but a holy school. Thirty-two years ago, I entered the holy school. The first training that I had in this school was in Cincinnati, for several years. I was kept in training for what has developed since, though I had no conception of what it all meant.

I want to relate one incident that occurred while in this school in Cincinnati. I had been having cottage prayer meetings which resulted in much good. I would entreat those who were the most dependable to meet at the Mission and have prayer before starting to the cottage meeting. One evening I felt strangely led to be somewhat more aggressive. I said: "Brethren, how many will clasp hands making a circle and enter into a covenant for at least one soul as we have seen no one saved or sanctified for several meetings?" I thought it time to take more aggressive steps. We went and had a fine time at the house of a sister who was a widow about my age; and I was also single.

Well as the meeting progressed one brother whispered to me, "Where is that soul?" as not a sinner was in the room. I said, "They will be here soon." So on went the meeting under a heavy fire. There was plenty of shouting, and we had a blessed time. Again the brother whispered, "Where is that sinner?" I replied, "He will be here." Finally the leader closed the meeting at 10:00 p. m. and those who had formed the circle began getting their wraps and prepared to leave. But I had remained sitting with head bowed, praying for that sinner.

Soon one who was not at that circle came up and said, "Aren't you going home?" It seemed that I was silenced, as several spoke to me and knew that the woman of the house was a single woman and I a single man. Glances were exchanged, and they finally all left, leaving me sitting there with that woman and she living entirely free from company. I felt the embarrassment but it seemed that I could not open my mouth, could make no explanation as to why I was sitting there after all had gone — all but this widow and her seven-year-old daughter. I dared not raise my head, and all that I could do was to pray and hold on. I said, "Lord, Thou didst impress me to make that vow and here I am."

While I wanted to tell the woman why I was waiting there, I could not get my mouth to do it. There we both sat, she disgusted and I perfectly dumb. The clock struck eleven. I said, "Lord, only one more hour left to our covenant for one soul." The half hour struck. I said, "Lord, just thirty minutes for that soul." The house stood out on the edge of the pavement and I had hardly gotten the last statement out of my mouth until rattlety-bang, and open flew the door. The woman jumped, screamed and ran into the kitchen, and in fell a drunken man, sprawling on the floor. As soon as I saw him tumble in, a voice said, "There is your man." So I jumped up, and tried to haul him in; but he was so drunk that he was about lifeless. The woman, seeing what had happened and being somewhat anxious about her carpet, came in and said, "Put that man out!" "Sister, this is in answer to prayer," I said. "Well, I will not have him in here on this carpet, with his filth." I said, "Sister, get on your knees and get hold of God! We have only twenty-five minutes to get this man saved." She said, "God can't do anything with a drunkard." I said, "Sister, pray!"

I dropped on my face with my feet against the door, and soon said, "O God, only eighteen minutes." She said, "What do you mean by eighteen minutes and twenty-five minutes?" I said, "Get hold of God for this man, and I will tell you later." Soon he raised his hand, and said, "Where am I? What am I doing here?" "You are reaching God here. God is going to make a sober man out of you." "Well, I believe that He has now," and he rose up, and said, "I have got religion." I said, "No; you have not." "Yes; I have," he answered as he rubbed himself. I said, "Get down now, and repent and cry mightily to God for salvation, as you only have that demon drink cast out of you."

We had some trouble to get him to see as we saw, but we prayed earnestly to God to show him, which He did; and soon the man was down praying for mercy. As I looked up, I said, "Lord, only eleven minutes. God, bring him to terms. Take this case through." As I lay on my face pleading, the glory struck us. The woman felt it and she shouted, and the man jumped up and grabbed me and carried me all over the room. All of this was finished just three minutes before midnight. Amen! So it pays to trust God. That man was a sober man for three years, and then God took him home to Heaven. This was the first venture on that definite line; but as God answered, several such feats have been done, all in His name, as He will do as He has promised.

I will give another incident in the work in Cincinnati. There I received clothing for the poor, and distributed it. I was out at Mt. Lookout, a suburb of Cincinnati, and a sister there gave me some clothing. In a few weeks I noticed that one of our strong members was not out for a week or so, so I went out to see what was the matter. I found her washing, and reminded her that several services had passed without her presence, which was rather an unusual occurrence. She was a poor woman, with three children, and had to pay her rent, but never allowed us to help her, as we were accustomed to help many others in similar circumstances. As she seemed loathe to give a reason for being absent, I noticed that she had on quite poor shoes, and finally I said, "Sister, are those the best shoes you have?" Blushing, she turned her back on me, making me feel that those were her best; but she finally said, "Now, Brother Bevington, I will have to admit that they are. I am expecting to get a pair next week, as I am to keep the children clothed and fed regardless of my need."

So I returned to my room; and that being Thursday evening, I began to plead a new pair of shoes for her, as I had none that I felt were good enough for her, and therefore I prayed the more. I just held on. Finally, I looked at my watch, and it was two minutes of 4:00 a. m. I had been there ten or eleven hours. Then I dropped on my face again, and inside of thirty minutes I saw a pair of ladies' shoes, and new ones, too. That was Friday, nearly 7:00 a. m. I went to my breakfast satisfied that all would be all right for a pair of shoes for the Friday night meeting; that was our regular evangelistic night service. When I came back, I was detained some, and did not get to the mission until about 10:00 a. m, and went into the prayer room. One of the kindergarten teachers came out, and said, "There is a lady wanting to see you." She came out into the main hall, and said, "Brother Bevington, I bought a pair of shoes this morning, but one is at least two sizes larger than the other. They look like mates, but they cannot be. The ones I tried on at the store fit me nicely. Then, as I was near here, I thought that I would run in and see the kindergarten children work; and while waiting to see you, I thought I would put on my new shoes and wear them home, but found one to be entirely too large." I said, "Praise the Lord. I prayed all night last night for a pair of shoes, and I guess these are the ones." "Yes, but, Brother Bevington it seems too bad to give such a pair of shoes as that to anyone, and I don't want to take them back." (She was most too proud to do that so she concluded to see if I could work them off to a good advantage.) I said, "She is a poor woman, and needs the shoes, and she can easily put cotton batting in the larger one, and the smaller one, I think, will fit her all right." "Here they are; you take them up."

But I wanted her to see this woman, as I felt that she might be able to help her in various ways. So I insisted on her taking them, as she would have to walk near that home to get her street car. Finally she took up the shoes and started for the woman's home, and found her busy with her ironing. She introduced herself, and said, "Brother Bevington sent me here, on a rather embarrassing errand." She set the shoes out, not telling the woman that one was larger than the other. All the time she was talking about the shoes and other things, the sister kept thinking, "What will I do, as I can't wear those shoes, as my right foot is nearly two sizes smaller than my left, and I hate to tell her." But she concluded to take the shoes, and probably could exchange them. The woman started home, but she was impressed that she must tell the sister, so she returned and she told about the shoes. The sister just laughed heartily, and said, "Which is the larger?" "The left one." Then she laughed more than ever, and said, "Well, well, well! God surely understands all things, as my left foot is nearly two sizes larger than my right. Here it is just as I want it. Oh, praise the Lord." Now, I knew nothing about the difference in the size of her feet, but God did, and see how He worked in order to answer my all-night prayer. Isn't that enough to convince us that God fully understands His business? I say, "Yes." What do you say? Well, Hallelujah!

The main thought in this volume is to set forth God as Healer, yet several other instances may find their way into these pages as an incentive to trust God as Healer, as well as provider in other matters; for if we are going to get healed or get anyone else healed, we must believe the Bible, we must believe God, as healing is set forth in the Atonement. I feel impressed to give some Scripture on healing, and the conditions before and after:

First, God's covenant with His people: Ex. 15:26; 23: 20-25; Deut. 7:17; Num. 21:8, 9. Second, Obedience vs. Disobedience: Deut. 28:1-30; Num. 2:4-10; Ps. 107:17-21; Heb. 10:28, 29. Third, God's will is to heal His children: Matt. 8:1-17; Mark 1:41; Luke 5:13; Heb. 10: 7; John 4:34. Fourth, Healing in the Atonement: Ps. 103:3; Matt. 8:17; Isa. 53:4, 5. Fifth, Proof of Christ's Divinity needed now as much as at any time: Mark 2:10; Matt. 9:28, 29; John 4:46-54; 5:10-19. Sixth, The children's bread and their right; Matt. 15:22-28; Mark 7:29, 30. Seventh, Christ's testimony of Himself: Luke 4:16-21; 7:19-23;

John 6:62, 63; 19:12-24. Eighth, Peter's testimony of Christ; Acts 10:38, 39. Ninth, Christ's commission to His Church; Matt. 9:35; 10:19; Matt. 28: 18-20; Mark 16: 14-20. Tenth, Direction to His church; James 5:13-16. Eleventh, Faith in God; 1 John 5:11-16; Mk. 11:12-27; Ps. 4:56. Twelfth, Believing prayer: 1 John 3:18-24; Mk. 11:24; Matt. 21:22; 28:19, 20; Mk. 9:17, 30; James 1:6, 8; John 11:22 Thirteenth, Faith, not sight; Matt. 8:8-14; Rom. 4:17-25; Heb. 11. Fourteenth, His earnest of His resurrected life; Rom. 8:11; 1 Cor. 3:16, 17. Fifteenth, Rejoice and act your faith; 2 Chron. 20:21. Sixteenth, Your faith will be tried; James 1:2, 4; 1 Peter 1:7. Seventeenth, Those who have failed to retain healing; Mk. 4:17-26; Luke 8:13. Eighteenth, A safe shelter; Ps. 91.

The tendency in this age, in many quarters, is to rule the supernatural out entirely, and to ascribe events to a natural cause. This rationalism goes under the head of scholarship, attributing largely to the human and barring out the Holy Ghost. So I hope that you will study the above Scriptures thoroughly, and see if you have a right to ascribe miracles to the Apostolic days alone. If the reader will not believe these Scriptures and the witnesses of these days, then I will say as Abraham said to the rich man, "If they hear not Moses and the prophets, neither will they be persuaded, though one rose from the dead." That there are false teachers against Divine healing is no argument against Divine healing, for there are false prophets today as there have been in all ages. There have been various professions of religion in all ages; but, thank God, there are a few who can see even beyond their vision, and catch the truths of the Gospel, and actually get healed in spite of opposition. I remember being called to a home to pray for a sister who had been on her bed for nine years. She was blessedly saved, but her husband was a radical unbeliever. He came in from the field, and ordered me out. I went out, but slipped up into the haymow; and in spite of him, I remained there about seventy-two hours. God raised the sister up so that within twelve hours after He touched her, she got dinner and called husband in, and went to the spring to get a bucket of water, so as to meet him. When she met him, he was actually all broken up, and came to the haymow and hunted me out. Then he prayed through and got salvation.

Healing is not only for the benefit of the subject but its influence is far reaching. The doctrine of Divine healing stands in spite of objectionable professors. When our Savior was on earth, He said that false Christs and false prophets would arise to seduce, if it were possible, the very elect. (Mk. 13:22.) Dr. J. A. Dowie, of Chicago, seems to be a fulfillment of this prophecy, as our

Savior more than intimates that false prophets may heal the sick, cast out devils, and do many wonderful works. We must remember that much good done, devils cast out, and bodies healed, by no means prove that a person is a true prophet, as false prophets may bear all the marks and will have the audacity to flaunt them in the face of Christ, possibly at the day of Judgment. (Matt. 7:22.) Another example of Bible prophecy fulfilled is the so-called Christian Science (false prophet). But in spite of all false doctrines and teachers, some people are actually getting healed through Jesus, and He is getting the glory. Christian Science takes the stand that there can be no such thing as sin; all is mind, therefore there is no pain, no suffering, no sorrow, no sickness. What seems so, is in the mind. That is the message of the so-called Christian Science. To the sick, to the suffering, to the sorrowing, we are to think all the evil out of existence. "How is your grandfather this morning, Bridget?" said a Christian Science practitioner to an Irish child. "He still has the rheumatism mighty bad, Mum," was the reply. "You think he has the rheumatism. There is no such thing as rheumatism." "Yes, Mum," responded the child. A few days later, they met again. "Does your grandfather still persist in his delusion that he has the rheumatism?" "No, Mum, the poor man thinks that he is dead. We buried him yesterday." So you have it. Divine healing and Christian Science are not related in the least. Divine healing is not imaginary. It is not simply the exercise of will power. It is not mind cure. It is not spiritualism. It is not immunity from death, or from sickness, as those who believe in Divine healing get sick; and when their work is done, they die. It is not mere presumption, nor a disregard of God's will. It is the direct power of God upon the body.

A man said to the writer some time ago, "Well, Brother Bevington, I suppose, from your teaching, that you are never going to die, as you say that God heals and that He answers prayer. So all that you have to do is to pray, and He heals you, and you are never going to die." I reminded him of an incident that occurred while I was working at the carpenter trade near Michigan City, Indiana. As we were coming home one Saturday evening, in the buggy, we noticed a man and his wife walking around an old log house. They seemed to be scrutinizing the old frame closely; and as we came near, the man shouted, "Hey, Jerry, come in here."

So when Jerry got out of the buggy, the man said, "Wife and I have been examining our old house where we have lived and raised our family of eleven. They are all gone now, married off. You know you have been fixing this old house up most every year for several years; and just look at the sills, and those posts, and the roof, and that gable end. They are all in pretty bad shape, and we were just saying that we believe the old thing is not worth repairing any more. So we want you to build us a new house."

We built one, and saw them vacate the old building and move into the new. They left about all the old furniture in the old house. I said, "Sir, that is the way it will be with me, as Christ has promised to keep this building that I am living in, in repairs; but the time is coming when the old thing won't be worth repairing, and I expect soon to see Him come down, take a walk around the old frame, and say, "Well, Bevington, the old thing is not worth repairing any more, so now vacate it and move up here into the new mansion that we have just finished for you. Just leave all the old furniture down there, as we have your new mansion all newly furnished in gold and diamonds."

I observe that Satan hates Divine healing, and is doing all he can to prevent it; and if one does get healed, he tries to keep him from telling it, and often succeeds in doing so. It is then that one gets in darkness over it, as Satan keeps the track well covered up. One more thought, and I will try to proceed to my mission. Divine healing is the fulfillment of those promises that cannot possibly be explained by those who take the ground that miracles ceased when the Apostles went to their reward.

There is a long list of promises ignored in most of our public teaching. It seems that revelations have by common consent been set aside, and when the thoughtful Christian in his daily reading of the Scripture meets with many of these wonderful promises made to believers, he often pauses to ask himself, "What can these words mean? If I am sick, can I ask God to heal me? Is prayer really a power with God?" It is not merely power, but it is a transcendent power, accomplishing what no other power can, overruling all other agencies, and rendering them subservient to its own wonderful efficiency.

I feel impressed to jot down some of these promises for the reader's consideration, for study, for meditation, as we must be governed by the Word; we must draw our conclusions only from the Word — not people's opinion, nor the failures of others; but see what the Word says about it. Start in with the Acts — Acts 2:39. Read it. We can readily make a plural out of that promise. It would be justified by many other passages. So these promises are for us. Now, Matt. 7:7-11; 18:19; 21:22; Mark 11:24; John 14:13, 14; John 3:21, 22.

Now we do not claim that all the foregoing promises apply literally to the physical realm, but we do claim that some of them do directly, and the others indirectly to the healing. Some of these promises are not confined to the spiritual realm alone but reach out into the physical as well. See James 5:14, 15. The Apostle illustrates what he means by prevailing prayer, by the example of Elias, a man subject to like passions as we are, as he prayed for rain and it came. We must forever settle the Bible authority on healing. We must see it in the Bible as in Isa. 53:4, 5. But read verses 2-8, and so settle on that, if God's Word means anything, it means there that there is healing in the Atonement. If so, why not have it? Yes, why not? I, for one, am going to hold onto that chapter. In connection with verse 4, read Matt. 8:17, 18; Heb. 9:28; 1 Peter 2:24, and Heb. 13:8. Paul says that Christ is the same yesterday, today and forever. Now, we think that we have given warning and invitation and Scripture enough to justify in accepting the following as being possible from a Bible standpoint.

I feel that Luke 13:16 ought to be inserted right here: "Ought not this woman whom Satan hath bound— be loosed?" Read the whole verse. We know of no stronger statement of the Lord's willingness; nay, more of the Lord's will to heal His trusting children, than this verse. The word "ought" expresses much more than willingness. It expresses obligation, right, something which would be wrong not to do. Oh, it places Divine healing on a high and solid plane; as not only a possible and actual intervention of God for the help of His suffering children, but as His normal provision for believers. It is something included in our redemption rights, something that is part of His Gospel grace, something that is already recognized as within His will, and that does not require a special revelation to justify us in claiming it. If God expects us to do what we ought to do, surely we may expect as much from Him. There is something startling in the positiveness and force of the expression "ought not." And surely no child of God should ever doubt again His perfect readiness to help and heal.

There is another important fact to notice in this verse. We have said that we firmly believe all sickness comes from Satan, either directly or indirectly; and we note here that Luke identifies it with the direct route from Satan. He says, "Whom Satan hath bound." So you may rest assured that when you undertake to see healing done, you have to walk right in on Satan's own ground, and demand of him his own property, as he is the author of all sickness. So you have a task on hand, as he claims a right to his own property, the same as you and I claim a right to that which rightfully belongs to us. He has met me several times at the threshold and positively forbidden me to enter his domain. He has called me a usurper many times; but I have credentials from God, and never cease to push my claim to the limit.

3

First Light on Divine Healing, Evangelism

I WENT TO HAMILTON, Ohio, once to hold a meeting, and, as usual, took my small drug store with me, consisting of four quart bottles of medicines, a box of pills, and two plasters. That was my regular outfit. I often think that I took up more room in my suit case for medicines than for Bibles and books. Well, I was assigned to a fine room in a hospitable home, and set my medical outfit on the mantel, so as to have them handy, as I took of all of the remedies every day. In this precious home there were several dear children, one of four summers. She came into the room, and spied that outfit on the mantel; and as it was something new to her, as her parents used no medicines, she ran out into the kitchen, and said, "Oh, Mamma, you des tome ere," as she tugged at Mamma's apron. But Mamma, being busy kneading bread, paid but little attention to the little child's appeal. But the little tugger was determined to have a hearing, so she kept pulling and jabbering.

Finally the Mamma said, "What do you want? Mamma is busy now." "Oh, Mamma, you des tome ere, and see att de preacher's dot." So, to please the child, she followed her into my room; and as the child came in the door, she pointed up to the mantel, at that curious outlay — strange looking things to the child, as I suppose she had never seen a bottle. Well, I raised my eyes just in time to catch the expression on the mother's face, which, had I been able to properly read, would have saved me much perplexity. However, that strange look, as she turned back for the kitchen, set me thinking.

Though I could not diagnose the meaning enough was visible to trouble me, as I could not get away from that expression. However, I kept praying and reading the Word, preparatory to delivering the great message that night. Well, the message was delivered; but it fell flat, like my first biscuits I ever made — flat and heavy. Of course, I had no trouble in finding plenty of excuses for the apparent failure. But next day, symptoms were somewhat alarming. Such peculiar feelings! I never felt just like that before; but was quite well adapted to excusing myself, as I had been sanctified only about a week, and hence had not entirely given up my ability as an excuse maker. This power seemed to have wonderfully revived on this occasion, so I kept at it. But my excuses seemed to fail in producing the desired effect, so that by noon I was in a terrible mixed-up mess; and the great difficulty was that I could not locate the trouble. I examined myself prayerfully, and I believe honestly, and came in on the animal from various angles, approaching the thing but not being able to get him landed sufficiently to get rid of him. So I preached, or tried to, that night. I thought that I did better than the night before, and gave the credit largely to a man and his wife who sat before me during the preaching, as they seemed to be praying for me all the time. So I said, "Now, if I can get that couple to come every night, I can preach all right. But that prop was knocked out from under me, and I was cast on a tempestuous sea.

The next day I was still worse, so I helped myself quite freely to the medicines on the mantel; but they, too, seemed to have gone off with the crowd, and were quite useless. So I went to my usual resort, the woods, and spent all day out there examining myself, thinking that maybe I was deceived, and had never been sanctified. But God showed me that I had been. Well, then, maybe I had lost out. So it was a reconnoitering, and digging and boring, and blasting all day; yet I could not get the thing landed. Finally, I went to the house, and said, "Brother, you will have to take the meeting tonight. I don't know just what is the matter with me, but I can't preach tonight. I will tarry here before God, and see if I can get located." So he said, "I will help you out." They well knew what was the matter with me, though they never even hinted that they were praying for me, over that outlay on the mantel. They were doing their talking to God, and He was doing His best to talk to me, and it was a time, sure. I did my best at treeing the critter, and kept getting farther out in the thicket, as it seemed to me.

I put in a restless, sleepless night, and the next morning went to the woods. I had not been there long until this sentence came to me, "I am the Lord that healeth thee." Well, I paid but little attention to that, as that was not what I was after; but the thing that brought this heaviness, as sickness had never done that. That Scripture kept coming at me; but I was not sure that it was Scripture, though I knew I had heard it or read it, (we are always sure to get in the brush when we give Satan the benefit of the doubt.) So I still persisted in throwing that sentence entirely out; but it would not be put out, and just kept coming at me. I stood this firing as long as I could, and went to the house, and said, "Sister, is there such a passage in the Bible, as 'I am the Lord that healeth thee?'

"She said, "Yes," and got the Bible and showed me the passage; but never said a word to show that she and her husband were praying for me relative to that outlay on the mantel.

Then I began to think that God wanted to heal me; but I had heard so many at the mission testify to healing, and then when sick, go for their doctor or medicines, that I had arrived at the point where that had but little effect on me, as I supposed that those whom I heard testify were fair samples of what healing is. But all that reasoning failed to bring relief, so I began searching the Scriptures, and of course found plenty of evidences that Christ healed, and also the disciples; and I found that healing was taught in the old Scriptures. But, of course, it must have been dropped back there with the disciples; if not, then why wasn't it preached in our Methodist Churches, as they were surely the nearest to the Bible of any. In fact many of our M. E. preachers had told us that Divine healing was only for the disciples; and of course that settled it, as the preachers had gone through colleges, and what they did not know would be foolish for me to undertake to fathom out.

So having that settled, I again proceeded with the investigation of that dark horse hidden away, causing me so much trouble. But, somehow, those M. E. preachers, with all their collegiate advantages, failed to keep that matter settled; it would roil up, and get me all mixed up. So I went out to the woods again, and there came another sentence to confuse me. Asa took medicine, and he died. Now that was the way it came to me. The medicine is not in that passage; but it says that he went for the doctor, and we all know what that meant. I went back to the house, and asked about the passage. The sister got the Bible, and that should have settled it. I went into the room, all tangled up, and said, "What does all this mean? I am not after the pros and cons of medicines; I am after the cause of this awful feeling," and yet I knew that I was a most miserably mixed up fellow.

I got down on my face, with my head near the fireplace board, just a little below where my young drug store was located. I said, "Lord, Lord, what does all this mean? What is the matter with me? What has all this Scripture to do with my case just now?" "I am the God that healeth thee," came as an answer. I said, "O God, dost Thou mean that I am to give up all these old faithful standbys? Why, how can I ever do it?" (And the tears were just pouring down my cheeks.) "Here are six different kinds of medicine that have been my guide, my strength, my all; and, oh, how can I give them up?" My hard feelings against those people who claimed healing, yet when sick took medicine, had affected me in such a way as to render it impossible for me to take Jesus as my Healer and still use this medicine. It seemed a settled fact that if I was going to take Jesus, I must drop the six great remedies. But God had His hand on me, and He had to answer the prayers of His faithful servants with whom I was stopping.

I was called out to dinner, and there came the husband, holding up a mashed thumb, and saying, "Wife, look here!" I noticed that she just smiled, and I thought, "Oh, what a hardhearted wife!" Why, I thought that she should have dropped dinner, and made a great fuss over that awful thumb; but, no, she never paid any attention to it, but just went on with the dinner, a-smiling, while to me it was a sickening sight. He worked in the tool factory at Hamilton, and had gotten his thumb between two heavy stones, some way; and there it was with two-thirds of the nail gone, and the other third a-hanging. I went to my room, and got my bandage paraphernalia consisting of soft rags, Castile soap, and so on, and said, "Now, while wife is getting dinner on, I will just do that up for you." He gave no signs of turning the case over to me, but just stood there laughing at my outfit. "Well now," I said, "maybe you think I am not an expert at this. Why, I have worked at it several years among the poor in our mission locality, and am good at it." Just then in came the wife with a steaming dish of mashed potatoes, and she, too, was laughing. I had the twofold object in view! First, to show them a kindness; second, to show my efficiency as a wound dresser; but they just laughed, as my explanations and references to my ability seemed only to add fuel to the flame. Then I began by giving the great healing properties of my salve, also of my soap and soft rags; but all this failed in making any impression to my liking. When they had laughed until they were laughed out, the wife kindly said, "Brother Bevington, we never use any of those things." "You don't? Why, what in the world do you do? Don't you wrap up a wound with something to heal it?" "No, no! " "Why, what do you do?" "We just trust Him," she said, pointing up.

Well, then for the first time it dawned on me as to what all this wretchedness meant, and where it had come from; and I just turned and went to my room, without eating any dinner. I fell down as before, with my head toward the mantel, and wept great tears. Finally I said, "Lord, Lord, oh, for such a faith as theirs!" Give me some evidence, Lord, that I can live without these six remedies— some unmistakable evidence, something that I can and will rely on." Dear reader, I was something like Elijah— I wanted to die. But I was not fit then for translation. Ah, that was a memorable day, marking one of the grandest epochs of my life, after sanctification, Glory to God! I tell you all hell put up a stiff fight in those three or four days of intense darkness; but, bless God, the light came, and I have been walking in it this thirty-one years, and they have been years of victory over that question of healing, as not a drop of medicine has ever entered my mouth since then.

Well, I will finish. There I lay fighting out one of the greatest battles of my life. I was waiting for some evidence, and suddenly I heard a noise, but never raised my head. Yes, I actually heard a voice; and down the mantel came those bottles on long legs as I had seen them in advertisements. They walked down the wall, turned and walked between my head and the mantel, and out of the window. Then came the plaster, and then the box of pills; and I heard the pills rattle as plain as I ever heard anything. When all had disappeared out the window, I took that as the evidence and got up and took the whole four quart bottles out, and smashed them up; and took the pills and the plasters out to the kitchen and consigned them to the flames. Thus ended the years of slavery to the medicines. I returned to the room, and oh, what glory flooded me! I just wept and shouted and laughed. The sister came in and I told her the whole thing; and oh, how she did laugh! We had an old Methodist Camp Meeting right there.

Now, in my haste I have left out one point that may be worth something to others. When the brother would not allow me to dress his hand, then Satan came in and said, "Now, he is just fooling you." As he came home at 5:30, I went out at 5:00 into the back alley, and hid behind a coal house to watch him as he came, supposing that he would have a rag on his thumb, but would take it off before entering the house, so as to fool me. Well, I lay there for three-quarters of an hour, with the sun pouring down on me, while I was waiting to catch him. By and by he turned into the alley some fifteen rods away. He was swinging both hands, and a-singing a song I had taught him, and no sign of a rag on his thumb. Well, I was ashamed, and slipped back into my room. I felt condemned, and pleaded for forgiveness, and got it.

I love to think of that memorable hour when, with my soul flooded with glory, I just walked the floor. I was willing to abide by the results. I did not know whether I was to be healed or not, but took it for granted that all that had been done was for my good and God's glory. If it was to suffer, He would give me grace to bear it. This all occurred about 2:00 or 3:00 p. m., and I was not out of that room ten minutes until I was accosted by Satan, who came as an angel of light, and informed me that I had made a terrible mistake. He said, "Now, Satan had you do all that, and you should have had better sense than to do as you did;

for you haven't money enough to replace that much-needed outfit, as it would take about $6.50."

Well, I was quite young in the work, and thought, Can this be God talking to me? It must be, for how could Satan be so interested in me? I was reminded of what those good old sainted Methodist preachers told us four years ago, and here I had ignored their noble efforts to keep me out of fanaticism, and had actually gone into fanaticism, trampling over their counsel. And that word "fanaticism," how it did penetrate my very being, as it was quite a new word to me. I had been looking it up since the smash-up, and had become terror-stricken at its definition, yet so unconsciously had been drawn under its mighty crushing influence. You see I had gotten into the maelstrom, and been engulfed by its power. I tell you I was astounded.

I went into the kitchen, and told the sister what I had experienced. She said, "You have done just right, and all this afterclap is of Satan." She then got the Bible and showed me that healing is for us, and gave me their experiences; and I began to feel better. She said, "Now, when husband comes in to supper, you will find that his thumb is healed." "What," I said, "that terribly smashed thumb healed?" "Yes, it will be healed." And I said, "Without a rag on it?" "Yes, all without remedies, as we never use them." And sure enough, when we came out to supper, while the thumb was red and tender, it was not a bit sore; he never experienced any inconvenience with it only as he would hit it, and then the hurt was very brief.

That night, at family prayer, I said, "Now, brethren, I want you to anoint me and pray for my healing." "Well," the sister said, "we haven't any oil, but God understands, and it will be just as well." So we got down. They had a sweet little tot (the one who had led her mamma in to see what the preacher had). She was sitting under papa's chair, and mamma said, "Now, honey, you lead us in prayer." She said, "Dear Jesus, I'se so dad tos papa smashed his fum, and dat de preacher seed it, tos it'll help him to trust Desus. Amen." Well, a very short prayer, but, oh, its length has never yet been explored. Thirty-one years have passed, and I am not yet to the end of that giant prayer of that little three-year-old tot.

Then they came over to me, and laid their hands on me, and prayed the prayer of faith for my healing. While I had no evidence of any kind, yet I just took God at His word. They said, "Brother Bevington, we believe that you are a healed man."

The last night that I preached before getting swamped, a young lady came to the altar for sanctification, and they postponed the meetings until the preacher should get shaped up. So I preached on the next night (Sunday) and this girl came again, but did not get through. I closed the meeting, expecting to go to Cincinnati on Monday. But this girl came, and said, "Brother Bevington, I want to get through. Can't you remain over and have a meeting at our house tonight, as I do believe I could get through then?" I said, "Why certainly." So we planned to have meeting at her house that night. I was invited to another home for dinner, and about 3:00 p. m. I felt the old symptoms coming on me. Of course Satan was there, and in thirty minutes I was as deathly sick as I had ever been. I stood on the promises, but kept getting worse.

As meeting time drew near, two young men came; and as they entered the room both stood speechless with amazement for several moments, and I was about as silent as they were just then, as I was, oh, so deathly sick, and the house seemed to be spinning at a tremendous rate. Finally, the silence was broken by one's saying, "Why Brother Bevington, what can be the matter with you? I am a doctor's son; I will go for Father, only two blocks from here, and I left him at home." "No," I said, "Well," one said, "you are as white as a sheet; you are in danger; the doctor's son says that you are in great danger." I said, "Well, boys, I took Jesus for my Healer last night, and I am going to leave my case in His hands." "Yes, but you are dying now." "Well, I am ready for the translation, and don't want to interfere with God's plans; no more doctors, boys." I said, "Lead me out onto the porch (as heart trouble was my trouble). They led me out, and it was all they could do to hold me. I was thrown violently at times, and this seemed to be one of those times.

They insisted that I must have a doctor, and I was just as determined not to have one. I said, "Hold on to me and lead me down the steps," as I needed some air. Just then the man of the house came, and he assisted them in getting me down the steps; and he, too, insisted on having a doctor, but soon said, "Well, I have no time to fool away with fanatics." So he went into the house. I was then blind. Only three times in my long fights with my weak heart, I went blind. I said, "Lead me to the fence." They did so, and I got hold of it, but seemed to be getting worse. The doctor's son said, "Well, I will run down and tell them that there will be no meeting tonight." I said, "No, don't do that, as there will be a meeting." "Why, man, you don't know the danger you are in," he said. "Well, there will be a meeting, for God told me to remain over for that purpose. Lead me out into the street, and keep a firm hold on me; don't let me go." Well, we had some great tussling out there, but they managed to hold me well enough to keep me from getting hurt. I began to plead the promises, and really felt that Jesus was going to deliver me. I said, "Boys, pray," as we went staggering and plunging down the street, a very unpopular sight on that street at that time of day.

After one block had been passed, I said, "Boys, we are going to have the victory," as I could see a little, though suffering greatly. I began praising God, and one said, "You don't look much like a subject to be praising God." I soon began to feel better, and my sight kept returning, and I praised God all the more. People stopped and listened to me praising God in my condition. Some thought that I was a drunken man, others that I was off in the upper story; but I just allowed them to have their own opinions, and kept praising God. One more block was passed, and I could see the house, so I just holloed as loud as I could yell. I soon said, "Boys, let me go," and I raised my right hand and praised God for real victory. Though I reeled some, yet I held on, and in ten minutes I was as well as I ever was. Oh, hallelujah! That was the last of the rheumatism or heart trouble for about fourteen years.

I now relate the incident which followed. We went into the house, and had a most blessed meeting. This girl prayed through, and received the Holy Ghost in all His fullness. She came and sat down beside me, and said, "O Brother Bevington, this is most wonderful, it far surpasses anything I ever dreamed of. I had a vision. Oh, such a sight; I saw hundreds of little faces, not as our children's faces are, but, oh, so many, and every child had its little hands out beckoning to me to come and teach them. There was a great long arch, and huge red letters on it, which read 'Fiji'." I said, "What?" and she told me again. "Why," I said, "that is a call to the Fiji Islands, to go as a missionary and teach them of Jesus." She rose, with both hands up, and tears of joy falling fast, as she said very softly, "Glory, glory! " In fourteen months she sailed for the Fiji Islands. Dear Brother Gamble helped us to get her there. She spent sixteen years on the field, and then went to Heaven from there. But many a time before going, she said, "O Brother Bevington, what if you had given up and taken medicine? — where would I have been?" She firmly believed that if I had taken medicine after accepting Jesus for my Healer, I would never have recovered from that sickness, and she would never have been sanctified. Let that be as it may, praise God that He enabled me to take the stand I did on that memorable night.

Now, reader, this volume is to set forth the power of God as might be manifested in these days of doubt and skepticism — not to set forth what was done in Christ's day. We are not living in Christ's day nor the Apostles' days. Let us grasp the possibilities of our day from a Bible standpoint, and from no other. The manifestations of the power of God all comes through consecrated prayer, earnest, believing, real solicitous prayer; prayer that moves Heaven; prayer that will not take, "No," for an answer.

Now, not having names in reference to dates and incidents, I may get some things slightly mixed up; but they will stand the scrutiny of Heaven, whether they run the gauntlet of the critics down here safely or not. I want to say that I did not find it so easy to mind God in regard to my call to the evangelistic field, as some seem to have found their calls. I saw my defects standing out greater than the power of God, and had quite a time before I could venture out where I could fully trust God; and also to get to the place where He could trust me, which is of the two most essential. But this healing was a great boon to me; it removed many hindrances that stood like mountains towering farther up than I could see, as these hindrances had engulfed my every effort to mind God in going out.

Dear Brother Nichols, a blind, sanctified preacher, took me up into West Virginia, and gave me some valuable lessons on trust. He gave me the boost that has enabled me to lift many a one out of a tangled wire net, as I spent the whole winter back of Huntington, in cottage prayer meetings, being with Brother Ails and others, and the power of God was manifest.

I remember being out in the woods in prayer, one night in the spring. I had been wrestling nearly all night for that locality, and I said, "O God, I must have some evidence that I am in the center of Thy will." And as I lay there, I just cried out in great raptures, as wave after wave of glory flooded my soul. I shouted and laughed and cried until I just had to get up and give vent by running and jumping over logs and brush piles for over three hours. The glory fell unmistakably, and I tell you I did not have to ask any one to come to the altar that night. The row of ten chairs was filled before I was half through preaching, and the seekers were in earnest. No one had to tell them to pray; it wasn't necessary to lift up their hands; we didn't have to shake religion into them. No, indeed, that all-night prayer had knocked off the scales, and they had a vision, and now they walked up to it. So it is prayer, not money, not congratulations, not large crowds but prayer, that brings victory.

I was in a meeting in Ohio, and there was a man there in the lumber business, who came to me, saying, "Oh, you ought to hold a meeting down where I live." "Well, Sir, where do you live?" "I live twenty-two miles from here." So I prayed over it, and felt somewhat inclined to give the matter further consideration. I asked him for the names of the leaders, and he gave me two. Then after the meeting closed where I was, I went to the woods, to get the mind of God, and was impressed to go. But as I seemed to be running up against some pretty hard problems in this hollow log, I concluded to wait longer before God, so as to be definite and sure. I spent forty-eight hours longer in this commodious hotel — the hollow log — making 120 hours, getting things straight from headquarters. Amen! I tell you it pays to know what we are doing when it comes to dealing with God, or minding Him. That is where the trouble is with so many, they jump at conclusions when they should go slow.

Brother Knapp taught that nine times out of every ten we get our impressions from Satan, so we need to wait, get still, get where God can actually talk to us. So I searched for the mind of God, and He gave me the clear assurance that He wanted me to go to this place. "Well," you say, "what was or is this assurance?" Well, read on, and you will get a fair sample here.

After I had gotten real still, free from everything else, He showed me the road that I was to take, and then a clump of trees and a road that was little traveled, running off to the left and down to a schoolhouse, so that between the main road and this branch was quite a grove of small trees. The schoolhouse stood down a slope; and back of the schoolhouse was a creek; and back of that a large cornfield, and away back of that a large farmhouse, a large barn and out buildings and a windmill. I said, "Amen, Lord, that is good enough." I backed out of that hollow log, and went down to the house, and told the family where I was going. I got some dinner and started out on the twenty-two mile walk, with two heavy suit cases, filled mostly with books to sell. I traveled until sundown, and then stopped at the house, and asked for a drink. I gave out some tracts, and talked salvation to the man, and told him where I was bound for. Well, we talked salvation until after dark. I got so interested in his soul and that of his wife; and did not know whether I could stay there all night or not. But he said, "You stay with us tonight."

The next morning he said, "Now, see here; you are going down there on uncertainties. I know that man you have to deal with; he is a German. Now down the road there is a church, but we have no Sunday School here, and no services. If you will stay here, I will give you the best room in the house, and you will have all the time you want to pray. Give us a meeting, and then go on to this other place, as you have no dates." Well that looked pretty reasonable and seemed to be good logic — a great trap that Satan sets, and he gets lots of victims too. Now this was a case where it paid to pray through as Satan would have stood a pretty good chance of side-tracking me if I had not spent hours in that log, getting the thing straight. Yes, it pays to get plain, definite orders, if it does take 120 hours. I said to this man, "I can't stop now; maybe I can come back." But he, knowing the obstacles and failures at the place where I was going, thought that I ought to stay sure. But I went on.

Now, I gave out tracts all along the road, and when I got within ten miles of the schoolhouse, I told the people where I was going, and what for. One woman said, as she looked very doubtful, "Oh, I do wish that you could get a meeting and a Sunday School at that place, as the people are getting desperate there; they are so ungodly and so wicked that they just go to the woods Saturday night, and play cards and gamble and drink beer and fight and have rooster fights until Monday morning. Oh, I wish you could, but -- ". Ah, how many get stuck on that "but!"

Well, I went on, and when within four miles I stopped to get a drink. I gave out tracts, and told the family my mission. The woman sat down and said, "Oh, I do hope that you can get something started, for they are so wicked down there, and their wickedness reaches all over the country." She said, "You see that girl there in the garden. She is thirteen and my only living child. This summer my husband goes every Saturday over to the rock houses in the woods, where they gamble and swear and chew and smoke and tell all sorts of smutty yarns; and he takes the girl with him to do the cooking, and she, being innocent of the danger, rather enjoys it. I have done everything I could to prevent it, and have tried to get the neighbors to help me break up their hellish work; but the men are all in it, and they like to have my girl there to do the cooking for them. I have become nearly distracted, for they leave here about one o'clock Saturday and don't get back until Monday. Often they do not come back until night, and I have all the stock to look after."

Well, I went on, praying and giving out tracts. But I forgot to mention another place where they wanted me to stop and have a meeting in a forsaken Baptist Church. These two opportunities proved to be important later. My burden increased as I journeyed on. I soon met a man and wife, and gave them some tracts. They asked my business; and when I told them, they shook their heads and went on. But they stopped, and said, "You had better stir up some of these hollows, for I tell you that you will be fooling away your time in that awful neighborhood." I said, "These are the ones that Jesus came for." "Yes, I know; but if you knew what we know, you would never stop there. There has been many an attempt there, but all have failed, and left the place worse every time.'

So I jogged along, thinking and praying, "O God, this is Thy work; what does it all mean?" "What's that to thee; follow thou me?" was all the consolation that I could get. Well, that was enough, too. Hallelujah to His dear name!

But this fellow wasn't satisfied, and he turned around and overtook me, and said, "Now over the other side of that hollow is where I live. We will give you a good room and all you can eat; and there you have a certainty, but up at that schoolhouse is a dark prospect, and if there is a place on earth that needs a meeting and a Sunday School it is our neighborhood; and we will see that you get some money, and you will get none where you are aiming for." Well, you see that was quite an inducement, but that was not the place. So I thanked him for his kind offers, and said, "I may come back when I get through out there." He said, "You will be of no account when through there, even if you come out alive." But I had received my orders back there in that hollow log, and preferred rather to mind God, and run the chances than to accept his invitation.

Soon I saw a faint road branching off to the left; and as I was looking for that, I at once saw that this was the place, as there was the diamond-shaped clump of trees, and this faint road ran down to a schoolhouse. Then I looked back of the schoolhouse, and there was the creek and the cornfield; then there was the large farmhouse away back, and the large barn and the windmill. "Well," I said "this must be the place." I went down through this clump of trees, and tried the door of the schoolhouse, but it was locked. I went through weeds higher than my head, to the back end of the schoolhouse, and there got down on my face, and praised God for landing me safe, right at the spot He had showed me back there in the hollow log twenty-two miles away.

"Father," I said, "I am so thankful that I escaped those enemies that I encountered on the way, who tried to get me off Thy line. Oh, dear Lord," I said, "I am so glad that Thou madest it possible for me to pray clear through, and get orders; and I am so glad that Thou hast so fixed me up that I am perfectly willing to run the gauntlet though facing some muscular giants, swaying their clubs, aiming to scare me off. Thou wilt enable me to run through without a scratch." Well, I lay there for some time, praising God and thanking Him until He let the glory right down into my soul. I had to get up and run.

I left that spot about 10:00 a. m. I think, and stopped in the next house and gave out some tracts. I then enquired where Mr. R— lived. The woman said, "In the second house on the right." I thanked her, and started on. Then she said, "Say, aren't you a preacher?" I answered "Yes, ma'am." "Well, are you going to hold a meeting in the schoolhouse?" "I expect to," I replied. "Oh, I do hope that you can, but —." There it was again, that "but." Well, I wasn't running on "buts", so on I went.

I soon saw the house, and the large barn on the left; and I saw a great big fellow out in the truck patch, cutting weeds, as there had been much rain, and he could not plow his corn. I set my suit case down, and said, "Good morning." He looked up and responded cordially. I said, "Is this Mr. R—?" "Yes, what of it?" "Well," I said, "I am a holiness evangelist." And before I could finish the statement, he had straightened up on his hoe handle, and said, "A what?" "Why, a holiness evangelist," said I. He repeated it, and then said, "I have seen all sorts of evangelists, but I don't believe that I ever saw one by that name." "Well, Sir, just come out here and look a holiness evangelist right in his two eyes." He came out to the fence, and said, "Well, what do you want of me?"

"Well, Sir, I want to get in that schoolhouse that you have control of, and hold some meetings, and get someone saved, and organize a Sunday School." "Well, Sir, I would be delighted to unlock that door and let you get in for that good purpose; but, my dear Sir, they have notified me from the wiggle tail in the puddle to the giant of the throne that I must not unlock that door for preaching, as the benches are just about all whittled up. I am sorry that I can't unlock the door, as my wife, I know, would be real glad, and she would take hold and help; I am of no account at that. But as it's about dinner time let's go up and have some dinner." So we went.

The wife felt so bad because John would not open that door. Nothing was said about his authority or power, but the meeting hinged on that door, and it was the all-important item the next nine days. Well, when dinner was over, he said, "Mr., I was down at the mill three or four weeks ago, and a friend, a trustee, over on the other road, told me that they have just finished their new schoolhouse, and if I should run onto a preacher, to send him over, as they would like to have a meeting there and have a Sunday School started." So he led me out onto the porch, and said, "That place is Pumpkin Hollow. You go back down the road until you come to the first pair of bars on your left; turn in there, and cross that bottom, go up a hill, and follow that road down across another hollow through a strip of woods, and on. 'Tis three miles. Well, I must go up the road," he said, "and I hope that you will have a good time over at Pumpkin Hollow." So I picked up my grips, and said, "Pumpkin Hollow, hey. Yes, but that isn't what I am after."

So down the road I started, and said, "Well, Lord, where am I going?" "What's that to thee; follow thou me," came as my only answer. So I kept going, and soon came to a hill, a long one on the right when a voice said, "This path is the way." So up that immense hill I started with my two suit cases. "Well, Lord, where in the world am I going?" "What's that to thee?" So up I went, asking no more questions. Finally I reached the summit of the hill, and dropped the suit cases under a large oak tree; and the same voice said, "This is the place." Now I want to remind you that the hindrance to having the meeting was that locked door. So I just stayed under that tree nine days and nights. I had nothing to eat; I did not want anything, as I got such a burden to get that door unlocked, for I knew that God had sent me there to hold a meeting, and that now Satan was hindering. My business now was to pray that door open, as 'twould be no use to try to break it down, and to go off and give it up would be disobeying God or disregarding His wish or orders. You may ask, why did it take nine days to get an answer? Simply because I could not get still enough any sooner.

After the first twenty-four hours, Satan came down, and argued the situation. I had a conflict with him most every day, then he brought up Pumpkin Hollow as a much better site than this where I was lying there under a tree contracting a cold that would break up all meetings that year, and probably land me in the grave, prematurely. It had rained three times, while I was under that tree, waiting to get that door opened. So 'twas, one thing and then another for the eight days and nights. So on the beginning of the ninth day, I began to see that I was getting still; and at the fifth hour of that day I rose from off my face, and held up the Bible, praising God that the door was going to be opened, and said, "Now, Mr. Devil, if you have any more material down in hell, just bring it on." I had met every objection that he had offered with the Word. And, Sir, he could not rake up another proposition, had exhausted all the resources of hell on me, and was completely whipped out.

So I dropped down again on my face, feeling sure that I was near the door's opening, and at noon, I saw that I was actually getting still; and, oh, how desirous I was to keep still — I did not want to breathe, and several times I held my breath until I had to pound my lungs to get breath — as so many times when getting close to the object desired I would hold my breath, and would just be able to reach it, while at other times I would not, and have had some difficulty in getting my breath. So I kept getting smaller and smaller, smaller and smaller, until I saw myself as a little worm not over an inch long, and began to say, "Glory," very softly. I repeated it and saw that I was not losing ground by it, but rather felt assured that victory was near. At 2:15 p. m. I was, oh, so still, and said, "Now, Lord, Thou wilt open that door." Suddenly I heard a key go into the lock, and heard it turn, and saw the door open; and as it opened, it left a circling mark where it rubbed on the floor. I said, "Oh, glory, 't is open!"

But I felt that inasmuch as this meeting had been such a hard pull from the start back there in that hollow log, I had a right to do as Gideon did — ask for two witnesses — so I dropped on my face again, and said, "Now, Lord, Thou didst answer twice for Gideon, and Thou wilt for me." I settled down, and in fifteen minutes was as small as before; and in five minutes more I heard the same as before, and saw the mark plainly. Then I jumped up, looked at my watch, and saw that it was twenty-five minutes of three. I stood there praising God for the wonderful victory of the nine days' conflict, picked up the suit cases, and went down the hill. I saw Mr. R— out in the truck patch again; and he saw me, and halloed, "Well, well, how is Pumpkin Hollow?" I made no reply to that, and he said, "You had a good time, I reckon." "I have been having a fine time." "Well, I knew you would," he said. "Well, we just got through dinner; go up to the house and get something to eat." So in I went, and his wife said, "Oh, I am so glad to see you." She said, "While we were eating dinner, John had to get up three times to answer the phone, relative to the meeting here."

Now, please note that in the first place I did my duty in giving out tracts all along that twenty-two mile trip, and telling the people what I wanted. So God then had some foundation to work on As soon as I reached that tree, God began to work on these people, and through them, by having them phone to Mr. R— as to the meeting. Then as I began to get still up there under that tree, God had three of them call him up and remind him that they ought to have a meeting there. Well, he got tired of that and, after answering the third call during that dinner, he said, "Wife, how is Nance?" Nance was a bald-faced mare that had been crippled about two weeks, and was on the pasture. "Why," said his wife, "she is all right, I guess, as I saw her running and kicking up her heels just before dinner." "Well," he said, "you get Frank (their boy ten years old) and tell him to bring her up, and put the saddle on her, and go over to Pumpkin Hollow, and tell that preacher that as soon as he gets through there to come over. " So when he said that was the very time that I heard the bolt turn in the lock, saw the door open, heard it rub on the floor, and so on.

Now someone asks, What is the witness? Well, here was the witness in this case, the witness, the evidence, that my petition was answered. I was there nine days to get that door open; and as soon as Mr. R— gave his consent, then God gave me this witness. So we can rest assured of some kind of satisfactory witness.

After I had done justice to a fine meal, Mrs. R— gave me the key, to go down and unlock the schoolhouse to air it. They would phone around as to the meeting that night. As I passed Mr. R— in his truck patch, he said, "Well, you go down; there may be some women and children out, we men folks are after the foxes, as they got to killing off our chickens. We met and organized a Fox Band, and I was put in as captain. We have invested a lot of money in hounds — we have about twenty — and we all go out, about thirty of us men, every night. So there will be no men at the meeting, but there may be some women and children and boys and girls." "All right, Mr. R— , I have the key, and that is the main thing." I went down and, of course, was anxious to see that circling mark caused by the door; and as I unlocked and pushed the door, it rubbed on the floor, and made the mark just as I had seen it. I said, "Oh, glory to our God!" I just stood there and wept and laughed and shouted for about an hour — had a blessed time rejoicing to know that God would take so much pains to show me so many things, all of which were to assure me of the right way.

Well, I closed the door, got down on my face behind a shoe box, and began a stampede on that organized Fox Club. I prayed for nothing else from 4:00 until 7:30; but stuck to that club of thirty unsaved men, souls for whom God sent His son. At 7:30 I heard quite a racket outside, barking of hounds and talking of men, and I heard the captain say, "Well, boys, let's go in and see what the fellow is a-doing." So they all dismounted, tied their thirty horses, and marched in about 7:45. I got up off my face, shook hands with each one, and at the same time gave each one a nice new song book, and said, "Now let's have a few songs."

"Well," said the captain, "we are not going to stay but just a few minutes." "Well, what time you are here help us sing," I answered. So I bowed my head and asked the Lord, "What song shall we sing first?" as I felt that the whole thing hinged on that first song and the Spirit said, "Will there be any stars in my crown." Well, I was not very partial to that song for a lot of sinners, but dared not to question. So I called for it, and the captain said, "That's it exactly." It was what they all wanted, and I tell you they did sing it. I called on the captain to lead it, and he sang well and got wonderfully enthused over it. Before that song was finished, the house was packed. So I called for another song, and that was a great favorite to all of them. I gave out seventy-five books, and saw that the children had books. How they did sing! Well, listen; that song service in answer to prayer burst up that great Fox Club. I didn't get to preaching until after 8:30. I preached thirty minutes, and then had another song service, holding the captain to lead and said, "Now, captain, we want you to take charge of this singing and have all of your songs selected before church; and can't you meet here at 7:00 to drill some? Well, that suited them, so no more was said about those chicken thieves.

Now, I won't tell of all that occurred there, but the meeting lasted nine weeks. On the fourth night, the captain stepped out as I closed my message, and with tears in his eyes he said, "Boys, we want and need this kind of salvation. Come on, let's have it." The whole thirty came and I tell you they went to praying. By twelve o'clock, midnight, the captain bounded to his feet; he was the first to pray through, and he did some wonderful jumping and shouting, and he preached there as he walked back and forth by those twenty-nine men weeping and praying until 4: 00 a. m.

Three prayed through; seven women also had come forward, three of whom prayed through, and the captain's wife was seeking sanctification. She was the only regenerated person in the neighborhood when the meeting began. In all over 200 knelt at the altar, and most of them prayed through as 'twas not quite so hard to get them to go straight and hence to get through. It would be quite interesting to relate many of the unusual incidents. So many said, "Oh, what if Bevington had failed under that tree!" So it pays to mind God, even if the way is somewhat befogged with conditions that we don't understand.

There was a large holiness hall built there, and they wanted me to take charge of the work; and I believe I should have done it, but I had so many calls. I said that I would come back often, and I did; but in a few years a sharp, shrewd preacher got in there and organized his church, and in three years there wasn't a sanctified man or woman there except the captain's wife who stood straight, and died a-preaching sanctification.

I was holding another meeting in Ohio, and was invited to another place. So, when through with this meeting, I went to the woods to settle this call. I crawled into a hollow log, as it was quite chilly, in the fall; and there God told me to go, so I went. I preached three nights, when I was notified that I could not preach any more in the schoolhouse. Knowing well that God had told me to come, again I went to the woods, and into another hollow-log.

I lay there five days, and then came a puzzling circumstance. I began to get hungry, which usually means that the fast is called off; but I knew that I did not have the victory I was praying for, so I decided to remain in there until I heard from Heaven, or died in the log. My hunger was increasing and I was feeling weak, both of which were usually good evidences that the fast was called off, or that I was through. I mention this to show the danger of getting in ruts, as God works entirely apart from ruts.

The log was somewhat small, so that I was slightly cramped, and occasionally stretched out as best I could, by extending my arms out in front of me. While I had been telling the Lord that I was hungry and also that I was not satisfied thus far, on the second twenty-four hour watch after I began getting hungry, as I stretched out my arm, my hand struck something unusual there. I found more like it and, gathering them up, I concluded that they were acorns, and was impressed to eat them. Well, I never was fond of acorns; but, oh, they tasted so good. But I said, "How could acorns get in here?" as these seemed fresh. How long had they been in there, and how did it come that I had not felt them before, as I had been extending my hand out that far for some time?

These questions came up and had to be met some way. Well, I ate the six acorns, and felt refreshed. This was at 6: 00 p. m. — I struck a match to find out the time. I lay there all night, and the next morning in stretching I found six more acorns. I felt all around but could find only the six. Now, I found six fresh acorns in that hollow log three times a day for four days, until I had prayed the matter through, making in all ten days that I was in that log. Well it became quite a curiosity to me to know how these six acorns got in there, so on the last day I crawled out of the log, left my shoes at the entrance as a pretense that I was in there, and went some distance to a hollow tree and there concealed myself. At 11:45 there came six large gray squirrels. Each one jumped up on that log and dropped his acorn down a knot hole. I said, "Wonderful, wonderful, my God, here Thou hast been feeding me through these six squirrels;" and I just wept for joy to think that He was so mindful of my needs as to have these dumb animals obey Him. I said, "Elijah isn't the only one who was fed by animals." I crawled back in, oh, so humble. I have often wished that I could live feeling as humble as I have felt at times like this!

Well, I spent four hours more there, and then saw thirteen men and women down a-praying just outside the schoolhouse that I had been put out of ten days before; and they did not know that I was in the neighborhood. So out I got; and as I started down the hill, here came the man who had put me out of his home and the schoolhouse. He was bareheaded, and looked like Indians I had seen in

Dakota, so wild and reckless. I didn't know just what to make of his actions. But I knew that I was in order, so we met, and he shouted, "O brother, pray for us. I am so glad to see you. Pray for us. I have been in hell these ten days."

So we got down there by a log, and if ever you heard a man pray he did. He surely was in earnest. We remained there two hours pleading his case, and he prayed through in good shape, and said, "Now, come into our home again, and we will open the schoolhouse tonight." So we had a blessed time there for three weeks. Many sought and found God, all because I stayed in that hollow log even if I did get hungry. Oh, folks give up too quick; they just do whatever Satan says. Satan drove me out of that man's home and out of the schoolhouse; and if I had done as many would have done — gone off and given it up — where would those souls have landed?

Someone found out by some means that I had been in that log and claimed that the squirrels fed me; and on the way to my lodging apartments he overtook me, and said, "Mr. Bevington, I understand that you have been up on the hill in a hollow log, and that you claim the squirrels fed you acorns there." I said, "How did you learn such stuff as that?" "Well, I got it straight, and I want to know the truth of it." "Well, I would like to know where you heard it." "Never mind that. Answer my question, please." "Well, Sir," I said, "I did and do claim that six squirrels fed me three times a day." He stopped me on the road, and said, "Mr. Bevington do you know that you are a thief?" "No, Sir, I don't know that." "Well, Sir, you are, and I can prove it to you. Those squirrels were putting up their winter food, and you ate it all up." Well, I tell you that staggered me. I said, "Could it be possible?" It looked like it, so I went home considerably worked up about that transaction. The next day, for a better under standing of it, I went up there at 4:00 p. m., and crawled into that log, and could not find an acorn. I kept that up for three days, but no acorn. So that settled the question, and left it clear that God had made caterers out of the squirrels for this special occasion. I felt just like lying low at Jesus' feet, and giving Him a chance, believing that He would work all these things out, as He knows best.

Now we will go back to the subject, Healing. I am pretty well convinced that a large portion of our sickness is on us just because we allow Satan to put it on us. When Wednesday night comes, Satan knows that all he has to do is to just affect us a little. He knows that there are only a few who will not allow him to do so. He deals out his aches and pains in quite large quantities, to those who will allow him in order that they may have some excuse to stay at home.

I tell you God wants us to get to the place where we will believe the promise,

"I am the Lord that healeth thee" (Ex. 15:16) and take a firm stand against Satan's bold attacks — stand for our "Blood-bought right." I have fought him face to face on this line. We produce no effect at arms' length, and he is too great a swordsman for us to tackle him on that line.

I was called to conduct a tabernacle meeting in Ohio. I prayed over it and went, and was met at the train and escorted to a hotel. In the afternoon I was waited on by six of the leaders, four men and two women, saying, "Now, Brother Bevington, when do you want your money, now, or at the close, or in installments? We are prepared to pay you all you want." Well, that was a great surprise to me, as I was not generally troubled with much money. I often had to walk away at the close of my meetings. I said, "What are you in the habit of paying?" "Well that depends on the number of singers the evangelist has, and as you are going to lead in the singing, we will give $80.00." "Whew! $80.00!" I said, "Where do you get this money from?" "Oh, that isn't for you to discuss or think about. You are just to conduct the services, and we are to see to the paying, as we don't want the evangelist to be encumbered with any of the expenses." $80.00, I thought; that was more than I had gotten at times in a whole year. Their liberality set me to thinking, and I said, "Well, how do you get this money?" "O brother, we don't want you to be bothered with that at all. The evangelists that have been here pay no attention to that. You just say whether you want it now or at the close." "Well, brethren, I feel like insisting on knowing how you raise this money." So one of the sisters said, "Well, in the first place we have gate fees. And then we have stands on the grounds, and get lots of money out of these." "What do you sell on these stands?" "Oh, candies, cigars and tobacco, soft drinks, popcorn and so on; lunches and meals, and most anything that we can make money out of." "And you have been conducting this camp on those principles allowing all of that stuff?" "Why, yes. How would you expect to make expenses from any other source?" "Well," I said, "my people, you have the wrong man here. I never could allow such as that." "Why!" they all exclaimed, "you don't set yourself up as so much better than those other noble, grand evangelists that have been running this camp for years, which stands out second to none in the great state of Ohio?" "Well," I said, "I have nothing to do with them. This is a personal matter with me. I cannot do anything here under those conditions."

That was Thursday p. m.. And Friday morning here they came, about twenty of them, and said: "Now see here, Brother Bevington, we have advertised these meetings extensively, at a great expense; and we can't afford to have them fail now; it would forever ruin this noted camp. And we never can meet the expenses unless we do as we have always done, which of course is perfectly right and legitimate as any reasonable person will admit."

They were positive, but I stood my ground. One woman on the committee rose up, and said, "Well, we don't want this crank here, as he would not preach to suit us and would meet with failures on all lines. We will send and get our old standby." (And I knew him to get drunk most every time that he held a meeting and got money.) Then they all rose up, and said, "Well you will have to pay your hotel bill, and walk out of town unless you have plenty of money." I said, "I am a good walker." They felt somewhat roiled up.

So I packed up, went down and paid my bill, and had eighty-four cents left, and thirty-six miles to walk with two heavy suit cases. But I started, walked about a mile and a half, and sat down under a tree, and said, "Now, Lord, I am able and willing to pack these grips the distance, but I feel like asking you to give me a lift." I felt like going back a little farther, some five rods, for a more extended prayer, leaving the grips under this tree by the road. I had a good prayer, a praise service — good rejoicing time — and then feeling pretty well muscled up for the trip, I rose and started down to the tree, and saw a man and a woman sitting in a two-seated wagon, eyeing my grips. As I came to them, I gave them a hearty handshake, and gave them some tracts. The man said, "Isn't your name Bevington, the one that is going to hold the camp here this summer?" "Well, my name is Bevington, but I will not hold the meeting. " Well they both laughed. "What are you doing here?" "Well, I have been having a prayer and praise service up there" (pointing to a log). They both laughed again and said: "We heard you praying up there and thought we would stop and hear what you were praying about."

He said, "We stopped down at the store as we came through, and they were telling what a crank they had engaged to conduct their camp. They were setting you out in great shape. So we drove up here. Wife said, 'I believe that is the noted crank. Let's stop.' So here we are, as we thought we would like to see the fellow that possessed all those remarkable characteristics; but we don't see that you look much different from any of God's children. But where are you going?" "I am going to L—." "Well, we are going through there, so jump in." So that man took me into his home, as he lived at L—; and he and his wife and daughter and a lot more got regenerated and sanctified.

You may say, "Did you not feel led to go to the tabernacle; and, if so, what were you going to do thirty-six miles from there?" Well, Sir, God had His thought for the whole affair. He wanted this man and wife and daughter to work for Him, and He had to take this circuitous route to get them. They went into evangelistic work; but had I compromised, this family probably would never have been saved. I have seen and heard all three of them testify on the platform at the Cincinnati Camp many a time, and they lived blessed lives with God. If God had undertaken to tell me what He wanted, He probably could never have made me understand it; so He sent me to this noted camp, and then on to the road. And then He had the man come along purposely that I could meet him. And instead of having the meeting at this popular tabernacle with eighty dollars staring me in the face, He had me go to Louisville with only a little change, and no visible encouragements.

4

Work at Cleveland and Chattanooga; My Rib Experience

WHEN I WAS IN Ironton, Ohio, in the mission there, I had a baby organ, but could get few to play it on the street. One night a nice looking man came up, and said, "Now, brother if you can get someone to pump the organ, I will play for you every night and start each line in the songs. I am a consumptive, and haven't strength to pump the organ." "Well," I said, "I think I can get pumpers and good ones at that." So we did, and he played for several weeks. But he soon said, "I am getting no better here in this climate that I was so much in hopes would prove helpful to me." (His home was in the south.) He said, "I am thinking of returning south." So in a few weeks he was gone.

The next turn in affairs was for me to go to Cleveland, Ohio, and open another mission. Well, I fought that hard, as I was getting to love those dear poor children at Ironton, that we had been wrestling with for sixteen months. So I gave little attention to this Cleveland impression. But some way the thing would keep coming up about every time I would go to prayer, until it claimed and actually had majority in the petition that I would send up. So I finally had to give up, though through many tears.

I don't know as I ever had such a time giving up a place as Ironton, as I had come up there through many a swamp and quagmire. I finally said, "Well, Lord, send someone to take my place, and I will go." So in two days here came a man and wife to take up the work. Then I pulled out for Cleveland. I had no money, and knew but one person in Cleveland; so the first thing to do was to get still and pray down a mission, as I left everything at Ironton, and I never ran in debt. I went to this home of the only party I knew in Cleveland and was taken in. I put in six days fasting and praying, and on the seventh I was ordered out. I then went to find a room, engaged it, and went to cleaning it up.

A man came along, and said, "A saloon I suppose." "No," I said, "it is to be a Holiness Mission." "Well," he said, as his face brightened up, when are you going to open up?" "Saturday night." And this was Thursday. "Got your seats

I suppose?" "Well, they are not here, but we have them." "Where are they? I have a team, and might haul them for you, as drayage is pretty high here in the city." "Well I will let you know, just give me your name and address." So he did. "Now," he said, "tell me your name and where you are stopping." So I did. And he got on the street car and went out to where I was stopping. The man was at work, so he did not see him but he had a talk with the wife. He said, "What do you know about this man Bevington?" "Well," she said, "I don't know anything about him. He came here about ten days ago a stranger to me; he said he was acquainted with my husband. So we bade him come in until husband came. We assigned him a room, and he went in there and just groaned. I suppose he was praying, and for about a week he went on at an awful rate. He would not eat a mouthful, but after a week he came out and said that he was hungry. That was this morning, and he said that he was going to open a mission by Saturday night."

"I suppose," said the gent, "that he has plenty of money, as he said he had his chairs, and an organ, and song books. But he would not tell me where they are. I could have hauled them this afternoon."

"Well," said the woman, "if he has money, I would like to know where he has kept it. Husband got a little uneasy about his actions, and we pulled his outfit out and went through all his grips and belongings, and all we could find was twenty-nine cents. We went through his pocketbook, and that was all he had." "He told me he had the chairs and the whole outfit," said the gent. "Well," she said, "he sure is a funny fellow. I can't understand him at all."

So here he came in while I was cleaning, and said, "Now my team is idle, and I could draw those chairs and anything you need." I saw at once that I had to explain myself, so I just quoted 1 John 5:14, 15. "Well," he said, "I don't understand you; you said you had those chairs." "Well" I said, "I have them according to that verse, as I prayed through on them and expect to open Saturday night." He said, "No chairs in sight! How can you do that?" "Why, on the Bible." I saw that he was puzzled, so I just left him and resumed my cleaning, and looking for the stuff, as I had put out the sign "Pentecostal Mission," and expected someone to bring the stuff and locate it by the sign.

Satan, as usual, came round, as he is so much interested in our work at times, and began reasoning with me, saying, "Now you are here a stranger, and you should make your wants known; that is the way all missions do. They go out and solicit help. And you will never open here till you do." But I had tried that once before, and had enough of that sort of work. So I just rejected his suggestions. I stood my ground, though facing a great reproach, as the sign was out for the opening Saturday night. Well, the Lord used the brother where I was stopping, so that by Saturday night the mission was seated. I also got fine benches, song books and an organ. We never went after a thing nor told anyone of our wants, just lay before God and let Him attend to all of it; and He did it fine, too.

A brother from the First M. E. Church, of Ironton, came along and said, "Well, what is going to be opened here?" I said, "A Holiness Mission, a work among the poor people." "Well," he said, "if you haven't chairs, I am sure I can furnish you good, nice benches." I said, "If the Lord leads you to do that I will be very glad." So in five hours here came fine benches with good backs; and while they were being unloaded, a sister came along, and said, "What is going on here?" "We are expecting to open a Holiness Mission here Saturday night," I said. "Well, I have an organ I would like to put in here, and will play it, if you want me to." I said, "Send it down." And next morning here it came with forty good song books. And she played the organ. So you see when we get out of the way, God will work; and the reason He doesn't work is that we get in His way. Oh! to tuck ourselves in some corner and get out of the way, then God will work.

Well we won't detain you any longer at Cleveland, but will probably come back again, as many valuable lessons are to be gleaned from our stay at Cleveland. After I had been there quite a while, I received a letter from Sister Allen, of Chattanooga. She was the wife of Brother Allen that played the baby organ for me while at Ironton, by having someone to do the pumping. She said, "By the time you get this letter Mr. Allen will be buried. The doctor just left and said there would be no more need of his calling again, as he bled over a quart and is now just alive. I can scarcely discern any life in him; and what I will do I do not know."

Well, I took the letter into my prayer room, telling the brother that was with me not to allow anyone to come in or bother me. Well, I lay eleven hours to ascertain whether he was still alive. I had much on my hands, hence it took me some time to get still enough to get the voice of God. Then I saw him lying, as a dead man, white as he will ever be, perfectly still, and thought sure he was dead; but was not permitted to break the vision, and lay there five minutes more. And I saw him raise his right hand, and smile. So I said, "Amen, Lord; now for his healing."

But I had to put in nine hours in finding out as to whether the Lord wanted to heal him or not. So there were twenty hours gone on my face. But I was then on the right track, and could proceed intelligently as I had the foundation laid. It took just forty-six hours more to see him a healed man. I then saw him sitting in front of a baby organ pumping and playing with all his might. So I said, "Praise the Lord, that is good enough." After lying in the dark room for fifty-six hours, I could walk out a conqueror in the name of Jesus. So I went out and got something to eat, and sat down to write him, telling him that he was a healed man, and that in two weeks he would be working. I told him the exact time that I saw him at the organ, a healed man.

Well, before he received my letter, he and his wife had written to me. Now, in Cleveland, I saw him get up, sit on the edge of the bed, and rub himself; I saw him feel his arms, pinch himself, get up and look in the mirror, and heard him say, "Yes, this is Allen, sure, no doubt about it. Pretty poor, just nothing but skin and bones, but it's Allen." Now in his letter he detailed every act, just as I saw it several hundred miles from him.

He went out on the porch where his wife was washing. (As she had some washings to do, she had gotten up early, as it gets pretty warm down in Chattanooga.)

She was startled, and said that she had hard work to undergo so sudden a strain, but held her poise. She insisted on his going back to bed, as she expected him to drop dead there on the porch. But he insisted that he was hungry and wanted something to eat. "Why, Mr. Allen, you are sure out of your head; you ought to know that the doctor would not allow you to eat anything, as it would be sure death." "Well," he said, "I am out of the doctor's care now. You must have written to Bevington, didn't you?" "Yes," said she. "Well, he has prayed through for me, and I am healed. Give me a square meal; I dare eat anything." She was still insisting that he was going to drop dead out there on the porch, but he was insisting on something to eat. She said, "I will not be guilty of murder to give you something to eat."

Just then his neighbor was coming in from his barn, going to his breakfast; and Brother Allen called him, and the man was thunderstruck. "But," Allen said, "I am as hungry as a bear, and wife won't give me anything. You tell your wife to bring me over a good big breakfast." Well he went in, and said, "Wife, just come here and see a sight. Allen is up and out on the porch a-begging for something to eat." So out she rushed only to see him as she had been told, and he begged her to give him something to eat. "I am not going to drop dead just now, I am healed," and he went to pounding himself. Then the neighbor ventured with a soft boiled egg, and he swallowed that down and called for more. As he still retained his equilibrium, and did not fall over dead, she ventured again, until he had eaten a strong man's meal. Well, in two weeks he went to work just as I had told him. That was in the spring.

I remained at Cleveland all summer, and in the fall would get inklings that I must go to Chattanooga. Well, I just thought 'twas because Brother Allen lived there, and I would not give it much attention. But the thing kept growing on my hands, until it got to be a monster, and soon had me under control. Chattanooga seemed to be rather a large dose for my limited faith, so as a more rapid transit out, I was switched off for Cincinnati. Well, that did not seem so hard a problem. I had become attached to Cleveland and did not want to leave there, so I did not listen to the Cincinnati call. It seemed to be calling loud, and incessant; so finally I said, "Lord, if thou wilt send someone to take my place, I will go," though I could not for the life of me see what for, as I was getting under good headway there. But in three days here came a man and wife. As soon as she saw me, she burst out in a laugh, and said, "That's the man; he's the one." And the husband said, "Yes he is. This is the place." Well, though I had been praying for someone to take my place, yet I was not on guard, and was wondering what kind of folks they were. I could see no trace of former acquaintance.

They soon cleared up my confused state by telling me what they had seen two nights before at Rochester, N. Y. I readily assented to their familiarity, and said, "Well, you must be the people who are to take my place." So I went into my room, fell across the bed, and broke out in tears and sobs, as I was not entirely weaned from that work. I lay there some time bathed in tears. Finally I said, "Oh, God I cannot doubt these people coming direct from Thee but, O Father, these tears, these moans! O God, I can't leave in this condition. If it is really true that you want me to leave, relieve me from this work, remove the burden." Soon the tears were all wiped away; the clouds lifted, and the sunlight broke in on me with such a beautiful mellowness that soon all desire to remain there was gone.

Well, now, that was settled, but I had no money to go on. I had a baby organ with the other belongings, and while in that room praying about my railroad fare to Cincinnati, a knock was heard. I opened the door, and there stood a Salvation Army sister who had helped me much in my work. She said, "Brother Bevington, we are informed that you are leaving us. Now these people that have come to take your place have a baby organ and won't need yours, and I want to buy it." "Well," I said, "I never did such a thing. (I had opened up fourteen missions, equipping them fully, but never took anything away with me nor sold anything.) Just then the dear brethren stepped in the door, and said,

"Well, we won't need the organ, and we both feel that you need the money; so you sell it at once." The sister asked me what 'twas worth, what I had paid for it. "Well," I said, "I paid $15.00 for it, and have used it four months. I reckon it is worth $10.00." "Yes," she said, "it is cheap at $12.00, I will give you $12.00 for it;" and she just laid the $12.00 down, and took the organ.

Well I needed some clothes. I had no clergy rates then, so had full fare to pay, which was $8.00. I bought $3.00 worth of clothing, which left $1.20 (I had 20 cents before).

Well I started. I landed in Cincinnati, and there got on a street car and went down to Constance. I stayed all night, and came back in the morning. I was running round town doing some business and while on Fourth Street was passing a large front window. As I looked in, I saw a large bulletin board with the words, "Your Last Chance." Well I just passed on, but that "Last Chance" kept nagging at me, and I actually had to return, though I saw no sense in that as I was in a hurry. But I minded the impression, and went back, and looked in the window again. Yes, there it was. But what did it mean? So I opened the door, and saw at once that I was in a railroad office. I said, "Sir, what does that mean," pointing to the board. "Why, Sir, it means just what it says." "Well, what is it for?" "Why, Sir, haven't you heard of the great reduction in the excursions to Chattanooga?" "No, I haven't." "Well," he said, "it is the great reduction in the excursions and this is the last chance, the last day." "What time does the last train leave?" "At nine this evening." Well, I started out, but thought that I had not ascertained the price, and so returned. "What is the cost?" I asked, "Why, Sir, round trip $3.75, clear to Chattanooga and back." I went out and up the street after my needs, not thinking anything more about Chattanooga, or the cheap fare, as I did not have a dollar.

But Chattanooga kept ringing in my ears, until I had to turn from my pursuit and start back — Chattanooga was all that I could hear. I got down near to where we took the street car for Constance, and the voice said, oh, so plain and positive, "Will you or will you not go to Chattanooga"? Well I was startled, but said, "Why, yes, Lord I will go — but!" (Yes there it is again that but.) Oh, how many have been stranded on this little word.

Well I got on the street car, to go down after my grips, somewhat dazed, but determined to mind God. I got a lunch and struck down for the depot. I had only thirty minutes, but I was sailing down minding God anyway. I saw a man coming towards me eyeing me closely, real scrutinously, and I said, "Well, he would not get much money if he should waylay me." But as I came nearer, he was smiling. When he met me he just threw his arms around me, and said, "Oh, this is Brother Bevington." I dropped my grips, and said, "Yes, but I am in a hurry; I want to make a train in twenty minutes." So he grabbed up the grips for me and we started down. "Now," I said, "who are you?" He laughed and told me, and then I remembered him. As we came to the depot, he said, "You prayed for my wife four years ago, and Jesus healed her. Then she said, "Now we won't have no more doctor bills, so let's give Brother Bevington our doctor's money. So in one year they had $5.00 for me, and he had packed it round for three years waiting to see me. God had him there from the country purposely to meet me. So you see that God understands His business, if we will let Him have His way. Oh, it pays, it pays to let God work; and again the cry comes up, O God, will we ever learn? Will we ever learn?

So we got to the train just in time for me to be shoved on the last coach. I sat down and said, "Now, Lord, here I am at your command; now what are you going to do with me?"

I did not feel that I ought to go out to Brother Allen's, as it was a long ways out, and they were very poor, with a family. Well as was often the case when I questioned God, I got the answer, "What is that to thee, follow thou me." I said, "All right, Lord, shall I pack those two large grips?" I was impressed to get them checked. This cost twenty cents, which left me, after getting my dinner, eighty cents. And there I was among strangers. Well I was impressed to go on somewhere, and was walking by a high board fence, and soon noticed a sign: "At 2:30 p. m, Sunday — every Sunday." I stopped, looked around and saw nothing that would indicate anything of that sort. So was walking along slowly, wondering what that meant, when I heard a call. Looking back, there I saw a colored man, as black as could be. There was a shine on his face, that assured me that he was a real child of God. He was coming toward me with a great big smile covering his whole face.

He said, "Laws, bless you man! You's de man; you's de man!" Well I hardly knew what to conclude. Was he a fresh escape from the asylum, or what? So I said, "Well what about it?" "You's de very man I's been a looking fo'. You's goin' ter preach in the mission down here on de corner. De man what's dere is done and broke down. And I wuz down fo' to see him three weeks ago, and he done tells me all about how he's no account and axes me ter pray fo' a man ter come and give him a lift. So I comes inter my home, gets down, and lays the case afo' de Lord, and He showed me you just as you is now, 'cept dar is two big suit cases, one black and a yaller one. Now, Broder, whar am dem two grips?"

"Well," I said, "I guess you have got the thing pretty straight." "Oh, I know that, Sah, yes Sah. I get 'em straight." So he showed me where to go. "As you is going jes gib me your two checks, and I will bring dem to you in my cart." So I did. As we were walking along another man called to us, and said, "I know you'se de man what Joe done tells me about. Jes come in my house and get a drink of cool water." So I turned in and got a good cool refreshing drink. "Now," he said, "let's have prayer." Well that suited me, so down we got, and he called on me to pray, and I don't believe I ever had freer access to the throne in my life than there in that colored home. As I left, he gave me a dollar bill. Then he showed me the mission I was to preach in. So down I went, and the man of the mission was sitting at the window on the second floor, where he could see down the road. He saw me and knew from the description Joe had given him of me, about three weeks before. Down he came, and gave me a hearty welcome, and showed me his young wife. (He was about forty and she twenty.)

I began preaching that night. This mission was run by the different churches, the M. E. one night, the Baptist another, and so on, each coming in once a week. There were five meetings a week. Well, I soon saw that some of these meeting-house folks were not taking to my way of preaching very well. The M. E. folks took me all right. On the second night three fell at the altar — that was the M. E. night. We had a good time.

On the fourth night was the meeting for the other church. Well, as I was preaching in came a drunkard; and, as had been their custom, he was signaled out. But he did not seem inclined to go out. So the head man of the church said to the leader, "Put him out!" He started, but I said, "Hold on there, don't put that man out." But the boss motioned him to obey orders. So I jumped over the rail, and said, "Please don't put that man out; Jesus came to save just such poor creatures as he." "Well", he said, "you don't know that man; he is the lowest down creature in town. He must go out!" I said, "Oh, no; please don't." But he said, "Put him out! " I sprang between the leader and the drunkard, and insisted on his remaining. But oh, what a terrible odor came from him! Well the boss and all his crowd left — taking out about fifty.

Then the leader said, "Brother Bevington, I know what Jesus came for. But we have been dealing with this man for ten years, and actually there is no hope for him." I said, "My dear brother, you will never make me believe that. Jesus can and will if we give him a chance." "Well," he said, "you and him for it. I will put out all the lights but one up by the pulpit, and you and him for it. I can't stand the odor." And he left. He went up the stairs but could not sleep.

I took the man up to the front of the platform and got hold of God for him. He did right well till about 2:00 a. m., and then got boisterous. He said that he was burning up, must have some whisky. He said, "You get me a pint, and I will get all right. I would like to be a Christian, but am in hell now." Well, I plead with him, but about three o'clock he was getting the best of me. He was much stronger than I, and was backing me toward the door in spite of all that I could do. By four we were within eight feet of the door, and I was getting exhausted and saw that something must be done.

I was impressed to call the man upstairs, but the Spirit rebuked me, and I held my peace and began to intercede at the throne more intensely. I soon just let go of him, and threw up both hands, and cried out, "O God, what did you send this man in here for? What did you send me here for? O God, come, come, come! " And at the third "come," the man fell prostrate on the floor. He actually crawled around under the chairs just like a snake and 'twas then that we plead to have the demon cast out. I said, "O God, cast him out, cast him out!" And in thirty minutes the man was as quiet as a lamb.

He got up and rubbed himself, and said, "Well is this Tom? I have got religion." I said, "You may have religion, but you have no salvation as yet." "Oh, I know better, why I have religion." I said, "Come on up to the altar and get saved." "Oh, I am saved right now." "No, you are not saved; you just had that whisky demon cast out. Now you are a candidate for forgiveness." Well he would have it that he was already saved. But finally at five-thirty we got him at the altar and he got down and prayed earnestly. Soon he saw that he needed salvation and at seven a. m. he prayed through, struck bottom, and of all the capering you ever saw, he did it there.

The woman came down and she was delighted. She called her husband, and down he came, and both seemed satisfied that Tom was really a saved man. Well I was somewhat worn after wrestling all night with that ferocious man, and wanted some rest. But I said to the leader, "Now you have some clothes to give out; so you get me a tub and a broom and a bar of soap, and a scrubbing brush. And you bring down some good clothing, and I will take him out there in the back yard and scrub him up. His wife sanctioned the suggestion, and brought me down some asafetida as a preventive; so I tied some on and went for him. I used up three tubs of water and a bar of soap, and succeeded in getting him fairly clean. They furnished some good clothing and soon we had him looking entirely different. He was a well educated man, but whiskey had floored him. But God gathered up the fragments and got them in their places and polished them up so that he was in pretty good shape by the time we were through with him. "Now," he said, "I want you to go with me down to my cousin's. I used to be his foreman in his lumber-yard, but he hasn't allowed me around for years." So we went down about 11:30, and the cousin was there waiting for dinner. Tom had me stand in front; so I knocked at the door and we were invited in. The cousin looked at me and then at Tom and saw that we were strangers. He seemed confused as we did not make our business known. After some suspense I said, "Mister, did you ever see that man?" At that Tom smiled. The cousin said, "This can't be Tom, can it?" And Tom sprang up, and said, "Yes it is; I am a new man, Bill. Jesus has saved me and this preacher has cleaned me up, and the mission man gave me this nice suit. Bill, I want to go to work again. I will join the M. E. Church with you, if they will take me in." We were then invited in to dinner at 12:30, and I tell you I enjoyed it.

After dinner Tom took me outside, and said, "Now Brother Bevington, Jesus has sure cleaned me up on the inside, and you on the outside. Now I want you to go with me to see my wife." "Have you a wife?" "Yes, I have or did have; I haven't seen her for eleven years. They say that she is worse than I was. She is down on Pokey Row with the very poorest, onerous, colored people that there are in Tennessee."

So we went down. The leader saw us coming, so came down to see if we had our dinner, and I told him our mission. He took me upstairs, leaving Tom down. He said, "Brother Bevington, I think I can get a fair reconciliation with the managers of the mission here, now that Tom is so different. But whatever you do or don't do, please don't get near that woman. It is unmistakably evident that God has undertaken for Tom, but that woman is a thousand leagues lower than Tom was or ever could have been. And if you undertake to have anything to do with her, it will kill all the prospects that now seem quite favorable for a reconciliation and for getting them all back again. But any movement toward getting that woman will kill all that has been done and will throw me out of this place and my health is not sufficient for me to make a living elsewhere."

His dear wife had listened to it all, and she came and set down a nice cold glass of lemonade. She said, "Husband, I am young and strong, and am willing to take in washing to make our living. I believe that Brother Bevington is on the right track, and that he knows his God, better than either one of us. If God could save Tom, He surely can save Lizz, as you call her. I say let Brother Bevington alone; keep your hands off. Let him and God and Tom do their best; and if it comes to getting out of here, I will work our way through." Well, I said, "Amen!" and took her by the hand, and said, " God bless your dear good heart." I just wept for joy, and admired her for her noble stand. The husband said, "All right," and he kissed his wife saying, "You are the better of us two."

I went out and said, "Come on, Tom," and we went down the street into the poorer vicinity, and soon turned up an alley, and of all the poverty and ignorance and filth I had ever been in, this beat it all. But I said, "We have started and we will trust God." I still had the asafetida on, but said, "I don't know as Jesus needs any help," so I took it off and threw it down. Tom said, "You had better keep it on; we are not there yet, and it's much worse where she is." But we went on holding our handkerchiefs over our nostrils.

Finally we got there. Now a greater obstacle was in our way, that was to locate her; as she, we supposed, had changed her name many a time, and we did not know her by the name she was going by. But we ventured in a yard and began to make inquiries. We found no one that would interest themselves in what we were after; they all wanted tobacco, or whisky, or opium, or beer. We saw a stairway going up to the roof of a shanty, so we climbed that and got up some twelve feet above the filth. We thought that there we might escape some of the awful stench and we began to call on God for information. Soon a big black Negro, oh so dirty, came out and saw us kneeling there. He wanted to know what we were doing there. We told him. He said, "I know who you are after; I will bring her out."

Well, in all our mission work at Cincinnati, St. Louis, Louisville, and Cleveland, we never had looked on such a vile, hopeless-looking case as this one. We told her what her name had been fifteen years ago. She remembered it and acknowledged it. "Oh," we thought, "could Jesus do anything for such a creature?" We talked to her and finally we called Tom in and presented him to her. She said, "Is that Tom?" and she gave a low brutish glance at him. Well, he told her what God had done for him and said that he believed He would do as much for her. But she just swore one oath after another and was smoking an old pipe the odor of which was almost unbearable. But Tom kept telling her of Jesus. Well, I was getting faint and almost wished for that asafetida. I crawled down that filthy ladder, and said, "We will come back tomorrow at 10:00 a. m. Make up your mind that Jesus can do as much for you as he has done for Tom, and that you can live a respectable life again."

We hurried out of that malaria; Tom went to his cousin's and I to the mission where I went to bed as I was about done up. It was 5: 30 p. m. Well I slept fine, and woke up at six o'clock the next morning I went down and got a nice breakfast, and related our trip. The young wife was interested and gathered up a lot of her clothes for Tom's wife, saying, "They are going to get her." The husband tried to persuade us not to bring her there to the mission. "Well," the wife said, "we will take her down to Uncle Ben's coal house, and fight the thing through there." Her uncle Ben was a saved man.

Well by nine o'clock here came Tom, full of hope and faith for the poor emaciated wife. So we went down and sure enough there she was away out at the head of the first alley a-waiting for us with a bundle of filthy rags to wear. We told her to drop them. The first thing to do was to get her cleaned up as Tom had been. We took her to the mission, and Tom took her into the same yard where he got his cleaning up. He used five tubs of water and two bars of soap, and got her pretty clean. Then nice clothes were put on her. The leader of the mission was not able to go, but the wife went with us and we took her to Uncle Ben's coal house, which was nice and clean.

Well I thought I had a terrible time with Tom, but it was nothing to what we went through with that wild, unreasonable woman. We wrestled there with her eighty-four hours, day and night. We had to have help; she had Tom all bruised up, and I did not escape her fury. She would grab me and use me quite roughly, until Tom would extricate me. She tore my clothes about to pieces, but we held her in, and fed her strong coffee and other food until the eighty-fifth hour, when she was knocked down by the power of God. She lay on her back cursing God and man. Froth foamed from her mouth, but she was powerless, perfectly helpless, and exhausted. Near the ninety-sixth hour, she got still and lay perfectly quiet. About 1:30 she raised her hands, and wept, and asked us to help her up. Her clothes were in shreds and so were Tom's. We had to get both of them clothes before they could go on the street. But we got the clothes and took her down to Tom's cousin. And next morning she prayed through most gloriously. She did not caper like Tom did, but just walked the floor with her right hand up, weeping and laughing, and all that she said was, "Oh, glory! " She kept that up for two hours, and then we all went to dinner at Tom's cousin's.

The next day the cousin fitted them up a three-room cottage with all new furniture. He also gave them new clothes. He put them in there and gave Tom his old job back again. Well, now, you see that God was in the real saving business. That was what Jesus came for, and He did a good job at it, too. I saw Tom and his wife three times at the Cincinnati Camp and they gave their testimonies on the platform — a blessedly saved and sanctified couple. We insisted on their getting the Holy Ghost, and they both did in their new home. Well that created quite a stir among the professors, as many knew of them, if they were not personally acquainted with them.

I would like to insert a few things here relative to the mission, as the managers had given orders for the leader to pack up his belongings and go. He and his wife had both stood by me, and when Tom was prayed through (that was on Friday) it was noised around. There was no meeting Saturday night, but I preached Sunday morning, afternoon and night (that was the M. E. Church night) and twenty fell at the altar and several prayed through. Well, they allowed him to remain, and then I went after him to get the Holy Ghost. He was somewhat scary of that, but God got hold of him; and in a day or two he was seeking in good shape. Then the wife came, seeking the same blessing. With these two and Tom and his wife, we had a busy time for about a week. But glory to God, the Lord got them all through!

I well remember that during the time the leader was seeking the Holy Ghost, several came down to break up all those proceedings and ordered us all out; and out we went. They discharged the leader, but he had gone so far in this that he just could not turn back, but went through. He had two bedrooms of his own furniture which he had held for a few days. But when the wife got through, there was a reconciliation made, and they were permitted to remain.

Some of the meeting-house folks pulled out, but the M. E. folks stood by him. But I was not allowed to preach any more, or they all thought it best not to, so I stepped down and out quietly. They gave me their spare room and my meals until I could get entertainment elsewhere. I have forgotten to mention the fact that I had the privilege of marrying Tom and his wife over again before they set up housekeeping. Neither of them went back into sin. They had three sweet children with them at the Cincinnati Camp, the last time I saw them. I now want to take you back to Cleveland. You remember I said I saw Brother Allen sitting at the organ, a-playing with his mouth stretched, a-singing with all his might! Well when I answered their letter telling them of what I saw there, I then told them that I saw him at the organ pumping and singing, and that I expected some day to see him just that way.

Well, the first Sunday I was at the mission at Chattanooga, we had no morning service. I was up in my room sitting by the window, where I could see the people passing to and fro, on the street. And as I sat there praying and reading the Word and meditating, I looked out, and saw a large man coming down the street, a-singing. He had a baby organ in one hand a-swinging it as I would a small grip. I looked closely at him, and said, "Well, I declare, believe that is Brother Allen;" and then he looked and I called. He dropped the organ, and began jumping and clapping his hands, and I knew 'twas he. I ran down to meet him. I had not seen him, or written him that I was there and at the mission.

Well he picked up the organ as if it were a peck of potatoes, and laughed, and said, "Now, Brother Bevington, I hold meetings every Sunday in the jail; and last Sunday I told them that you were here and that I was going to bring you out. So I want you to go out with me." Well I was delighted to go, and we had a rousing time. When I got there, I heard the organ going in the hall, and I looked around and there he sat just as I saw him in Cleveland, about eight or ten months before. I just threw my hat and gave an Indian whoop, and stepped up and told him that was just what I had seen in Cleveland. You see God doesn't give us visions on uncertainties. So we had a blessed time and I went out the next Sunday, and five claimed to pray through. Well, by this time we were out of the mission.

There was a business men's prayer meeting in a first floor room which they rented for this purpose. They ate their dinner there, and then had a prayer service for thirty minutes. Often there would be fifty or sixty out, and it was beautiful. They would read a short lesson, and give requests for prayer. Then they would all get down and pray, sometimes everyone was praying. The leader of the mission took me there. So I went the next Monday after Brother Allen's first visit. The leader introduced me and told of Tom and Lizz, as they were known.

Well, next day they gave me the Bible, and I read Romans 4:14-25, especially emphasizing the verses which tell of Abraham. They all seemed delighted, and invited me back to read another lesson. I went back and read and talked on faith and obedience. We could have only twelve minutes to read and talk. They had given in their requests for prayer, but the man who had the management of this group told about a long standing trouble he had. He had related it to others often but said that he wanted me to hear it. Well, when he got through, I talked ten minutes. Then I said, "Dear brother, I am sure Jesus can heal you, and I believe He wants to." "I wish He did," was the reply. He said that he had not walked to his office for thirteen years, and had to hire everything done in his office. He kept two girls and a doctor all the time, and he had not slept a natural sleep for ten years. We felt that we should pray for his body, so we got down and got real still before God; and more and more our faith took hold for him .

I laid my hands on him, and got blessed and praised God for it. Then I said, "Brother, you are a healed man." Our time was up, so we arose from our knees. I said, "Didn't you feel the touch of Jesus?" "Well," he said meekly, "Brother, I am sorry, but I will have to tell the truth. I have felt no change whatever." "Well," I said, "you are a healed man, and you will sleep tonight as good as you ever did, and that without remedies. And that isn't all; you will walk to your office tomorrow morning." I noticed when I said this, that there was a general exchange of looks all around, and some jeers were visible; but they all walked quietly out. They were in the habit of having a handshake every day at the close; but not a handshake that day. All went out with bowed heads; no one shook hands with me, and I returned to my room.

Now listen what Satan gave me. He said, "You go too far down here among these Southerners. You are not up North. These people won't take a strong diet as you gave them today; you go too far." Well, I had to go on my knees to ascertain as to the source of this, and soon felt convinced it was of Satan. I went back next day, but was a little late, and had to take a seat in the rear. They had had their song and the manager got up and read a short message. Then he called for requests, and several were given. Satan said, "Now you see it is just as I told you. You went too far yesterday, as he isn't healed, for if he was he would have said so. You see he never mentioned a thing about the case. If you hadn't brought up the walk to the office and that he would sleep like a baby, why you would have been all right. But you see you went entirely too far."

I said, "You are a liar, Sir, I never did; and if it were to do over again, I would go farther." There was no visible sign that my prayer was answered or my assertions carried out. We went to prayer and several prayed. Then he closed with prayer, but never said a word about his being healed. So Satan was there to remind me that I should learn discretion and common sense in my dealing with Southerners.

I said, "He is a healed man." "Well, it looks like you haven't as much sense as I gave you credit for, as anyone knows that if he had been healed, he would have been the first to tell it." Then we had it there in that back seat. But I stuck to it that the man was healed. Well we got up, and the leader was supposed to have five minutes for closing remarks; When he rose, I said, "Now, Lord, make him confess it; break him up." He undertook to talk and his lips began to quiver.

I saw that he was determined to be a coward, so I just pressed my claim all the heavier. He soon began to cry, and said, "Brethren, I have a confession to make." Raising his right hand and pointing to me he said, "That man's prayers were answered last night. This morning I can't do otherwise than admit that I am a healed man. Last night I never thought about my medicine till I was almost asleep. Then I thought that I would get up, but I was oh, so sleepy, which was something entirely new to me. Then I was reminded of what the brother had said, that I would sleep well and that without remedies. So I just dropped off to sleep, and the first thing I knew wife came in saying, 'Well, what is the matter with you this morning that you are not up? Here breakfast is ready and waiting. You will not get the first car now'." Well he got up realizing that he had slept, just I had said he would. He got out just in time to see the car speeding away and 'twould be an hour before another car.

And right here let me mention another thing that may help someone. When I made the assertion that he would walk to his office, I had no idea that he lived so far from it. I was under the inspiration of the Spirit and was not consulting even facts — just said what the Spirit gave me. Had I known that he lived near Missionary Ridge and would have over three miles to walk, the Spirit no doubt would have had trouble in getting me to make that assertion; but as I was ignorant of the distance, He could work through me; so it isn't always best to be too wise.

When he saw that the car was gone, he said, "Well, I feel so well, I guess I will walk down the street a ways." He did not think then of what I had told him, that he was going to walk to his office. Well he just kept a-going slowly and was gaining strength every square, and several times said, "Well, I must be healed, I feel so well." And he said, "I just kept on a-walking. I was all the time a-speeding up quite a bit, and got within five blocks of the office when I looked back and here came the car. I thought I would get on, but soon was reminded of what the Brother said. So I just walked in. One of the girls did not come to work, and I took her place and have been working all day thus far. I 'phoned her that she might stay home all day. And brethren," he said, with both hands lifted. "I am without a doubt a healed man."

The glory fell, and oh, what a time we had! They tore loose from all conventionalities and programs, time, and everything else and it was after two o'clock when we left the room, and they were supposed to leave four minutes before one. I tell you they all shook hands with me that day. They all went out a-singing, some shouting and some dancing, and all had their heads up. So we need to learn to take a stand and then to stand. Find out where we are and stay there. Oh! how Satan tried to get me to back down. And it surely looked as though I would have to; but I knew God, and He had satisfied me the day before that I had not gone too far.

I will now proceed to tell you about my three broken ribs. As I stated before I was out of the mission. So a dear brother came to me and said, "Now I have been going out in the suburbs for several years holding some services. I have a Sunday School out there, and I believe the Lord would be pleased to have you go out. I will take you out tomorrow night; that is our regular night out there." So we went. He preached to them in a home, and kept it up for several nights. Four were saved and two sanctified and three healed. Soon the homes would not hold the people. So three sisters came and said, "We have rented a storeroom near here, and will fit it up for you to hold meetings in." I said, "All right," and turned in to help them. We had the seats and the stove, as it was in the fall of the year and somewhat chilly. On the second day I was polishing the stovepipe; was standing on a cloth-bottomed chair, and not wishing to soil the cloth I stood on the outer edges of said chair. I was rubbing quite hard, and stretching and reaching just about as high as I could, when the chair turned and I fell, striking my side on the chair, mashing the chair to pieces.

I lay there for some time, don't know just how long, but when I came to, that building was a-spinning at a tremendous rate, and I was so sick. I undertook to get up but saw that I could not, so fell back on the floor and lay there trying to pray. I was in such misery that I just could not do much at praying. Finally I got some better and by the aid of three chairs got up on my feet. But, oh, my side! What in the world could be the matter with it? I found that by putting my hand on my side and pressing quite hard that it was easier.

Well I preached that night, but had to keep my hand pressing hard on my side. I never told anyone how the chair got mashed. The next morning I was in a fair way for a pull sure, as the only way I could get any rest was to take the machine cover and put it at my side, and lay the sheet over me. By having the sheet rest on the box, this kept the weight off my side. I would pray and get relief and drop to sleep. But at any move I would waken. It felt as though a thousand needles were running in on that side.

Well Brother Allen heard of my fall and came to see me the first day. He worked only five blocks from where I was stopping. So he got his meals down there and just stayed with me. He took my bed as I could not lie on a bed; I lay on the floor, and as

I had two rooms given to me for use, I occupied the front room and Brother Allen the bedroom at nights. He went to his work each morning.

"Well," he said, "Brother Bevington, I know that God healed me, but this seems to be a different case. There is surely something wrong with your ribs, you must have a doctor." I said, "No doctor for me." But the next day, the fourth day, I seemed to be impressed to go and see a doctor. "Why," I said, "Lord, I don't want any doctor, as Thou art my healer." I stuck it out another day and was still strongly impressed to go and see a doctor. So I went. This was the sixth day, and I had not had anything to eat during all this time; I didn't want anything.

Women would come with eatables, but I could not eat anything, could not swallow even water without being thrown into a paroxysm of pain. I got up with the aid of two chairs, and got my hand on my side. I had a belt made to go around me, and would crowd cotton batting in under the belt as it seemed to give relief. Well I got a stick for a cane and ventured out in search of a doctor. After hobbling three blocks, I saw a sign, and as the sitting room opened onto the sidewalk, I had not much trouble in getting in. I stood by the door, and soon the doctor came out and offered me a seat. I did not want to take it as I knew I would have a time in getting up, so I stood there. But southern hospitality would not permit him to endure my standing there, and I had to stand a-leaning some, so he came out and insisted that I sit down. So I did. But, oh, how I did suffer there for about forty minutes, awaiting my turn! But it came, and he stepped out and motioned for me to come in. "Well," I said, "Doctor, I don't think I can get up alone." At that three men were at my side, ready to assist me. They got me up and over to a settee.

"Well," said the doctor, "you seem to be somewhat crippled up." I said, "I have been having a little trouble with my left side here." So he laid his hand on it and I, not prepared for the act, halloed, and came near going down. I would have, no doubt, had not the men held me up. "Well," the doctor said, "there must be something quite serious." Then he laid me down on the settee, and put his hand on my side. I said, "You can examine it now; I was not prepared before." He said, "I will give you a sleeper." I said, "No, doctor, nothing of the kind, please. You just go ahead and make your examination." He felt my side awhile and said, "You are not able to undergo such an examination as will be necessary. Let me give you a sleeper." But I objected. He said, "Well, what is the matter anyway? Some mule kick you?" I said, "No." I didn't want to tell him; I wanted him to find out.

So he said, "What is your business?" I said, "I am a Holiness evangelist." "Do you live here?" "No, I am from Kentucky." "Oh ! you are from the north. Were you holding meetings here?" "I have some, yes." "Where abouts?" "Well, I first started in the Wilcox Mission." And he stopped and looked at me critically, and said, "Are you the man from the north that saved old Tom and Lizz?" I said, "No; I never saved anyone." "Well," he said, "I had it pretty straight from a friend of mine that passes here every morning going to his work. What is your name?" I told him. He repeated it, "I tell you that sounds like the name. You must be the one." "No, it is a mistake." "Well now, I got this pretty straight. Then it was in the papers. That sounds like the name. Didn't you hold a meeting in the Wilcox Mission?" "Yes." "Well, you are the man." I then explained to him that it was Jesus that saved them. "Oh, well I know. Well, well, and you are the party that fasted and prayed and stuck to them till you got them actually saved and remarried. Both, they tell me, are doing well." "I guess they are," I said.

"Well how much money have you? I would like to put the Xray on you." I knew that in Cincinnati they charged $10.00 for that, so I said, "I am not able for an Xray." But at the same time I felt that was just what God wanted me to come there for. "Well," he said, "this Xray is not mine. I have to pay one dollar for every time I use it. So if you have a dollar I will use it." Well I knew I did not have a dollar, but I bowed my head and soon said, "I tell you what I will do. I have a friend that will give you a dollar. So if you will, you may turn it on." So he slipped in a silver dollar, and blindfolded me. He soon jerked off the bandage from my eyes, and said, "My good man, you are all torn to pieces." "Oh, I reckon not." "Well you are. I don't see how you have lived these six days in this condition. Sir, your first rib is separated three-fourths of an inch, the second, half, and the third one about a quarter. What has caused you so much pain is, there is a sliver torn from your first rib, just the size of a horse shoe nail — looks like a large horse shoe nail. And that lies right across your ribs. "I can't do anything for you," he said, "but I have a cousin at Nashville who has charge of the largest, finest hospital in Tennessee. He and I were talking over the phone the other day about Tom and Lizz. He wants to see that northern fellow. Now I am sure that I can get you in there real cheap. Ordinarily it would cost you five hundred dollars, taking about seven months. But tomorrow I will see what can be done for you."

Well, I went back saying, "Five hundred dollars and seven months." I said, "Lord, Thou canst beat that," and went into the room, and resumed my position

4: CLEVELAND AND CHATTANOOGA; RIB EXPERIENCE 69

on the floor, and at every move suffered tremendously. But I would soon get victory. The floor seemed to be getting harder and harder at each move. Well, night came and with it Brother Allen. I told him what I had done, and where I had been, and he said. "Well, what doctor did you go to?" I told him. "Why," he said, "that is a dear friend of mine, a saved man. He is the one that bought the baby organ for me to play at the jail and on the street. He does all the doctoring at the foundry where I work. Everybody recognizes him as a Christian. He always gets down and prays at the foundry before examining patients. I will see him as I pass by his office as I go to work." So the next morning he gave the doctor the dollar. And that dear doctor worked faithfully all day. To a casual observer he did a tremendous day's work for me.

That night when Brother Allen came in, he was all perspiring; he had run those three blocks so eager to break the news of the wonderful developments of the day, through the insistent efforts of the dear doctor. He said, "I just stopped in at the office to see what the doctor had done. All things are ready, all planned out. They will have a fine stretcher here with four men, at nine o'clock in the morning. They will bear you to the depot, where a special has been chartered for you, to take you to Nashville; where you will be cared for, as but few are, at the remarkably low price of just what the material for the artificial ribs will cost. This will not exceed eighty dollars. All the work and care and board will be given you; hence you will be having donated to you nearly seven hundred dollars. And," he continued, "I am so glad. Oh, the doctor is a dear man; I just love him more than ever for all these favors granted you."

"Well, Brother Allen," I said, "that is a great favor. I surely do feel thankful to the doctor for what he has done; but, Brother Allen, I can't go to a hospital." "What!" he said, "You won't go to the hospital?" "No," I said, "I can't do that." "But Brother Bevington, you must remember that you are not in the north now. You are here in the south, where gangrene springs up in all cases such as you have, and spreads rapidly, inoculating the whole city, and the Board of Health will have to interfere. You will be sent to the pesthouse. And Brother, I never can endure to see you sent to that place." I said, "Brother Allen, didn't the Lord heal you down here in this very city?" "Yes, but yours is altogether different. In the first place you are older than I; and then I had no ailments that would produce gangrene." "Well," I said, "is God circumscribed to conditions or places? Is God's power conditional? Have these earthly matters got to be analyzed before God can operate?"

"Oh, well, Brother Bevington, you must exercise judgment. You must remember that you are not dealing with northerners now. It is hot-headed southerners that you are, and will be, dealing with and that right soon too." I said, "Brother Allen, according to that God's power is limited to places and people. Now Brother Allen, possibly you may believe that, but you will never make Bevington believe it. No, never, my dear man! I can't go to the hospital. could not turn my back on my Doctor. No, never! He has done too much for me."

He said, "But you will inoculate the whole city, which they would not have done for millions of dollars. You will have all the officers in town after you, and the pesthouse is where you will land. Then you ought to know what will be the result of that move. No one will be to blame but you." Next morning he went to work, and met the doctor, who said, "Well, I suppose Brother Bevington was delighted with what has been done for him." "Well doc, that fellow is a crank sure." "Why?" "Well, he doesn't want to go to the hospital. He has it in his head that the Lord is going to heal him." "Nonsense," said the doctor. "Well," said Brother Allen, "he has said positively that he will not go." "And, then, do I understand that he has turned down all that I have done for him?" "Yes, I am sorry to say he has." "Well, well!" And off he went. His southern blood played to the tune of the "old man". So about ten o'clock, here came three officers, and I tell you they raked me over the coals quite briskly. They gave me twenty-four hours to further consider my decision, leaving me well informed as to the pesthouse. Well the time limit would bring it up to about eleven o'clock the next morning. I went to praying as best I could.

The next day here they came at 11:30, ready to take me to the pesthouse. But I prevailed on them to give me till seven the next morning. They had a doctor with them, and he said, "Gentlemen, there isn't the least sign of gangrene — a remarkable exception. And there is no inflammation, strange as it seems. It is a clean wound." Brother Allen came in feeling desperate over my obstinacy, especially as I could not sit up nor lie only in that one position.

I said, "Now Brother Allen, just keep quiet." I was getting somewhat weak, and nervous. I had never been troubled that way to any alarming extent. I said, "Now Brother Allen, you just stand still and you will see the power of God." I was well-nigh convinced that God was arranging to give the people there an object lesson, which they would not forget soon. My suffering seemed to increase, but I held on. About four o'clock next morning, I saw myself actually sinking down, getting smaller. I could see that I was on the trimming lathe, and was being trimmed down. So I began to praise the Lord. I did not dare to exert myself, nor did I want to, for fear of breaking the chain that was being woven round and through me. And I did not want to disturb Brother Allen. But I kept quietly saying, "Glory! Glory! " At each utterance I could see the shavings a-flying and felt that I was getting the victory. So the "Glorys" would come regardless of Brother Allen's sleeping in there and needing rest — out they came, louder and louder.

When I saw that it was time for Brother Allen to get up, I did not hesitate to open my mouth. I also saw that what little exertion I had made did not hurt me in the least and as I had not taken a long, down-deep breath for so long, I just wanted to so bad. So I tried it, and oh, what a relief! And best of all, it did not hurt me. I had wakened Brother Allen, and he lay where he could see me. Soon I raised my right arm, and felt no pain whatever. I then shouted, "O, glory 'tis done!" I jumped up and began pounding my fractured ribs, and at that Brother Allen bounded out of bed, ran in and grabbed me, frightened at my actions. I said, "Oh, Brother Allen, I am healed! " "Oh, Brother Bevington, you will kill yourself!" "No, I am healed!" And in spite of his trying to hold me, I was pounding those ribs with all my might and feeling no hurt from it. I forgot to say that as I lay there realizing that I was healed, when I said, "It is done; I am healed." I heard those ribs come together; I felt them rub together. God surely was in their coming together.

Brother Allen could not believe that I was healed. He actually thought that the suffering and the failure of getting healed and the prospect of the pesthouse had so worked on my mind that I had actually gone crazy. But Hallelujah, it is done, a most wonderful work of the supernatural! And I tell you as I relate it, I feel the same glory, the same power, as I felt then. So here at Ashland I rejoice in a Christ that heals. Hallelujah to His dear name. Oh! let us magnify Jesus; let us exalt Him above all other agencies and powers. Well, I was hungry, so I went and had a good early dinner. I had had but one meal during the eight days of struggle. I came back to the room and oh, how different things looked! I just fell on my face on the very spot where I had been healed, and sent forth my heart's contents. There was a great landslide came into my soul, and I just laughed and shouted and jumped for about three hours.

Well, after I had gotten somewhat quiet and was getting adjusted to the remarkable change, I thought that I ought to go and let the doctor know what had happened. So up I went. I stepped in, and took a seat, and soon he came to the door. I spoke, but he gave a sort of grunt. His southern breeding had been insulted, and the "old man" in him was making a fine display of his goods on the inside.

When it came my turn, he stepped to his door, and motioned for the next one, ignoring me. But I jumped up, feeling that he could not fail to see the difference in my movements to what they were the first time he saw me. So my quick getting up had the desired effect. He stopped and looked at me in amazement, saying, "Well, what has happened to you?" "Well, Sir, Doctor, I am a healed man." It was readily seen that he did not take much stock in that. But yet there were some facts staring him in the face; that much he could not very well reason out of. There I was, pounding my ribs, and he was staring wildly at me.

The first thing I knew I was shouting right there in that doctor's office, with a lot of onlookers gazing at me and the doctor a Presbyterian. He laid his hand on my side. I said, "pound it, Doctor." He did, and then dropped his head on my shoulder and wept and trembled till he shook my whole frame. He reminded me of an aspen leaf in the wind. He stood there weeping for several minutes. Then he said , "There must be something in this healing power. I never saw anything like it. And you say that Jesus really healed you without any remedies?" "Yes, Sir, and now doctor, here is another dollar, for I would like you to turn the Xray on.'; "Oh, I will gladly do it. I am interested in that sliver that lay cross your ribs." I said, "You will find that splinter in its place." So when he turned the Xray on, he just stood speechless, while I laughed. And again he laid his head on my shoulder, and wept and trembled.

I said, "How about that splinter, Doctor?" He said, "There is no splinter to be seen, and no trace of its ever being there." And again the glory fell on me and I had to walk the floor. I didn't dare to be too noisy out there in that office; so I just walked or rather flew, for it seemed my feet never touched the floor.

He said, "Brother Bevington, I want you to come to our church, (a Presbyterian) and give your testimony; I can stand for it. My church is on Lookout Mountain. I will come after you in the morning with my car." I said, "All right." So we went. There seemed to be no objections to my testimony. It took me an hour to tell it, though it was pretty dry to me, and no one seemed to be interested in it but the doctor, his wife and son and daughter. The daughter was nineteen and the son twenty-three. Then the doctor wanted me to preach that night. The pastor did consent, though somewhat reluctantly. However, I preached. I said but little about holiness, yet they all saw where I stood, and what I claimed. At the close, I said, "I feel that there is someone here that would like to get saved, get the old-time salvation. But I see there is no altar here." But the word "here" had scarcely left my lips, until the doctor had two chairs put out. His son and daughter fell there and began praying. This did not suit the pastor, as they had been the stand-bys. But we held them over hell just the same. The pastor soon pronounced the benediction and had the lights put out, leaving most all of the congregation in the dark, and we all had to feel our way out.

I was happily surprised on Monday morning to see the doctor. He threw his arms around me, and said, "Brother Bevington, the children want to get through." So they came in and kneeled down and about 3:00 p. m., they both got saved. I went up to their Wednesday night prayer meeting and the son and daughter gave their experience. And the doctor got up and said, "I move we invite Bevington up here to hold a meeting." Well that move never got a second. It was not only pigeonholed but was kicked out before it had a chance to show itself. So Thursday morning here he came, and said, "Brother Bevington, I want that blessing you preach about." I said, "Doctor, are you sure you do?" "Yes, Sir, I am." I said, "Do you want it bad enough to get down here and die out?" "Yes," Sir, he said. "Then," I said, "Doctor, die out to that Presbyterian Church!" "I have already done that. Last night's action settled the Presbyterian Church with me." "Can you die out to that proud wife of yours?" "Yes Sir, for she will be after the same thing." So down he went in my bedroom. He remained there three days, groaning and pleading and wrestling.

Then I heard a knock at the door. I got up and there was the wife. I was somewhat fearful, but the second look at her allayed all fears, as she asked, "Is the doctor here?" in a more meek and humble attitude than I had ever given her credit for. The doctor called out, "Come in, Honey." So in she went ahead of me. He was in the bedroom, and she had one room to pass through before reaching him, so by the time I got in there, she was down with her arms around him, crying and kissing him. Well, that was a happy surprise to me, as I really had expected just the reverse. She rose up, and said, "Brother Bevington, I want this same blessing." So she went after it. She stayed there all night. Next morning she proposed to go to their own home and fight it out. Well I was a little scary of that, until she said, "We will take Brother Bevington with us. I don't like to have the children alone there too long."

So I agreed with her and went with them. We were on our faces forty-two hours in their home, no one eating anything. In fact the doctor nor I had not eaten anything since the Thursday we came down, and this was the following Tuesday. They got through about 2:30 p. m., Tuesday. The four of them went to their prayer meeting on Tuesday night, all on fire, and all testified as to what God had done. They were sung down, and, at the close of the meeting, their letters were handed to them. So they were delivered from that ice chest. Then they both went on the street with me and were a power.

The doctor said, "I am going to pray over the matter. Wife is impressed to make a radical change of which I am a little afraid." So he and his wife put in three days waiting on God. The doctor's office was locked up now over a week. The following Monday they both came down, and said, "We are impressed to sell our place here, get a rig and drive through to California, preaching the old-time Gospel all the way. Would you give us an idea as to what we will need? We will want to eat, sleep, cook, travel and preach from this wagon." So I made a list of the things needed. They sent to Studebaker at South Bend, Indiana, and got their outfit. The outfit complete cost them over $1200.00. They sold out and started, and were on the road eleven months, preaching and distributing tracts. The children, as they called them, were sanctified three weeks after they left. I feel impressed to state that I heard from them all the way through. They have sent me money, and I have met them at the camp meeting since.

5

Important Truths

Divine Healing: What It Is Not.

1. IT IS NOT healing by remedies.
2. It is not imaginary healing.
3. It is not the exercise of the will power.
4. It is not the power of magnetism.
5. It is not mind cure, or metaphysics.
6. It is not spiritualism.
7. It is not faith cure, or prayer cure; faith and prayer being simply the avenues leading up to healing.
8. It is not immunity from death, but strength for life.
9. It is not presumption and insubordination to God's will.

Divine Healing, What It Is.

1. It is the direct, supernatural power of God upon the body.
2. It is in accordance with the Holy Scriptures, and founded on them.
3. It is founded on Christ's sacrifice and work of redemption.
4. It is through the resurrection life of Jesus Christ.
5. It is through the personal indwelling of Jesus Christ in the body.
6. It is through and by the Holy Spirit.
7. It is through the personal faith of the sufferer, or his faith united with the faith of others.
8. It is submission to the Divine will, requiring our repentance of any disobedience, and consecration to God.
9. It is for the service and glory of God.
10. It is a fact of Church History from the Apostolic Age to our age, and is confirmed by innumerable testimonies in our own day.
11. It is a sign of our Lord's approaching advent.
12. It is a testimony to the Word of God, and the truth of Christianity in this day of unbelief.

It is not our business to save people, but it is our business to lead them to Christ. And so it is not our business to heal people, but it may be and should be our business to lead them to Jesus who has promised to heal them. Divine healing is not the most important teaching in the Bible, but it is a truth, and God has shown me and we cannot avoid it without detriment to our spiritual development. Divine healing is not doctrine or theory, but a living fact, thoroughly established in the Word of God. Divine healing, in its deepest, truest sense, is a life of utter abandonment to God, and an incessant dependence upon Him, a dependence on the power beyond ourselves in the most trying places. Here is our source of strength if we keep our eyes on God at all times. Amen ! May God help you to see Him as He really is, and what He will be to those who meet conditions.

I will now give you some evidences and facts. While holding a meeting near Hopewell, Kentucky, I was called to Bro. Jim Felty's to pray for his wife's healing. She lay as a dead person, had been in bed, I think, two or three weeks, not expected to live. We asked Jim if he could go down with us for victory for her healing, all in the name of our blessed, compassionate Christ. He said that he could, so we got down and prayed; we were there some three hours when her brother, Less Bradford, came in, so he got down with us. We lay perhaps two hours longer waiting on God. Finally we were led to go out. I said, " 'Tis done!" Brother Less said, "I know it," and he got up, and we went outdoors. In less than five minutes Mrs. Felty was out of that bed, reeling like a drunken woman. We all felt the power of God. She assisted in getting supper, and went to prayer meeting that night, setting the congregation on fire by her testimony. Sometimes it takes much waiting on God; other times not so much.

Another woman (I have forgotten her name) back of Grayson, Kentucky, had been confined to her bed several weeks. She was almost an invalid, and could not walk, only as assisted by her husband and son. I was invited to pray for her, and next morning, at church, I was told that she was out of bed, walking without assistance. That night she came horseback some two miles to the meeting, getting off her saddle alone, which set the crowd to rejoicing. The woman was perfectly healed.

There was another case, several miles from Grayson. I was called to pray for a certain woman who had been a great sufferer, and had become weak-minded through her suffering. I prayed for her, pleading the promises, believing that God was able to heal her without assistance in the face of every darkness; but I left feeling somewhat bothered over the conditions there, as I did not have the liberty that I thought I should have, but stood my ground for her healing. Next night we had a cottage prayer meeting. Quite a large crowd was there, and Satan was there also. He said she wasn't healed or she would be there.

Several had shaken hands with me, and especially one sister had given me a very hearty handshake. I noticed it, but did not think much about it. As soon as all were in, I slipped over to a brother, and said: "I sent that sister here that we prayed for yesterday." He burst out into a hearty laugh, saying, "Sister, Brother Bevington doesn't know you." Then she hurried to me with a handshake similar to that she had given me. I never would have known her—such a radical change, so instantaneous. That is the way God has been working, praise His dear name!

If Brother Black were living, he would gladly tell of how God answered prayer in his remarkable healing, while we were holding a meeting at Honeywell, this side of Grayson. He came through on his way to Cincinnati to be operated on for a complication of diseases of several years' standing. He thought he would stop off where I was, over Sunday, as we were having quite a good meeting. When he told me where he was going, and what for, I said, "It might be that you could get a shorter cut than Cincinnati, one by way of the Throne." When we went to prayer, I had no trouble in reaching the Throne in his behalf, and that afternoon God wonderfully healed him. He was a living witness in all that community to the healing power of God.

Bro. Tom K., back of Anglin, is another case. He was so crippled with rheumatism that he had to use two canes or a crutch and a cane. He also came to this meeting at Honeywell. It took three of us to get him up stairs to my room; but he came down alone, and that without the use of a cane. He went home to work getting railroad ties, down on one knee and then on the other, but it did not bother him. He was an unmistakable witness to the mighty power of God to heal.

I think there were seven or eight cases of healing in that county, all of which were of persons about given up by the doctors. To Jesus be all the glory! He is no respecter of places or diseases. All He asks of us is obedience and faith. Hallelujah!

I will now endeavor to chronicle one more marvel of God, just about bringing me from death to life. I was painting a house for Rev. John Fleming, and stayed there three weeks. 'Twas in the fall of the year, and quite cool, so I slept on feathers and between blankets during those three weeks. I want to record this as a warning against thoughtlessness on the part of people entertaining evangelists, as to putting them in unhealthful beds. Being quite accustomed to the feathers, and being past sixty, I found it somewhat hard to make the change. Well, I went from this feather bed out near the Michigan line to hold a meeting. I got there on Friday night, and preached in the M. E. Church to a good crowd. One girl came to the altar.

I got up next morning feeling very bad physically, so sore, and I ached all over. I went out into the kitchen, and said, "Sister, about how long has it been since anyone slept in that bed you gave me last night?" "Well," she said, "let me see. Grandpa died in that bed sixteen years ago, and no one has slept in it since." I said, "Has it been aired, or the sheets been changed? I am afraid I have caught a tremendous cold." I returned to the room and wrote in capital letters my whole name on the sheet. I then called her, and showed it to her. She seemed surprised and somewhat mortified, so she put on a dry sheet, but the mattress was no better.

I preached that night with some difficulty, and then slept what I could sitting in a chair. Sunday morning I could not speak above a whisper and, oh, I was so sore. No preaching that day. Sunday night I remained in the chair, and a dear faithful boy nine years old kept the fire up, as I could not move without severe pains. Monday morning I was still worse. John, as that is all I can remember of his name, said, "I am going to send the doctor up as I go to work this morning." His wife said, "I don't believe Brother Bevington believes in having a doctor." "I don't care what he believes. I am not going to have an old crank die on my hands, and have seventy-five dollars to pay by not having a doctor."

I then could hear nearly all ordinary conversation, but this severe cold had deafened me so that I couldn't hear, so this sister wrote everything down for me. Well, I began praying as best I could that no doctor would come; but I was so sore and having such severe pains that I could make but little headway in praying, though I did my best that no doctor would come as I was pretty sure I would not take any of his medicine.

John returned from work, but no doctor had been there. I was still worse, not being able to move a limb. The boy kept a good fire for me, the weather being quite cold. The wife, I believe, was saved, but not sanctified. John belonged to the meeting house, and that was about all, as I saw it then, and as I found out later. John was too tired to make a trip after the doctor, so my prayer was answered up to that time. Though I was suffering with a high fever, yet my feet and limbs were cold. Tuesday morning about 5:00 the doctor came, but he came in the back way through the back door. As he stepped to the door of my room, he threw up his right hand and halloed. He then turned to the sister, and I could see that he was giving her quite a tongue lashing, I suppose censuring her for not sending for him Saturday. He said? "That man won't live forty-eight hours." He never came to me, but remained standing there ten minutes, eyeing me very closely. Then he stepped to the kitchen table and left five kinds of medicine. One was the strongest that he ever gave, and must be taken every ten minutes for about five hours; the others were to be taken every forty minutes until used up. And he said: "If he isn't better in four hours, he is a gone man, as he has typhoid in its worst stage; and at his age everything is against him."

As soon as the doctor was gone, in she came with a glass of water and the ten minutes concoction. I said, "What is that?" "Why," she said, "that is what the doctor left to help you." Then she handed me what the doctor had said. I read it all. "Well," I said, "I can't take that medicine, just throw it outdoors and I will not take it." I could see that she looked much disappointed. She informed me as to her husband, and told me why he was so against holiness preachers. She said, "There was a holiness preacher here four years ago, who preached holiness as straight as you do; but when he left he took a man's wife with him, leaving three children under ten years. So John has no use for holiness preachers, though he consented to allow you to come here after much praying and coaxing; and now if you should die it would cost him seventy-five dollars for not having a doctor, and for harboring a law violator. So, Brother Bevington, for my sake, please take this medicine."

Well, I tell you to resist man or the doctor was a small thing, but to resist such a plea as that was about the hardest thing I had met for a long time. But I reasoned with her, and said, "I don't believe I am going to die, or I would have gone before this." But the fact that I was getting worse all the time was poor encouragement to think that I was going to get well. I was then alive only because of my will power, as she thought; but I persuaded her to take that truck out, live or die.

Nine o'clock came. That was my time limit, and the doctor had ordered her to phone him by 9: 00. But she had no good news for him, so she did not send him word. At 9:30 he phoned. "Well, doctor, he is worse, I guess, if such a thing is possible; and he refuses to take any medicine." Well, that infuriated the doctor, so he went to the officers, and the best he could do was to get the black Maria next day. It was being repaired, so he phoned out that if I did not take the medicine at once as prescribed, they would be out tomorrow and take me to the pesthouse. So she informed me as to the conclusion. I knew that if I could scarcely keep warm there in that warm room with pillows and blankets and a large fire, I never would survive a mud road on a twelve-mile jump to the pesthouse.

I tried to rally to pray, but it seemed I could not get still. I said to the boy, "Now, you get that chair; and if your mamma can spare another comfort, put it on the chair." When all was ready, I said, "Now, honey, you will have to go slow; take your time." The boy was so kind and tender with me, but I fainted before getting a limb on the chair. However, I soon rallied and persuaded him to renew the attempt. He hesitated, until his mamma came in, and together they got one limb up; but while getting the other up I fainted again, and this time it was nearly an hour before I came to. The mother, coming in, pronounced me dead.

After rallying, I had some trouble to get them to renew the effort. I said, "I feel I must have that limb up there for two reasons: First, to arrange so as to lay my Bible on my limb; and second, then it will be warmer for me." So they went to work at it with a board under my limb, and finally got it up. It was then about 4:00 p. m., Wednesday. "Now," I said, "lay my small Bible carefully on my limbs," which they did. "Now draw my right hand down on it," which, when they did, I fainted; but rallied in forty-five minutes and had them try again and by 6:00 p.m. my hand was on the Bible. At 7:00, I said, "Now raise my hand carefully, just the tips of my fingers." They did so, but I fainted again, and it was after 8:00 p. m., before I rallied.

Well, I let them rest until morning, the boy sleeping in a chair beside me, keeping a fine coal fire all the time. Then I could see but little, but I thought I was able to plead the promises. I was saying, "Thou art my Healer." Right here, if anyone does not believe in a personal devil, I want to say there is one sure, for I saw a dark form and heard a voice saying, "Yes, you have a fine Healer. I would like to have such a fine Healer as you have here. Here you are and can't move an arm or a limb. You have pneumonia in its worst stage, and are getting worse all the time — can't even move your head." Well that last word "head" impressed me. I had not even tried to move my head, but I yelled out, "You are a liar," and undertook to move my head, but fainted, and for one hour I lay as dead. When I rallied, I could see better out of my right eye, though the left one was useless.

I was reminded that this was the last day, as they did not say what time they would be there to take me to the pesthouse. I prayed that it would not be until after dinner. Well, Satan had me in pretty close quarters. I could not move my head, but I coaxed the boy to work my fingers; and I noticed as he raised them an inch it hurt scarcely any, so I felt that I was getting the victory. I could then see real well out of my right eye. At 10:00 a.m they phoned that they would be there at 2:00 to take me to the pesthouse.

Well, while I could not move a muscle and was in such pain, yet I could plead the promises better. So I just stuck to it until 12:00, and by the use of a goose quill, I took some soup. At 1:00 while pleading the promises, and without a pain, I said, "Now raise my hand." The boy did so — one inch, two inches, three inches. I shouted, "Hold on," and began praising God. The sister came in, and I said, "I am getting the victory." I said, "Let go my hand." He let go, and it dropped, but there was no pain. "Raise it again." He did so— one, two, three, four, five, six inches. I shouted, "Oh, glory, raise it up," and up it went twelve inches high. "Now lay it back on the Bible."

Then I felt the power of the blessed Lord coming through my body, and my left eye open, and I could see as well as ever. I raised my right arm, but fainted; and the woman came in and again pronounced me dead. She seemed to be determined to have me dead, but in thirty minutes I revived and began pleading the promises with greater energy than at any previous time. Satan again came to me, with the same words as before. I said, "I can move my neck." I offered up a prayer, repeated 1 John 5:14, 15, moved my head; and it did not hurt. I raised my left arm for the first time, and felt no pain. I raised my right arm again, shouting, "I am healed." I kicked the comforts off my limbs, and was out of the chair leaping and yelling like a Camanche Indian, but was weak.

In this exultation, I was soon exhausted and would no doubt have fallen to the floor but the sister caught me and got me seated. She then looked out of the window, and said, "There they are." Well, that would give me at least thirty minutes to rally, so I plead the promises for strength. It did not come as rapidly as I wished, but I kept repeating 1 John 5: 14, 15. Here they came through the kitchen; and if I ever saw a demon, the first man was one — so unsympathetic, so crabbed, so hard looking. He stopped in the kitchen door; and the sister was talking to him. As I had gotten my hearing back, I could hear what she told him. She said, "He claims to be healed. He was just up and out of that chair, but overexerted himself as he is weak, having eaten nothing for six days."

I seemed unable to speak, but could see the fiendish look on his face. Just behind him was another man, oh, such a nice looking man — so pleasant and so sympathetic. I just longed to get to him, but could not move. I could see the main officer shake his head, and hear him say, "I take no stock in that nonsense," referring to the other man who preached holiness, who broke up his brother's home, and drove his brother to the insane asylum (I presume the fact that he had those three children on his hands hurt him worse than all else). I soon rallied, and said, "Men, I am a healed man. I am healed, but I lack strength."

He had said that he would not go without me, as he would have to come back after me, which would incur the expense on him for the second trip. I said, "Here, Mister, I have a watch that will sell anywhere for twenty-five dollars. I will let you have that, and if I am not at your office tomorrow at 10:00 a. m., and you have to come after me, the watch will pay for the second trip." At that, this pleasant looking man stepped in, and I offered my hand as I wanted to get to him so bad. He said to the officer, "You try him; take his watch. I believe he will be there." So he persuaded him to go without me. I noticed them out at the gate talking. This nice man said, "You don't want that man's watch. I really believe he is all right. Now let me take his watch back to him, as I believe he has had a hard struggle and needs some sympathy and love and encouragement." Well, if ever a man spoke the truth, that man did at that time, as it seemed that if I could have had some sympathy shown me, I would have given most anything. "Now if you have to come back, I will pay the extra twelve dollars," he said. So in he came with the watch.

Well, I felt all melted up, and got hold of his hand and even kissed it and squeezed it the best I could, just to see the confidence he placed in me. I never will forget how that act helped me, as everybody had been against me, even the sister; though she wanted to help me and be kind, yet as she had never seen anyone healed, and John was opposing me, she was so fearful of trouble that she was miserable all the time. So this act was a great stimulant to me.

Well I rested all day, and slept good that night. That was Friday night, and Saturday I started out; but being weak, I was very sensitive to the cold. I had to put on two overcoats, which loaded me down. The boy went with me. We stopped sixteen times to rest in going the three miles, but got to the man's office just sixteen minutes before ten. As we came near the office, we saw we had nine steps to go up, and I stopped and said to the boy, "Oh, how can I ever make those nine steps?" I will never forget how the boy looked up so appealingly, and said, "As k Jesus." Well I did. This nice man was sitting at the window and, seeing me, he came down; and just as we got to the steps two men were passing, and he said, "Gentlemen, please help us get this man up these steps." Now note how God was there and saw me through. They had a doctor there to examine me, and he said, "There is nothing the matter with this man, only he is very weak." So they let me off. The kind gentleman said, "When I got home yesterday, I told my wife about you; and she was very much interested, and said, 'I believe that man will be there on time, and you take the horse and buggy down to the office with you, and bring him up here for dinner!'" As soon as we got into the buggy, I said, "Are you a saved man? " He began crying and said, "Oh, no, I wish I were. My wife is a backslider, too. We are both backsliders. We have tried and tried and tried, but haven't been able to get back to the Lord. We have been going to every altar for years. We have heard of your meeting out there, and had planned to come out."

As we came near the gate, out she came running to the buggy, and gave me her hand, and helped me down; and she just carried me right into the house. "Oh, I knew that God would answer your prevailing prayers, and heal you. I am so glad. I am a miserable backslider, and I felt that God would heal you, and then you could prevail for husband and me to get back to God. And I have a sister living half a mile from here. I went to see her yesterday, and she just broke down and, weeping, said, 'Bring him over here.'"

Well, while I was very hungry and weak, and the dinner was on the table, and steaming, I said, "Do you want to get back to God badly enough to fall down here and stay until you meet the conditions?" She said, "Yes," and down she went, and the husband also, and I with them. We plead the promises, and at 4:15 he arose with shouts of victory. He grabbed me and carried me all over the house, yelling at a tremendous rate; and at that she got the victory, and jumped up and danced about. We had a blessed time. We had dinner — the first meal I had eaten in six days — and got the dishes washed up at 6:00 p. m., then we got into the buggy and went over to her sister's. As the wife jumped out of the buggy, she shouted, "Hallelujah," and kept it up until the sister came running and crying. She threw her arms around her, pleading for us to come in and pray for her.

We all dropped down on our faces in the kitchen, as it was nice and warm, and went to praying. At 8:00 p. m. the husband of the unsaved sister came in, all black from his coal digging. The wife jumped up, and threw her arms around him, saying, "I am trying to get back to God; help me, help me!" He began to cry, and got down with us all; and they did some good digging, meeting conditions. He got through first, about 10:30; then he dropped at the wife's side and pleaded as few have ever pleaded. At 5:20 a. m. she got through. This was on

Sunday morning. I was much stronger, and walked the floor and praised God until breakfast was ready. Oh, how precious the Savior was then! He had not only healed me but reclaimed four inside of fifteen hours. We just magnified Jesus. I sat down to the table, but could not eat; had to get up and walk, bathed in tears of joy. Jesus was so real, so precious, that I just feasted on His presence. We all fell on our faces in great adoration, until each one had poured out his heart in praise. That was a most wonderful prayer and praise service, closing, or rather stopping, to be continued at 11:30. Then the hostess said, "Now, Brother, you must eat something, as you did not eat with us this morning. So I did eat; but there was a continual bubbling up, a spirit of praise going up from my heart. It seemed that was the first that I began to realize what God had done for me. So as strength returned, so did the volume of praise.

Well, now came some very remarkable workings of God. I remained there over Sabbath, preached that night, or rather had a meeting; for everything ran into a praise service, so there was not much preaching done. We retired at twelve o'clock Sunday night. All of those four who were saved were seeking sanctification all day Sunday.

When I got up Monday morning at seven o'clock, I found all four in the kitchen; they had been wrestling all night, and the girl that had got saved in our first meeting on Saturday night was with them seeking sanctification. I remained all day Monday, wrestled all night Monday night, and by nine o'clock Tuesday morning the five had swept through to complete victory. I remained there until after dinner, and felt strongly impressed to go back to John's; and on my informing these people, they all remonstrated, and said, "Brother Bevington, we want you here for a month yet." While we were at the dinner table, the M. E. preacher, having heard what had transpired, stepped in and joined them in pleading for me to remain, offering his church for as long as the Lord would lead me to occupy it.

Well that was somewhat perplexing, as these five who had been reclaimed and sanctified had relatives there who were backsliders, and the plea seemed to be based on good reasonings. But I went out to the barn, and weighed the matter carefully and prayerfully; but "Go back to John's" was all I could get. The M. E. preacher said, "Let him go; when he gets through out there, we will have him come back here with us. In the meantime we will circulate what God has done, and will be in better shape for God to work."

So on Wednesday morning this nice man took me back to John's, and we gave out tracts and advertised the meeting on the way out. We got out to John's just as he was coming in from work; and of course he had to admit the power of God in my healing, and said, "You are not expecting to hold any more meetings here are you?" I said, "Yes, we want a meeting tonight." He said, "Are you able to preach tonight?" Now, here came an opportunity to use a little strategy. He had told his wife several times that he would never go to hear another holiness preacher, but said that evening to his wife, "You may go, but I will not; " and she told me what he had said. I said: "John, I am somewhat weak, and I don't contemplate any failure in my attempt to get there; but you know there are a lot of sightseers around, and sport-seeking boys, and I have three-quarters of a mile to walk over a rough road. Now, John, I want to ask a favor of you. I want you to go along and take my arm; thus you will make it possible for me to have much more strength than I otherwise would have." I said, "You will not have to go in," though that was my object in having him to go with me. So he, being a kind-hearted man, could not very well refuse. Well, I prayed all the way down to know how to get him into the church. Then at the door, I said, "Now, John, we have gotten along fine, and I feel quite strong enough for the service; but I might fall on the platform, which would have a tendency to break up the meeting, and you being a cool, level-headed fellow, could catch me and prevent a commotion." He scratched his head, and finally had to submit. I had him wade through all the obstacles of holiness preachers and mourners' benches to the meeting, and now set him right down on the front seat at the side of the platform.

The next night I got him to do the same thing; and the next night, Friday night, I didn't have to ask him; and before I was half through preaching, he was at the altar. He prayed about as good as any man I ever heard. Saturday night he and others were at the altar, and stayed until four o'clock Sunday morning, some of them getting through. John's wife was among them, seeking sanctification. We remained there all day Sunday, and until about six o'clock Monday, making about thirty-six hours of praying, praising, preaching and shouting. Someone told me that the souls who actually had prayed through averaged just one an hour during the whole time. So you see it was a pretty fair meeting.

And now comes another way that God has of leading His people. Sunday and Monday I felt that I must go, but said nothing, and preached, or rather tried to preach, on Monday night. But the meeting was all prayer and praise, and all the time I felt that voice saying, "Go, go, go." Well, I supposed of course the "go" meant to go to my next meeting. Next morning I told John and those who were there. John said, "Brother Bevington, your work has just begun here. We

are all planning for the greatest meeting that has ever been in this community."
Well, I retreated to my usual place for solving problems (the haymow). But from the first there was that "go" and after three hours I had to give in.

The next morning, John hitched up to the jolt wagon to take me, as we supposed, to the depot some twelve miles away. I bade the wife and dear, faithful Frank good-bye; but the wife said, "I can't think that your work is done here," and she would not bid me good-bye. I had about one-third of my anticipated railroad fare, but off we went. We had gone about three miles when John looked back, and said, "I declare I believe that is Jim." I said, "Who is Jim?"

Now I have left out some things that will need to be entered here. When John's wife first wrote to me to come out and hold a meeting, she stated that there were fourteen sanctified people here, the father and mother of each of seven families. So on the first Saturday night, the last night I preached until after I was healed, I thought that, inasmuch as there were fourteen sanctified people there, it would be safe to venture on a testimony meeting; so I turned the services over to their class leader. I could hear some then, but not sufficient to get their testimonies clearly. I could not understand the proceedings and as my wonder increased, I finally said to little Frank, "Who are these people who are testifying?" "Why, they are all members here, the superintendent, the class leader, and the officers of the church — all sanctified." By the time the seventh one got up, I was in doubt as to their having a right to testify, and noticed the woman laying a quid on the bench as she got up. I suppose the quid would have bothered or hindered the display that she had planned. I endured until the ninth one, and could not stand it any longer, and said, "Mister" (yes, I said, Mister; I did not feel clear in addressing him as Brother) "You sit down." He said, "I don't have to sit down for you."

I rose to my feet, pointed my right index finger, and said, "You sit down there," and I tell you he dropped like a shot calf, but grabbed his hat and started for the door, and all but eleven followed him — about eighty went out. The girl that had gotten sanctified in that home back of the village, and ten more remained. Well, I did my best at preaching and dismissed. As we were going out, John's wife said, "Now you keep behind me as that crowd is all out here, and I don't know just what for." As we stepped off the porch, here rushed up the man I had called down, and of all the tongue lashings a man ever got I got it there; but I said, "Come on;" so we started out. He and others followed for some distance, calling me about all the names in the catalogue of vengeance.

Now we will return to where John, in the wagon, said, "I believe that is

Jim." When I asked who Jim was, he said, "The man you called down. He is my cousin. I see that he is bareheaded, and yelling for me to stop. But, Brother Bevington, you need not fear as we have this loaded whipstock here, and I will protect you, even if he is my cousin."

Well, here he was coming horseback, yelling like a cowboy, "Stop! Stop! Wait!" and so on. So John stopped, and here he came, looking more like an Indian than a white man. He rushed up to the wagon, threw the rein over the wagon brake, plunged into the wagon, threw his arms around me, and said, "Oh, Brother Bevington, pray for me. I have been in hell ever since that Saturday night." I said,

"Do you really want God?" "Oh, yes! " I said, "Bad enough to get down here in this wagon on this public road, and plead your way to the Cross?" "Yes, Yes." So I said, "Drive up along the fence, John." He did so, and we got down, he on one side of the wagon and I on the other. In about an hour he burst out, "O God, O God, have mercy, have mercy! O God, save me from this awful hell that I am rushing into!" And he said, "Oh, Brother Bevington, come over here! Oh, come over here! Take my hand, I am slipping into hell right now, Oh, come over here!" I said, "No, I won't come over. You repent! " "O Brother, I am going to hell ! " "Well, if you had your just deserts, you would have been there long ago. Repent! Repent!" Well, we were there by the fence from about 9:00 a. m. until 4:30 p. m. Three times some of his relatives came along, but they could not get him out of that wagon. One of his cousins, a wealthy farmer, came along with a flock of sheep, and said to John, "Who is that in the wagon?" "Why, that is Jim." "What in the world is he doing in there?" Jim yelled out, "I am getting God." The cousin made all sorts of threats against me and all of us; but Jim stayed in his place until he actually prayed through. Then he jumped up, yelling like a coon dog, grabbed me, landed us both on the ground, carried me all around there for nearly an hour, then jumped on his horse, and started back. "Well," I said, "I can't make any train now, so I guess we will go back to your house." That is just what he was expecting.

Now many will say, "Why, Brother Bevington, I thought you were going to the depot. How would God lead you to the depot, and not get you there?" Now comes an important lesson for all. We must remember that we are only human beings, and God does not always reveal His plans ahead, but leads us as He sees best. Had God undertaken to explain to me that He would have to get Jim out there in that wagon on a public road, subject to all the embarrassing scenes that it would be necessary for him to go through, in order to knock his churchanity out of him, his long membership, his testimonies that he had been giving for the last ten years, his antipathy against the holiness preacher who broke up that peaceful family, his good standing in the M. E. Church, and all arising therefrom — had God undertaken to explain all this to me, He would have landed me in the brush. But just see His wisdom. He told me to "go" and allowed me to interpret the "go " as I saw fit, as that would make no difference to Him. You see He took a short cut to make the many points necessary to getting Jim saved. God knew that I was nowhere nearly done in that vicinity; but He knew that it was necessary to get that leader completely transformed, broken all to pieces, so that He could use him.

Now as Jim was on horseback, he could make better time than we. So as we drove into John's barn yard, here came Jim and his wife rushing in. She jumped off the horse, and cried and sobbed, saying, "Oh, Brother Bevington, forgive me. I have been in hell ever since that Saturday night." We went to the house, and all went into the dining room and fell on our faces.

Now came one of the most remarkable seven weeks of my life, right there in that man's house. I never took off my clothes, and never preached a sermon; but just lay day and night on my face, praying, weeping, groaning, pleading, imploring, beseeching, besieging the Throne in behalf of the M. E. membership consisting of 300.

Some would get through, and strike out for their friends, and they would come in wagon loads, bring their provisions and feed and often their cows, and stay until the whole load got saved and sanctified. Then they would strike out after someone else. That was kept up seven weeks, day and night; no one eating but one meal in twenty-four hours, and yet someone was out in the kitchen cooking all the time. I got such a burden that I would not get up, but just lay there; and they would come in at times and feed me like they would a baby. Well, they claimed there were over 400 down there, and most of them prayed through. Of all the times I ever saw this beat anything: Some were praying, others crying, others testifying, others preaching, others shouting, others making restitution; but I just lay on my face, bathed in tears, and when it was all over I looked as though I had gone through a hard six weeks.

I think the most remarkable case was that of Jim's wife, as she had been of a boisterous nature or make-up. Before this meeting she would run and shout and yell when giving her testimony. She was the first to get through, and she lay under the power of God some sixty hours, and then was, oh, so different, none of the bold hilarious conduct; but she was so meek. She just walked the floor, bathed in tears, wringing her hands, and not a word fell from her lips, just like a little country girl of eleven summers; and I tell you she lived salvation after that. She and her husband and many, yes many, more lay there until they were sanctified. Of course, news soon reached the village that I had come back there; and here the people came, the preacher as well and he got sanctified, as did his wife and many of his members. So you see it pays to mind God and trust Him.

I love to rewrite these experiences, and do hope that they will prove the blessing to many that they have been to me. Real, steady, unselfish prayer will move things; and we need to mean what we say. A little girl said to her papa, who was saying that Jesus didn't mean all He said in the Bible, "Papa, if Jesus didn't mean what He said, why didn't He say what He meant?" I shouted "Amen, that's reason." I have seen ministers get down and pray for Jesus to heal some of their members and seemingly they prayed in earnest; but if their prayers had been answered, they would have been more surprised than those folks were when Peter stood knocking at the door for entrance. I remember one who prayed thus, and then I heard him deny that Jesus heals.

I was holding a meeting years ago, near Lexington, Kentucky, and God instantly healed a sister there of a disease of eight years' standing. Their preacher stood up in the pulpit and denied that Jesus had anything to do with her healing, though she had not stood on her feet for five years, but walked to the church the evening of the day she was healed. (O Consistency, thou art a jewel!)

I was holding a meeting once in Ohio, not far from an insane asylum; and as I so often did, I went to the woods. Supposing that I was out of hearing, I got somewhat noisy, prayed pretty loud and brandished my hands and arms, making gesticulations that looked sort of queer to a passerby. It seems that one of the inmates had escaped out of the asylum, and a reward had been offered for his capture. Well, two men were going through the woods and, hearing me, they took notice, and at once pronounced me that lunatic. As the reward was sure, they said, "Now we dare not tackle him, so let's run to the village, get the officers, and capture the fellow." So they hurried away, and reported their discovery, and officers were dispatched with three conveyances, with ropes, cuffs, chains, wires, and a grand display of safety equipments, and out they came. Well, it seems I had gotten through with my gymnastic performances, and had gone to the house; and as this was a somewhat secluded place, the lady of the house was some what confused as she saw seven men in all, and three conveyances drive up to the woods and unload all their equipment, so she called upstairs and said, "Brother Bevington, did you notice those men going into our woods?" I said, "No." Then she called me down to see the crowd out there. Well I didn't know what it all meant and went back to my room. Soon one of the officers knocked at the door, and said: "Do you know of a lunatic who has recently escaped from the asylum, and was seen in your woods this afternoon?" The woman made a few inquiries as to appearance, dress, and actions; and as the officers were describing him, she burst out laughing, as she had seen me praying, and she said, "Yes, he is in my house now;" and she stepped to the door and called me down. As the officer had been out twice to hear me preach, he at once recognized me; and they all had a big laugh, except the two who were planning for the reward. So our praying means something. Taylor was once praying and wrestling and pleading for Africa, and finally God said, "Taylor, you pack up your grip and get for Africa." You see he got into this by praying. Well, I came near getting into the asylum, but they let me off.

Now, I would like to say right here that if any of those parties who attended those seven weeks' meetings just described should get this volume, they will at once recognize the meetings, and I wish they would write me, giving the names of as many as possible, as all their names are gone from me, and 'twould be a comfort to me to write to them. I remember Jim's and John's given names, but not their surnames. Write me at Kingswood, Kentucky, and mail will be forwarded to me wherever I am, if this side of heaven. I expect to meet a lot of those people up there.

I went to the Cincinnati Camp one year, and while there was invited to come down the river to hold a meeting. I don't remember much about the meeting; but a sister there was unable to attend the services, being confined to her bed. I went to pray for her, and soon saw that there was something hindering, but couldn't tell just what. I wanted to know if 'twas the same as is recorded in Daniel 10, so I went to the barn and from there to the woods. She had been healed once before through our prayers. In about forty-eight hours God showed me that she had never testified to the other healing, so I went in and reminded her of negligence. After a pause, she said, "Brother Bevington, who told you that I had never testified to it? Whoever did, told you a lie."

I said, "Sister, you never testified to it here in this M. E. Church where you were well known." "Well, no, I never did here, but did once at an open air meeting at the Cincinnati Camp." "Yes," I said, " 'twas no trouble there where you were not known, no sacrifice there, no danger of any one's pointing the finger at you there." I said, "Sister, you were too big a coward to stand here and tell what God had done for you, and Jesus said, 'Whosoever shall be ashamed of me and of my words, of him shall the son of man be ashamed'." She said, "I would like to know who told you that." I said, "God told me out in the woods." "Yes, 'tis true, and, Brother Bevington, will you ask God to forgive me?" I said, "If you can convince God that you will stand here amongst these scoffers and tell it, I presume He will heal you; but you will have to convince Him, which may mean much. You might easily convince me, but you are not dealing with Bevington on this case; you are dealing with God, the all-seeing Jehovah. God has no use for cowards."

So I left her and went to the woods. I remained there about six hours, then slipped out the back way from the woods, did not go near the house, but went about four miles to hold another meeting, while she was getting worse all the time. I conducted a fourteen days' meeting, in which several found the Lord, and two were healed. She heard where I was and sent for me. I went, and she said, "I am in heaps of trouble. I have told the Lord I would tell it here in this neighborhood, in this church." I said, "I think He knows you are lying, as you did before," and grabbed my hat and made for the woods. I remained there about four days, as I was very desirous that she should get where God could trust her with such a boon as healing would be to her, as she had means and talents that God could use if He could get hold of her. Well, she was dumbfounded at my actions, and about concluded that there was something radically wrong in my upper story. But I was up on the hill under a large oak, pleading with God to wake her up, and get her where He wanted her; and God was doing His part. On the fifth afternoon, He said, "Go to her at once." And I went.

Such a sight as met my eyes! she had been crying for forty-eight hours. As I knocked at the door I heard her between sobs, say, "Come in." As I entered the room, she threw up her hands, saying, "Oh, I am so glad you came! And God has answered prayer. Forgive, oh, forgive me for feeling so hard against you, and saying so many bad things about you. Oh, I am so sorry, as I never knew I was so mean." Well, that was what I had spent those hours in the woods for, as that proud heart had to be subdued. You see she had never had anything more than a meeting house religion. I was fully convinced that she had never received the Holy Ghost; for, that a person could lose regeneration and retain sanctification always was a pretty hard thing for me to believe. So I felt that she was an entire backslider, but did not consider it wise then to so inform her.

She had just said, "Brother Bevington, I have lost my sanctification for, had

I been sanctified, I would never have felt toward you as I did." Now in such a case is where wisdom is needed, as I am quite sure that if I had said, "Now, sister, you are a backslider," she would never have accepted it. So I went to the woods and pleaded with God to tell her, as He seems better capacitated for those emergencies than we. I spent five hours in the barn after coming down from the hill, and cried, "O God, don't let her be deceived." That five hours of struggling in the barn caused the Xray to be turned, and she said: "Brother Bevington, I am sure you will be very much surprised at what I am going to relate, but I feel that I must tell you. I am an entire backslider; so don't pray any more for me to be sanctified, but pray that I may be reclaimed."

So it is to be seen that perhaps nine times out of ten, we make an awful failure of work for which God is so much more qualified than we. In three hours she was blessedly reclaimed, and was so happy, and said, "Why, Brother, I wonder if I didn't get sanctified when I got reclaimed here; I feel so very happy." I said: "Did you ever see anyone that was sanctified at the same time he was regenerated?" "Well, but I am so very happy." I said, "You ought to be happy. A woman that is mean enough to slam the door in the face of as good a friend as Jesus is, and treat Him as you have treated Him, and have Him tenderly forgive you for that treatment, and throw His loving arms around you, and restore your former joy, ought to be a very happy person indeed." She said, "I guess you are about right; and now can we pray for my healing?" "The Book says, 'Seek ye first the kingdom of God, and his righteousness'. Have you His own righteousness now, being only a regenerated woman?" "Well, I reckon not, but what must I do?"

I said, "Don't you want to be sanctified?" "Why certainly I do." "Well, why not pray for sanctification?" "I thought that after I was healed, I could pray through better and get sanctified." "Well, you settle that squarely from the Word." I grabbed my hat and started out. It had now been nearly seven days since I had anything to eat. I went into the kitchen, and told the daughter I was hungry. She got up a nice dinner, and I ate heartily. They had a little girl about seven, who saw me in the kitchen. She went into the mother's room telling her what I had said about a little girl in Cincinnati. The mother said, "Tell him to come in here," as she didn't know what had become of me. She said, "I have no more terrible feeling about you, and do you believe that Jesus will heal me?" I said, "He may after you get the Holy Ghost." Well, she drew a long deep sigh, but finally said, "Well, I want the Holy Ghost all right."

So I went to prayer. 'Twas then about 4:00 p. m. I remained there four nights and three days, holding onto God for her to die out. Neither of us ate a mouthful during this examination. God answered, as she seemed to be about the deadest living person I had seen for some time. Her husband was an unsaved man, but a firm believer in entire holiness, and he encouraged me all the time. He was also a staunch advocate of Divine healing, as he told me several times that if we could get her where God could have His way, He would heal her. So on this fourth morning she bounded out of bed. No one but the daughter was up, and the mother was shouting: "Sanctified and healed"! and, "Oh, I have the real thing this time! " I saw her twice after that and saw that she was an entirely different woman.

Well, the husband wanted me to stay one more day, so I went to the barn as I was somewhat fatigued; and there I plead for him. I came down at 3:30 p. m., and he was in one of the stalls in the cow barn, praying like a good fellow. Well, that was what I had been pulling for during those several weeks of queer actions, but they all counted; and that night about 10:30 he got through. We have heard him, on the platform at the Cincinnati Camp, give unmistakable evidence of having just what he had been advocating for some time. So listen! Is there anything too hard for God? Can't we afford to be misunderstood, talked about, lied about, misrepresented, and often ostracized, if in so doing God can bring the people to themselves? It isn't necessary for us to understand all the "whys" and "wherefores," but it is our business to mind God.

While I was not perfectly satisfied as to the all-round state of this woman, but just minded Him, as time went on certain revelations were given removing all doubt up to the present; and as He had so revealed up to that time, why, of course, I could trust Him for further guidance and developments, and He brought out all these facts just as fast as 'twas necessary. So God seldom tells us His whole plan, relative to certain persons whom He has specially delegated us to work with. He wants us to go through but one step at a time. God had this woman's entire sanctification and her healing, and the salvation and sanctification of her husband all in view, mapped and marked out. Now, He had to have someone who would allow Him to bring forth some very unreasonable things (from the human standpoint) in order to accomplish His designs. Well, He saw that Bevington could be trusted with that important work, so He assigned it to me, taking in round numbers about seven weeks to do it; and most of that time I spent in seclusion, in the woods or the haymow. That is when God accomplishes His greatest feats, when He can get us in seclusion.

6

Personal Dealings of and from God

WE LOVE TO THINK of John Wesley, and I would like to insert a lot of his sayings and doings by the hand of God. The resources of all heaven are at God's command. He has but to speak, and the elements are subservient to His will. How true, "All things are possible to him that believeth!" If our faith in God is unlimited, why "whatsoever we ask for, we receive." Amen. Those wonderful instances recorded in Wesleys works were not confined to his day; hence we have the same privileges Wesley had.

I was spending a few months in northern Indiana with my then only living brother, R——. Since then he has gone to his reward, leaving me the only one on probation out of a family of thirteen children. He had a boy staying with him that had been brought up a Catholic. We were going to Michigan City, several miles away in a wagon, and neither of us had any wraps nor umbrella, and it began to sprinkle and soon was raining. I said to Harry, "I don't want to get wet, as this wind off the lake here would be most too chilly for my health if I get wet. Now, see if it continues to rain, as I will offer up a prayer." And in less than five minutes it stopped. "Well," he said, "that is wonderful, I never saw anything like that. My folks all go to church, but I never saw anything like that done there nor anywhere else." So God gave me an opportunity to enable Him to display His power there in the presence of that ignorant boy.

I had something growing on the lid of my eye, it had been there about seven years. At times it would draw up as small as a large kernel of wheat, then it would seem to lengthen out about an inch. It had not bothered me much, so I had not bothered Jesus much about it. But soon after this miracle of the rain, I was several miles from Jerry's, holding a meeting, and the last Sunday that growth spread out larger than ever. It bothered me in reading the Word, and was quite sore. I put up with it until I got back to Jerry's on Monday, and it was so large that Harry couldn't help but see it, and he was amazed when he saw my eye was swollen and inflamed. He said, "Uncle Guy, why don't you ask Jesus to take that off. He stopped the rain for you;

wouldn't He take that off?" "I think He will," I said.

So when I went to bed, I knelt down and offered up a prayer of faith that the thing would be gone by morning. I went to sleep, and got up in the morning before Harry did. I went down to wash, and had not thought of it since praying for it the night before, and it had been hurting me when I would wash. Soon after I got up, down came Harry to see about that thing on my eye. I had not thought of it until he came bounding out on the porch, saying "Oh Uncle Guy, how is that thing?" "Well," I said, "look and see." Lo, there was no trace of it, not even a scar! He called for my brother to get up and see what Jesus had done for Uncle Guy. The boy said, "I don't see why my folks don't do that way. I had a sore knee and had to remain out of school four months, and they paid out a whole lot of money."

I also had a sore on my body that had been forming about six years. It had never bothered me much, so I didn't bother with it; but this summer while at Jerry's, it was getting quite sore, and was about the size of a twenty-five cent piece, and had rims of different colors around it. It got so bad that I could not rub near it, and it was very painful to the touch, so that I could not sleep on that side. I got tired of that as it was growing larger and more sensitive.

Well I went up to my room, called the boy up, and showed him the sore. He thought it was awful and pronounced it a cancer. I told a doctor about it and he said it was a cancer without a doubt. Well, I laid my hand on that sore and prayed the prayer of faith, asking for its removal, and in six minutes the soreness was all gone. I could rub it, pinch it, and there was no pain. The colors were still there, but the next morning they were all gone. So this boy had three good lessons, given him just through faith. He wrote home to his people and asked them if he couldn't join Uncle Guy's church, telling them what he had seen in answer to prayer. It resulted in the conversion of the whole family. Oh, glory, how blessed to have such a God!

After this I was called on to pray for a sister that had been sorely afflicted for eight or nine years. I prayed and she went to sleep. So I retired to my room. Next morning she said she had slept better than for eight years, till about four a.m. when she was suddenly taken with the malady, and suffered terribly, till they called me up, and after I laid my hand on her and prayed she was soon asleep again. We got our breakfast and she was still asleep. Her husband had but little use for a holiness preacher, as he had the meeting house for his support, which seemed to fill the basket, so he believed in letting good enough alone. I took my Bible and went to the woods.

I heard the dinner bell and came in. I found her still suffering. I resumed prayer and she was made free again. After our dinner I returned to the woods. The bell rang again at three-thirty. She was again suffering, so now I dropped down on my face, and lay there till they called for supper. I said that I didn't want any, but I got a good hold upon God and was enlarging my vision of His power. I just lay there pleading the promises and believing God though she was still suffering. Her husband came in and said, "I want you to take this medicine; I just can't bear to see you suffer this way, under this crank's supervision." I said nothing but prayed that she would refuse, which she did. She said, "I am going to take God, as He has wonderfully delivered me three times since Brother Bevington has been here, and I believe He will heal me entirely." "Well I would like to see some signs," was his response.

I just lay on the floor, praying with all my might. At nine p. m. I rose and laid my hand on her forehead, raised my right hand, and with the Bible laid on it, said, "In the name of Jesus Christ, depart, depart!" I opened my eyes and could see that she was still suffering. I held on, demanding the instant departure, still holding the Bible up, and pleading the promises. When I looked at the clock it was 4:15 a. m., and she was still suffering, but not quite so bad. We still kept holding the Bible changing it from one hand to the other.

Her husband got up from his bed, and saw that she had had a hard night. He was accustomed to waiting on her, hence had gotten so that he could tell by her looks how she was. He grabbed the medicine, shoved me out of the way, and demanded her to open her mouth and take the medicine. She opened her eyes and with a smile shook her head. But I could see that he was boiling, and determined that she should not suffer any longer, as they had the needed remedy. He turned to me and said, "You leave this room; take your traps and leave this house!"

I went outdoors still pleading and believing, and she still refusing to take the medicine. I was out under a tree and was actually getting hold of God when the husband came out and gave me a pretty hard kick, saying, "I told you to leave this place; now I mean it, and will not tell you again." I continued praying there, getting hold of God and did not want to move or utter a word. I felt sure victory was coming. I was so still, though the waters were raging about me; and there was such a sweet, calm, quiet assurance that she was going to be healed, that I just lay as still as I could, fearing any move upon my part would break the connection. I didn't want to breathe, in fact, held my breath at times. Then her husband came out. I turned over, and said, "Let me remain here one hour." He said, "I told you to leave." "Give me one hour and you will see the power of God." "Nonsense, that has been the cry for twenty hours", and he went to the barn to get the large horsewhip.

I got up and went into the house, having the assurance of victory. As I entered, the woman raised her right hand and smiled all over her face. "We have the victory Brother Bevington," she said. I shouted "Amen," and went out of the door. I had not gotten off the porch till I heard her feet strike the floor, and she ran out to the barn yelling at the top of her voice. Her husband was coming in all infuriated, with his whip, to give me a good thrashing. But he was melted as she dropped on her knees, praising God, and praying for him. Then he called me. So I went out and we had an old-fashioned prayer and praise service there in the weeds and grass.

Yes, we had a scene there that three worlds were witness to, till he prayed through and actually got salvation. Oh, what blessed times we had! Then she went to their church and set the whole congregation to weeping and laughing, and some a-shouting. The preacher did not get to preach any at that service. So it pays to hold on to God as He works quite different than we do. Well, Hallelujah. Amen!

This is the twelfth day of April, 1923. I am at South Ashland, Ky., all under the blood, glory to Jesus. Jesus hath redeemed me, hath cleansed me, hath healed me, and hath taken my sickness with Him on the Cross. Glory! He doesn't want us to suffer as He hath delivered us. Hallelujah! Oh, let us praise Him, hold Him up so the world can see Him through us as the world can see Jesus only as they see Him in and through us.

Well, another time after the Cincinnati Camp I was impressed to go down the river to see how the people were getting on at Rising Sun. I went to the depot to wait four hours or more, and while waiting there, a voice seemed to say, "Go out to Mrs.— " She lived about three miles out. Well it seemed so plain that I had to give it some attention, and soon said, "Well, I can walk out there and back for this train." So I took my suit case and grip down to a drug store, and asked permission to leave them there. I then started up the walk, but soon the voice said, "Go back and get the grip." Well, that seemed so foolish that I just took it to be Satan, and said, "Oh, no, you don't come that on me; don't get me to pack that grip out there and back in two hours," and went on.

But that voice still kept calling me to go back and get my grip. It got so plain that I had to stop and give it consideration. But as had been the case so often, my wonderful reasoning faculties had been at their best and were about to carry the day as far as I could see, but that voice could not be silenced, and I had to turn around and go back and get the grip, much to my disgust. Well, I went out to where they last lived to my knowledge but found that they had moved. The party living there could not tell me much about where they lived, so I said, "Now, see, such foolishness as packing this grip these six miles, and back to town! " I started, and at a pretty good speed. But that first voice said, "Go out to Mrs. M—'s." I said, "I can't go out there if I don't know where she lives," and was making good strides back for town to catch that out-going train. But, "Go back, go back, go back!" kept ringing in my ears, till I was stopped as though a man had grabbed me, and the voice said, "Will you, or will you not go back?" Well, I was dumbfounded; what could it all mean? But I turned back, and went to the next house; and the people there told me where they lived.

I went there and found the woman sitting under a tree, and as soon as she saw me, she exclaimed, "Oh, I knew you would come, I knew you would come!" "How did you know?" I asked. "Oh, I heard from headquarters," she said, pointing upward. "I have been suffering a long time from a running sore on my limb, and have been trying to do my work here, but oh, how I have suffered day and night trying to do the work here for my husband and my two boys on this farm! But I heard that you were at the camp, so I just began praying that the Lord would send you out here, and yesterday I saw you coming. So I have rested quite easy on the matter. However I looked for you earlier than this." She had not known, of course, what a time I had had in minding God. I saw at once what it all meant, and threw off my coat, and went into the kitchen to wrestle with the pots and kettles.

That night I prayed for her, and she went to sleep while I was praying. Her husband nudged me, and said, "She is asleep. It is the first time I have known her to sleep without drugs for a long time." The next morning I went to get breakfast, and prepared to do a large washing. At seven I found that she had been suffering severely since three o'clock, though she never woke up till that time. She said, "Oh, Brother Bevington, I am in such misery; please pray for me!" So I started to pray, and in ten minutes she was asleep again. I washed until dinner time, and got dinner for the three men. I then went in to see what she wanted for dinner and found her suffering again. Well, this kept up for over a week, I could get victory for her every time I would pray, but the pains would insist on coming back again.

I got tired of that sort of doings, and went after the case roughshod. I prayed until I struck fire, and she was completely delivered. The second morning, she said, "Brother Bevington, I have two daughters that I haven't seen for several years, and now won't you stay here for three weeks and do the work and let me go and see them? Well, that surprised me, but after praying over it, I saw that it was for me to remain. This Scripture came to me. "In honor preferring one another." So she packed up and went, and had a good three weeks' visit, and came back a different woman, having never felt the soreness of the limb. To Jesus be all the glory!

The multiplication of man's machinery means the diminishing of God's power, for in just the proportion to man's mechanism just in that proportion will God's power decrease. In many places so much of man's ingenuity has been introduced into the workshop of God's house that there isn't enough power to run it, or at least God won't hitch His power onto the bunglesome, weighty, clumsy machinery of man's methods and wisdom. So as prayer taps the reservoir of power, all that is needed is the right kind of prayer.

> *It may not be my way,*
> *It may not be thy way;*
> *But yet in His own way*
> *The Lord will provide.*

This Gospel of healing is one of good tidings. It is for all classes. While all hell is turned against this Bible doctrine of healing, it thus behooves us to be wide-awake, to be at our best, if we expect to get our prayers through.

We were holding a meeting at R—, and a young lady of beautiful character attended all the services that she could, but was hindered by a misfortune in the form of epilepsy. I was informed why she could not come regularly, so went to her home, and prayed the prayer of faith, and she never missed another service while I was there. I have heard her testify several times to her healing at the Cincinnati Camp. So I magnify Jesus as it was He who did it. A brother at this place came to me saying that he had been a sufferer for years from neuralgia, and asked, "If Jesus could heal those two, why can't He heal me?" I said, "He will, if you will allow Him to." "Well, I sure will do that." So I anointed him, and in twenty minutes he said the pain was gone, and he has told me since that it never came back. Oh, glory to Jesus! Will we ever learn to trust Him? Stop, ask that question over again, meditate thereon.

A sister in Ohio where we were holding a meeting was sadly afflicted: She had to be in bed half the time for eight years, and had quite a family of children to look after. I went to her home, anointed her, though it seemed quite dark and much of an uphill pull. I had many misgivings, took me some time to get where I would not allow my eyes to rest on the condition nor the atmosphere. I had to get up and abruptly leave her without any excuse being given. I went to the barn, and lay there several hours. I was then impressed to go back and anoint her again, which I did; and in about forty minutes she raised her hand, and quietly said, "'Tis done; I am a healed woman." Then she got up, dressed herself, and got a fine dinner. That settled all her trouble. So let's shout Amen, and see the devil run, as he can't stand these heaven-sent Amens.

Once while at Ironton I went to hold a meeting in the country. As I often had done before, I went to canvassing the homes, giving out tracts, and telling the children about the extra Sunday school we were to have Sunday. I prayed, too, where I was permitted to. I went in one house where there were several children, the eldest about ten, and the house looked as though it needed a mother there. I was telling the children about the meeting at the schoolhouse, and also about the Sunday school.

Soon the mother came downstairs with her head all bandaged up, and gave evidence that she was and had been suffering. She offered as an apology for the looks of the kitchen that she had been suffering with acute neuralgia for several days, and had been unable to do anything. She said, "I heard you say something about a Sunday school and children's meeting. I have several children here that need such training, and I just said that I must get up and go down and see what he is talking about." I said, "So you have neuralgia. Are you a saved woman?" "Yes Sir." "Well, don't you believe that Jesus can heal you?" "I know He can if I have the faith for it." I said, "Let's all get down and get hold of Jesus."

Well, we got still and in forty minutes I saw rags a-flying. She had torn every rag off, and said, "There is not a pain in my body." Then she jumped up and began walking the floor a-praising God, while tears of joy and gratitude just rolled down her cheeks. She hugged all the children, and I had a good time seeing her appreciate what Jesus had done. She said, "Now Brother you go into the other room, and I will clean up, and get you some dinner." Well, as it was only 10:30, I said, "I will go out an hour, and give out more tracts, and then I will come back." So as I returned at 11:45, she had the house nicely cleaned up, oh, how different she looked than when she came down those stairs! We had a fine dinner.

I taught the three girls a new song, and let me say right here that the youngest of those three girls is out preaching holiness now. She went one or two years to God's Bible School, Celia Bradshaw is her name, and she is a dear precious girl. They had a Sunday school up at the school, and from twelve to sixteen attended; there were hardly ever the same ones two Sundays in succession. But as I went around and had several children meet, I taught them new songs, so that by the next Sunday there were 156 children at the schoolhouse. The superintendent did not know what to do with them all, as he had no teachers, so we divided them in two classes. I took all under twelve, and he took the rest. Now, I mention this to show what a little personal work will do.

Well, before I left there this mother got sanctified, as also did her mother, and her mother was delivered of a serious goiter, from which she was suffering. And though both of them have gone through fires innumerable, yet they have been, and are still, true to Jesus and sanctification. All glory be to Jesus! Now, I believe that all of this came as a result of that mother's healing. So blessings don't stop at healing, but go on and spread out. That is why I still believe in and preach healing.

While holding a meeting in Ohio, I was told why a certain sister did not come to the meetings. She had been in bed several months, and her daughter did the work. They were farmers. I am not much in favor of going to pray for the sick; that is, to pray for their healing, only when asked, yet I felt impressed to go to see her. So I went one afternoon, and saw the condition. I felt that there was a case on hand surely, as she had never seen anyone healed, or heard of anyone's being healed. It was so comforting to her to take her four kinds of medicine. But I knew that Jesus sent me there, and that my God was charitable; so I did not give up the case, but I prayed there in the room without kneeling. Then felt that I must go to the barn and fight the thing to a finish. I knew it would take some time to get her where God could talk to her, and there was our meeting that night.

There was no one to take my place, as the meeting had arrived at a point where I considered it unwise to be absent. So being somewhat confused I went in, and asked her for a private room. I was shown one, and there I fell on my face. In about twenty minutes I felt that I must go to the woods. Well, what would I do about my meeting? But it was, "Go to the woods"; so as I had learned not to question God's ability, I said, "All right," and got up, though a little confused, as I had gotten nothing definite as to the night's meeting. I started downstairs however, with a determination to mind God, whether I was able to see or not. I went out into the hall and out onto the porch, leaving all with God. Glory enveloped me, and I just had to stop and weep as I looked up to praise God, for this was an evidence of approval of my obedience. I looked down the road, and there came a dear brother whom I had not seen or heard of for over a year, and he was walking as fast as he could. He was a Holy Ghost evangelist, and I just shouted "Glory;" threw up my hat, and said. "Well, dear Brother, where in the world are you going?" He just burst out laughing, and said, "Now it is all clear to me why God has been talking so strange to me for the last twelve hours. I had planned to be elsewhere at this time, but about ten hours ago God began to try to tell me something that I could scarcely grasp, as it was breaking into my plans. Now I am sure that God wants me to preach in your place."

Well, I just wept there, threw my arms around him, and we both wept for joy to see how God so minutely carried out His plans, though so foreign to us. He said, "I closed my meeting twenty-one miles from here day before yesterday, and intended opening another meeting tonight; but yesterday God began talking to me about going elsewhere and made me walk all night. I did not know where I was going, yet felt real sure that I was in Divine order. So here I am. I had been led to a certain text for tonight, though I could not see where it was to be delivered, as I was in an entirely new country. I told God that I would preach from that text. I did want to know." Well, you see God could not very well tell him as he know nothing about this place, nor that I was there. But he minded God, hence filled my place, and enabled me to take up the other case, as that seemed to be a case demanding speed.

He said, "I stopped at a friend's yesterday at 3:30 p. m. I got something to eat, went to the barn, and this text was crowding on me, and it was not at all appropriate for an opening service, nor for the place I had in mind." He went to the barn, and cried out to God. "Where art Thou aiming to send me?" All the answer he could get was, "What is that to thee? follow thou me." So he went out and started down the road, like Abraham, not knowing whither he was going. You see that was none of his business. He said, "Here I am, and now, Brother Bevington are you willing for me to preach tonight?" Well, I had a hearty laugh. Then I told him of the struggle that I had been going through for the last ten hours. So you see how God will work, if we will give Him a chance. So Jesus had quite a time in getting me to let go of the meeting, as well as in getting the brother to come and take it. Oh, what trouble we would save our blessed Lord if we would just relinquish our hold, and let God; yes, let God! Here God opened the way that we both could meet on the plane of obedience, fully realizing that the puzzling features would all be obliterated, if we would get out of the way.

Now, this woman's husband was a close observer of all the rules of their church there, but had no use for holiness preachers, so I found out why she had not sent for me, and why we had to go there much against my rule, so to the woods I went. I said to the evangelist, "Now, brother, be sure and mind God; don't leave here till you have unmistakable orders to do so, as I may be in the woods a week, or may leave there in the morning." I had no opportunity of notifying anyone of the change, nor the reasons for it, as God seemed very anxious that I should get to the woods, and leave the whole thing in His hands. That seems so hard for us to do, as we seem to have such wonderful executive and judicial properties in us that God has a terrible time in getting a chance to display any of His power.

I got under a tree, and wrestled all night, and I never saw the brother until camp meeting at Cincinnati. He started out and walked thirteen miles to the station, as no one there was interested enough in holiness to invite him home with them. I was somewhat used to that, as many times I lived in the woods for days, no one inviting me home with them. But when I knew that God sent me there, why I would go to the woods, or to the haymow, and live on acorns or sassafras bark, until God could get someone saved.

So at five o'clock that next morning I saw her sitting up in bed a-clapping her hands, so I jumped up and ran all the way to the house, as I wanted to get there before she got through. As I neared the barn, I saw the daughter in the door, calling, "Papa, come here quick; oh, hurry up!" So he had started in just ahead of me. I passed him, ran around to the front door, and found the wife out of bed, jumping and clapping her hands and shouting, "God has healed me! God has healed me!" She saw her husband and ran to him, and said, "O dear husband, Jesus healed me! Now won't you love this holiness preacher for staying with us until I was healed?" She said, "I saw Jesus come into the room at the foot of the bed just as the clock struck five, and He said, 'I have come to heal you.' And O husband, such a wonderful sight! Oh, I never saw such a face, oh, so sweet, so loving, so tender, so sympathetic. Oh, husband, I wish you could have seen Him as I saw Him, and before leaving He touched my body; I felt it go through me like electricity." And as the tears of joy fell in great drops, she continued to say, "I am healed, I am healed!" She did not know where I was, and supposed I had been to the meeting and was then upstairs in bed. I have seen her twice at the Cincinnati camp, and she had a good testimony. She never took another drop of medicine, for at least about nine years, as since then I have lost track of her.

So all we need is to mind God. I was well aware that God sent me there to conduct that meeting, but could not understand why He wanted to interfere (as we are too apt to say) with His own plans, by sending me to the woods, and sending another to take my place. So the essential thing is to get where we will know the voice of God, and then obey Him, whether it conflicts with the arranged program or not. But you can see that though He broke into the original plans, the work was not stopped or hindered, and resulted in a good revival, where some twenty actually prayed through, and several were healed. On the night of the day that this woman was healed, she came to the meeting and fell at the altar for sanctification, and her husband fell at the same despised holiness mourners' bench for salvation, as his meeting house religion didn't seem to harmonize with what he had seen and realized. He had held every office and position in said church but that of pastor and janitor. It took him four days, as we knelt right behind him and held him foursquare to the Bible, so he could not back out without crawling over us. He said several times in his testimony:

"I would have backed out several times had it not been that Bevington was close at my heels. I could not get up without making a display there." He said, "I do thank God that Bevington had the grit to stick to my back, shaking me over hell until I made a complete surrender, and hence got something that enables me to know that I am saved." Later he got sanctified. And their proud society daughter, a vain girl, had to succumb to the prayers of us three, as we turned all the forces of heaven on her, and she finally yielded. So all this came just because I was willing to be a laughing stock for the whole family, which resulted in her healing. I tell you it sets my soul on fire as I write about these wonderful manifestations of God's power.

I held a meeting in Ohio, and several got saved; so two years later someone sent me money to come back. As the meeting progressed, I kept missing one sister who had been such a power after she got saved in that first meeting. I kept wondering why I did not see her. "They must have moved away," I thought. I could not, or at least did not, ask anyone about her, as it seemed I would not think of it only when I was absent from those that would know until several days had passed. Then I was praying and this woman came to my mind.

So I got right up, and went out into the kitchen. "Sister, what has become of Sister D— ? Why doesn't she come to church? Has she backslidden?" "Why

Brother Bevington, haven't you heard about her?" I said, "I guess not; why?" "She scalded her foot; is laid up in bed, and has been there for nine months. They got a doctor. Three or four of us went and reminded her of what you had preached on Divine healing, but she clung to the doctor. We wanted her to write to you, but she held onto the doctor. She went to the hospital, and is there now. They have spent $700.00, and they are talking of taking her limb off above her knee. She has suffered terribly." Now note all this, as I want to show you the difference in doctoring down here (going down to Egypt) and in doctoring with my doctor.

Here was a woman who knew that God healed; as her niece was instantly healed the first time I was in the neighborhood; and this woman rejoiced so much over that healing. But you probably say as she said, "Oh, well this is different, a different case, a different cause, and so on." How Satan loves to hoodwink God's children by getting their eyes on the conditions, instead of on Jesus. Do you reckon that Jesus' power is confined to conditions, or surroundings? Is Jesus confined to certain conditions? I want to record right here for the glory of God, that for the last thirty-two years I have not seen a peculiar case, I am not looking for them; I will not allow myself to look at the peculiarity of the surroundings. I just see Jesus and Him alone. He says, "I am the God that healeth thee."

I want to show you the difference between trusting God, and refusing to trust Him, as this woman was a great sufferer for sixteen months, and then had the limb taken off above her knee, costing them nearly a thousand dollars. Now here is the other side. When I was keeping house about two squares from where I am now typing here in Ashland, I was having some boiled potatoes for dinner. I had a large quantity of water on them so as to prevent scorching the kettle. I was pouring the boiling water off, and by not having sufficient rags, I suppose, the lid slipped off, and over a quart of that boiling water went into my shoe. I was practicing economy; hence had on a pair of shoes that were intended to be good ventilators. Of course it was painful. I set the kettle down, laid my hand on the steaming shoe, and said, "Now, dear Jesus, I was thoughtless no doubt, but did not intend to be."

At once Satan reminded me of that sister in the country, who had spent nearly a thousand dollars. I said, "Now I have no money and wouldn't go down to Egypt if I did have. I can't afford to be laid up sixteen months and then lose my limb, (and mind you all this time that foot was just paining terribly) and the pains had shot up to the knee. Of course Satan was there to give vent to his sympathy for me in that sad event. He was trying to get me to hurry up. He said, "Get off that shoe quick; it will burn down to the bone, as the shoe and sock are retaining the heat." I tell you the tears were falling as a result of the pain, but I was waiting on God. I was nearer Him than to Egypt.

Of course there was logic in Satan's suggestions; but I ignored them as I felt like giving Jesus a chance at the foot. So when I had gotten still, and fully given the case over to Jesus, committed all to Him, I laid my hand again on the steaming shoe. Sickening pains shot up to my knee, but I said, "Now Jesus, as I take off this shoe, please do not allow any of the skin to come off, if it is better not to. So I took off the shoe. Satan said, "You have been so slow that it has burned clear to the bone; that is why those pains are flashing up to your knee." I came to the sock and laid my hand on it, and said, "Now Jesus, Thou art my Healer, have been for years. This is quite serious, and Satan is on hand to remind me that the sister had only a pint of water go into her shoe, and her shoe was not full of holes either;" but I said, "Lord, as I pull off this sock, please allow the skin to remain at present."

I was to have a street meeting that night, and had three-fourths of a mile to walk over cobblestones. I closed my eyes, as I began pulling off the sock. It came off with much pain, and before opening my eyes, I said, "O God, Thou art my Healer! Please stop this awful pain." I was still holding my hand on the foot, and with my eyes still closed, I said, "Yes, Lord; yes, Lord; yes, Lord." And as the last "Lord" fell from my lips, the pain stopped. I still had my eyes closed, and just sat there weeping for joy. I raised my right hand and went to praising God for being my Healer. Then I opened my eyes, and not a particle of skin was off. The foot looked very red and disfigured, but there was no pain. Satan said, "You better send word to Brother Stapleton to be sure to be there, as you can't walk that distance tonight. You won't dare to put your shoes on this week, give it a chance so that you will be ready for Sunday school next Sunday." (This was Tuesday.) He said, "It will be very unwise for you to attempt to put a shoe on and go there and stand on that damp ground. You will catch cold, have a long, serious, painful time."

All this was quite logical, of course. I am just as confident that if I had listened to that plea and recognized it as coming from God, as about nineteen out of every twenty do, that I would have been as bad as the sister. Satan tried to get me to wrap the foot up, put some soft cloths around it! But I refused all his suggestions, put on a dry sock, and put on my shoe. After dinner I went to the street meeting, and stood on the damp ground. We had a blessed time;

hands went up for prayer, and that night was the starting point for two precious souls to find Jesus. Oh, how God did bless my soul, as I testified to what Jesus had done! I went to prayer meeting in our church the next night, testified to my healing there, and oh, the hearty Amens that rolled up! Rev. John Fleming, the pastor, just threw his arms around me, and wept for joy. I could feel that he heartily approved of all I had said. Sister Walker had a spell, and a number of others were greatly blessed. All said that it was a glorious meeting. So you see that was the end of the scalded foot. I saved $1,000 and sixteen months of suffering, and also my limb. So can you see any difference in the two processes or choices of doctors? Which would you prefer? Well, I still hold to the old family doctor, Jesus. Hallelujah to Jesus!

Now that old skin all came off, and it was terribly shriveled up flesh; but it all came out clean and new, and I never missed a service and never experienced any pain or inconvenience. The old skin would not come off until there had been new grown on under it. I never pulled any of the old off, just let that be for my doctor to do. So many times there would be loose skin, and Satan would say, "Now pull that off; it will irritate the foot and prevent the new from coming on smooth." But I would not do any such thing, as I convinced Jesus back there in the kitchen, with the potatoes lying on the floor and pains shooting up to my knee, that I would turn the case entirely over to Him; hence dared not to interfere, or even suggest. Amen and amen! I dared not look at the symptoms.

I am reminded of something that I feel should be recorded right here, relative to symptoms. When I first took healing I was taught that in order to exercise faith and get direct results, I must deny the symptoms. Well, of course, I tried that, but I would get confused. One time I had a severe toothache, "Well, just deny it." I did, but the fact was against such proceedings, as I knew very well that I had the toothache. Well, I dropped on my face, and said, "Now, Lord, these people here tell me to deny that I have the toothache. What am I to do? There must be some better way out of this than that." I lay there over an hour waiting on God. The answer came, and this is it: "You need not deny the symptoms, but you can deny their right on your body." Then I saw at once where I had been wrongly instructed. So I jumped up, and said, "Yes, they are there, but according to the Word, they don't belong to me; this toothache does not belong to me. I will not have it. I belong to Jesus. This body, this head, with every tooth, belongs to God; 'tis His property, as He says, "Ye are not your own, for ye are bought with a price; therefore glorify God in your body, and in your spirit, which are God's." So I took that stand, and in twenty minutes the toothache was gone. I have followed that plan up ever since, and always come off conqueror. Hallelujah!

I will give you one instance directly on this line. Although I was healed at Hamilton of rheumatism, yet that does not imply that it would be impossible to ever have another attack of it. I had been holding meetings in the woods, under a large tree down below Portsmouth, O. There was much rain, yet the people would come, and several nights someone would hold an umbrella over me while I preached. And there was someone at the altar every night. They would put in dry straw each night, yet by the time of the altar service, it would be damp. We would be on our knees on the damp ground for hours, till our clothing would be wet. Each night my limbs up to and above my knees would be damp. I might have exercised more zeal than knowledge; but let that be as it may, I got the rheumatism quite bad. That was several years after the healing at Hamilton. Well, Satan was on hand as usual, and of course brought in his logic, relative to my indifference to God's laws by getting my limbs so wet. I had quite a time with the pain all night, and slept but little. Satan came nearly swamping me on the grounds that I certainly could not expect Jesus to heal me after I had deliberately violated all laws, knowingly.

In the morning I was suffering quite a bit, and had a time in getting out of bed. I ate nothing until about 4:00 p. m. I prayed and wrestled as best I could, and finally came to the place where I saw that if I preached that night there would have to be something done, and that right away, too. So I began to plead the promises, but made slow progress at that, and soon said, "Yes, not only the symptoms but the real thing is here. I can't deny that. "But just then I caught an inspiration, and said, "Mr. Devil, this rheumatism doesn't belong to me, Sir. I will not have it!" Well, I heard his chuckle, plainly, and he said, "Ha, Ha, you can't help yourself." I said, "You are a liar, Sir, I can be helped."

I got hold of two chairs and got up. Again Satan gave me the laugh, saying, "You look like walking across this room." I said, "I will do it;" and started with the two chairs. I made slow progress; was just an hour and forty minutes going from one corner to the other but, thank God, I made it. I said, "Now, dear Lord, I believe that you inspired me to make that assertion; you will help me just now to put this foot in the corner, and then victory is assured." And for the first time I felt strong enough to raise my foot without the aid of my hands, and planted it in the corner, so that the toe of my shoe struck the corner. The moment it did the pain was all gone and added strength was given. Oh, how the glory did fall as I praised God, while the tears flowed freely! You see I had to contend earnestly for every inch across that room; but I did so though it took an hour and fifty minutes. That was about the best hundred minutes I ever put in since I was sanctified. I never had even a symptom of the rheumatism since. So I repeat, It pays to go through with Jesus and trust Him. Where there is no opposition, there is no advance made.

Now I feel impressed to give one instance of prayer answered, and the results of holding onto God. I was holding a meeting in Ohio, in the country. That seemed to have been our field of operation, among those that did not have big meetings very often. The presiding elder came and preached on Sunday, and also preached for us on Monday night. He gave a good message against the saloon, showing that the majority of fallen girls and wayward boys came through the saloons. It was a heavy blow on the saloons, but of course could not be too heavy.

When he had finished this remarkable message, he said, "Well, Brother Bevington did I hit them too hard?" "Oh," I said, "I suppose not." Well, that answer and the way I said it rather shocked him; he thought that I was going to pat him on the back. He gave me a surprised and somewhat curious look, which made it necessary for me to explain myself. So I said, "No; I guess not," and then I said, "You and your people put that man in there and gave him license and authority to sell the hellish stuff. You, Sir, and your fellowmen told the government to put that man in there and let him sell the stuff to make lawless men and women, and you demanded of the government that they should protect him in his nefarious business." Well, he disagreed with me. But I held that if the professors, even of the M. E. Church, would vote prohibition, that would throw out the saloons. I said, "The saloon keeper was put in there by you people. He pays his rights, at your approval." He didn't like that very well, but did not allow it to interfere with his mission. He and I were going to the same place for lodging that night, about a mile from the schoolhouse where he, as I supposed, had given the fatal blow to the saloons.

The next morning he said, "I understand Brother Bevington that you put quite an unusual amount of time in prayer, often go to the woods, and spend hours in prayer out there. I was told that you generally remain there until God answers. I heartily approve of that and wish I had the time to put in at that kind of work. Now, my object over here is that I may get you interested in a puzzling case. It has baffled all efforts in trailing the matter out. There is a beautiful family over where I came from yesterday, a most precious family. They are highly cultured, all very refined, studious, careful, prayerful, and quite well off. They are the most humble people I ever met. They have an only child, a daughter of estimable character, and loved by all. She is now seventeen, and a year ago she gave birth to a baby girl, and she still is unmarried. This has been a terrible blow on the family, nearly crushing their lives out, and none of them have been to the church since, or for sixteen months. They will not be persuaded to come, as the calamity seems to be more than they can face. This girl is still there caring for the baby, and the great trouble is, no one can see her, and but few the mother. They keep secluded. He is trying to sell, as they want to get away from the scene that has brought them down to the lowest plane, as they see it. And the people are doing all they can to prevent his selling.

Now that I have given you the facts in the case," he said, "and as you have been accustomed to ferret out such cases through prayer, by the way of the throne, I came over here purposely to get you on the trail, and trail it out." I want you to remember that he used the word "trail". He said, "Get onto the trail Brother Bevington, and the pastor and his board and I will stand by you; will be right at your back. You just stick to the trail, and don't give it up until you have uncovered the matter." The whole thing is founded on that word trail. So as a trail-finder and sticker I will proceed.

Now I will take you back about a year, to where I was holding a meeting near Chillicothe, Ohio. The man with whom I was staying had several fox hounds which he valued highly. One was my favorite. He was very intelligent. Well, one night I heard a terrible yelping, and heard blow after blow laid on the dog, until I just could not stand it any longer. I got up, went to the window, and called out, "Who is pounding that dog that way?" When the answer came, I recognized it as from the brother with whom I was stopping. I said, "Why, brother, what in the world are you pounding that poor dog like that for?" "Well, Brother Bevington, he is my main fox dog, and I get money from others in training their dogs by this one. I was to get $5.00 tonight; but this dog got off on a rabbit's track, and nothing was done." "Well," I said, "does he knew the difference?" "Why, most assuredly he does, and that is why I am whipping him so." "Well, will it do him any good?" "Yes, Sir; it will be a long time before he will take up an other rabbit's trail." Please remember, too, that the elder told me to be sure and stick to the trail. That dog got a terrible whipping for getting off on another trail. So you see, if I failed to stick to it, I might get what the dog got. Now keep these things in view, as they are to play an important part in the coming events.

6: Personal Dealings   111

Now we will go back to the elder's trail. When I closed my meeting over there, I went to the woods, as that is my college. When I got comfortably quartered in a hollow log, I said, "Now, Lord, dost Thou want me to take up this trail? Thou knowest the father of that baby, and all about it; is the case demanding a ferreting out? What wilt Thou have me do about it?" Well, I lay there several hours, before I could get much light, yet dared not crawl out of my apartment house. "Wouldst Thou be getting any glory out of it? " I repeated several times. The trouble was I had several places awaiting my appearance for a meeting, though no definite dates were set, as I always avoided setting times for a meeting to begin or close. That was always left entirely for the Father to attend to. Many have said, "Well, Brother, where are you going when you get through here?" The only answer I could give was, I don't know.

So it took me several hours to dispose of these prospective places, as some of them would be liberal in their offerings, and my pocket-book had been laid on so much that it had gotten pretty well flattened out, all of which would be used of Satan to keep me from getting at the point of issue. So it took me nearly nineteen hours to find out whether God wanted me to take up this trail. After these hours on my face, I was clearly impressed to take up the trail. Well, it was somewhat difficult to get on the trail, to get started right, and to know that I was right. It took me fifty-four hours to get still and small enough so that God could handle me, and get me on the trail.

So many of us are so important, so big, so great, so clumsy, so awkward, that it takes God quite a while to get us on the wheel, so He can trim us up some, as He has some pretty small places for us to get through. He has to grind off a lot of this importance, as He can't handle that very well in developing the cases, whatever they may be. I finally got to the place where He could actually pick me up, and set me over there on the trail, much to my dissatisfaction, as I could not discover a track, nor even scent the presence of one; but having received so many thrashings for setting up my ideas, I just got down and soon had the scent, and was making good headway.

Now let's go back to what the preacher and the official board said, "Be sure and stick to the trail." So I will draw on my imagination somehow, as I have always reserved that right in demonstrating things, and in this case it will help you in getting the case clearly set up in your minds. The four told me to stick to the trail, and I had a right to assume that they meant it. They were on hand to do all they could in getting me to the climax. So now here comes the imaginative help, as they said, "We will be at your back," so as I am on the trail, I want you to see them following me up in the rear: and as the trail goes through some pretty dark places, somewhat difficult to trace out, they call out occasionally, "Ha, Bevington, are you still on the trail?" I answer back. "Yes, still on the trail, and making headway, though slow." "Well, stick to it as we are at your back; we want that thing ferreted out."

Well, I will not enter into all the details that I faced during the nine days; but I stuck to it day and night without anything to eat, and had only two drinks of water during that time. I would get so close at times that I dared not leave the trail to get a drink, while occasionally there would ring out the words "Ha, Brother Bevington, are you still on the trail? " Of course, I would assure them that I was. Now on the ninth morning, as I lay there at 3:30, I saw a large church. Now remember I was on the trail of the father of that babe. Yes, there was a large church with a deep porch in front, and steps going up on said porch from each end, one for the ladies and the other for the gentlemen. There was a door at each side of the church on the end and a space in between these two doors, perhaps two feet wide and three feet long and a marble slab in this space, with the name of the church in large letters, and the time it was built. Now, all of this I saw with my eyes closed, some fourteen miles from the pla ce; and there is where the trail led me.

I was then hungry, for the first time during the nine days and nights; so I got up and found that I was very weak, and quite exhausted. I had to rub myself some time in a sitting posture before I could stand on my feet or get the use of my faculties, but I succeeded in getting down to the house where I had been staying. They did not know where I had been, and I said, "Sister, is there such a church?" giving her in full the description I had seen on my face. "Why, yes, that is our charge here, a nice large church, and a strong congregation. Why, have you been over there?" "Well, — Yes, I saw it." Well, she said, "I was wondering where you were (my grip was there). Yes we often go over there as it is only about fourteen miles, and good roads. There are some fine people over there, but — " and then she stopped, bit her lips, and changed the conversation.

Well, I knew what was on her mind. She asked, "When were you over there?" I said "I just came from there." "Well, that puzzled her, as it was only about 6: 00 a. m. So I told her what the elder and the official board said and that I had trailed the thing to that church. Well I saw at once that that was a blow, and that if she had had a spark of confidence in me, it was all knocked out then and there, as what I had told her was the height of folly.

Now I want to go back to that hollow log, where I saw, in addition to the church, a path from the back of the church going down a slope to a fence where was a grove, in the midst of same grove a large spring. I saw all this behind that log and told her of it. "Yes," she said, "that is all there." I had never been nearer than fourteen miles of the church. Then I told her of that wonderful sermon the elder preached against the saloon, and how it ought to be exposed as all degeneracy was started in the saloon. She looked at me sternly, and said, "Well, Brother Bevington, do you really believe that all this disgrace was wrought through that church?" No one had ever been able to glean any information, relative to where or by whom it was done. "Yes ma'am, it was through a box social, as the Lord has shown me." "Oh, I can't believe it." "Well, I can't help that." "Well, what is to be done about it? They will never give consent to such a report as that, going out against that grand old church. You will have to let it drop; say no more about it, and you had better get out of here before it gets noised around." I said, "No, I can't let it drop, as the four cautioned me to stick to the trail." "Well," she said, "the pastor from that church is down here five miles visiting a member who recently moved from near this church. Do you think it best to see him before you go away? If so I will have the boy go after him in our buggy." "Yes, I wish you would." So off he went.

Soon here comes the pastor, and he got there about 3:00 p. m. He threw up his hands in horror at the report, shook his head defiantly, and said, "I will not accept that at all." "Well, Sir, you have to accept it, whether you want to or not." He rose and said, "Mr. (He did not address me as Brother, but said sarcastically, Mr.) you have seen this church or have gotten all this from someone, and now you want to bring this awful calamity within its pure, unstained portals. Sir, you shall not do any such thing, and more than that, Sir, I want you to get out of here; and if you haven't money, I will take you to the train and loan you money until you see fit to pay it, and if you never do, it will be all right." I said, "Do you remember what you and the other three said, that you all would stand by me, and that I should stick to the trail? Do you remember that?" So off he went, drove forty-four miles for the elder — "going to have that crank put where he won't be bringing such disgraces in the churches!" Why, they had me branded as a genuine church splitter.

So next day, here they all come — pastor, elder, official board — all denouncing me, except the elder; he didn't seem to have much to say, and I felt that he was thinking it possible, though maybe hardly probable. They gave me twenty-four hours to get out of that country. Well, I had gotten accustomed to threats — threats of rotten eggs, clubs, tar and feathers and rail, dungeons, insane asylums, pits, and jails, and even the whipping post. So I was not badly frightened, and made no move towards packing up and getting, as they had ordered. They said, "Aren't you going to get ready to leave?" I said, "I will not be too hasty about this; I will have to wait on the Lord to get orders."

The pastor rose, and said, "Here are your orders." I said, "I will have to wait on the Lord, and when He says 'Go,' I will go, and not before." The three said. "It will never do to have such reports go out relative to this grand old landmark." Well, for the first time, the elder spoke up and said, "Well, Brother Bevington, i t may be possible that this is all true; and suppose that we admit that it is true, would it not be better to drop it, and we will pay your way to your next place."

"Well," I said, "you told me to stick to the trail, and if I should do as you say, then the question would arise with me at least, What did you do? Did you stick to the trail? It would necessitate my telling a lie, by saying that I lost the trail. I said, "It was done there in that grove, at one of your box socials." I said to the elder, "Do you remember that sermon you preached against the saloons?" "Yes." "Well, there you said that every crime that was started in the saloon ought to be published, and the saloon keepers made to face it. Expose the saloon keepers as the cause. Now," I said, "when a girl loses her virtue in and through a church, is the crime or disgrace lessened any, just because it was done through the church?

" Well, he had to admit that the crime stood as horrible in one case as another, but said, "It must not be exposed here." I said, "If a girl is ruined in and through a saloon, then go for the saloon keeper hot and heavy, but if the same act is committed by and through the church, then it must be crushed." I said, "O Consistency, thou art a jewel!" and continued. "I cannot keep still on this matter. 'Tis now reported that I lay up in the woods nine days on this matter."

"Well," they said, "you can't prove it, as she will not allow anyone to see her."

Well, I just left them, and went to the woods and got into my former commodious quarters, and said, "Now, Lord, Thou hast permitted me to go this far and now here I am to get permission to see that girl and get the whole truth from her." That was quite a large proposition, as she would not allow anyone to see her. Well, it took me just seventy-two hours to keep the buzzards off, and get still, by getting them entirely out of the way.

The troublesome buzzards were not confined only to the prophetic days, but seem to have quite a numerous following these days, swooping down upon us, and devouring the offerings of revelations. After fighting seventy-two hours, and keeping all hell off, I got still, and saw myself approaching a house from the back, going down a hill, crossing a creek, going up a bank to a garden fence. Then I climbed over the fence, went through the garden, through a gate and then up on the back porch. I knocked at the door. When the door opened, there was the mother of the babe, and she invited me in.

Now this was all seen as I lay on my face, up in the woods. So I got up, and ran right into the path that led me through all this that I have here described. I then came to the brow of the hill, saw the house, and the path to the creek, and thence to the garden. I just stopped, got behind a tree, and there poured out my heart in gratitude to my blessed Leader. I praised Him that He had granted me the privilege of outwitting all men's efforts. I then counted it all done, and went just as stated, and the mother of the babe opened the door, invited me in, and gave me a chair there in the kitchen. Well, seeing that I was a stranger, she was quite embarrassed, and called her mother. The mother came in, and was surprised to see me there with her daughter, but she gave me a hearty shake of the hand. They both broke out in tears and wept, perhaps, thirty minutes. Nothing but the deep sobs could be heard; not a word was uttered. I wept too, as I could read between the sobs what it all meant to their precious hearts .

While we were there wrapped in silence, getting down to where the real life was, the father came in. He took in the whole situation at once, and threw his arms around his daughter, and there was another pathetic scene. Soon he released his hold and clasped my hand. His tears were flowing, and his frame was trembling, until my whole body was under its influence. We wept as if our hearts would break. I felt that I was never under such a holy, pure influence as pervaded that kitchen! It seemed that the great weight which had been crushing them was being applied to me. And I don't remember of ever having such intense heart throbs of sorrow as then. We all cried and cried, and it seemed that we could not quit. I wanted to go to the barn, but seemed to be held by an unseen power. Oh, reader, the blessed Holy Ghost was there, in the midst of that shame. Oh, it was so beautiful! I felt that underneath were His everlasting arms, so real were those arms 'neath all four of us that I just burst out between the sobs, " Oh, dear beloved, God is here; His arms are beneath us!" At that the father released his hold of my hand, reeled back and fell into his dear wife's arms, and they both fell on a sofa, and gave vent to heart burst, which I will never forget.

Oh, reader I can scarcely type these lines, as tears flow freely, as I go over that scene. But I had to break the long silence. I still cried, "Dear beloved, His arms are beneath us now, yes, now. Oh, we are emerging from the awful darkness that has hung like a death pall these seventeen months." I began to praise God; and the mother of the girl rose and clasped my hand, weeping for joy, as she waved her right hand above her gray hairs. Oh, I never saw gray hairs that looked so beautiful, as she stood before me, face radiant with the glow of heaven. She said, "I know that thou art a man of God. You are the only one that has been in this home for seventeen months."

The father said, "All sit down," so we did. The mother of the babe rose, oh, so beautiful, not in outward appearance as she was not possessed with what the world calls a beautiful face; but I was getting glimpses of her inner being, and there so meek, and lovely, she told the whole thing from beginning to end. At the time of this box social, the father was very busy in the wheat field, and could not go, neither could the mother; but seven of the nice girls came and importuned strongly for them to let the girl go. They said, "We all will go together, and remain together, come home together. We have change to treat ourselves." So the father and mother consented, and the girls went. But as soft drinks, and cakes with a ring in them, were gambled off, excitement rose pretty high, and girls were put up at twenty cents, a vote for the prettiest girl, and so on, until they all got coupled off and parted. This girl with the rest.

Well after they had been eating and so on, her company suggested that they take a stroll down to the spring and get a drink. She did not like that very well, but finally consented, as he said that they would return in a few minutes. As they came to the spring the young man said, "Now there hasn't been any school here for some time, and the water may not be just right. As I am passing here daily I like to get a drink, but the doctor told me that I should use a preventive; so he gave me a powder to purify the water; so we will use it now."

He gave her the first drink, and she said that was the last she knew, until the next morning when she woke up, in her own bed. She thought it very kind in him to be prepared against impure water. All the time she was telling this, she was in tears, and had her head bowed. Finally she looked up, and said, "I wonder how this all came about! I never could allow myself to see even my dearest friend. Oh," she said, as she placed her hands over her ears, "is this a dream; what have I done?" She seemed bewildered, but continued, "I have told you all, all that I have ever lisped, even to my dear parents who stood so nobly by me in my fall." And at that she fell into her mother's arms.

Oh, reader, such a scene; I wish I were able to picture it! She said, "Oh, this is a mystery!" The father rose and clasped her in his arms, and said, "Daughter, this is no mystery; God has answered your mother's and my prayers by sending this man of God here to get at this." Then they asked me how it was that I had come. So I told them all that had been told me, and how I had been in the woods nine days, and then again about seventy-three or seventy-four hours, and how I had seen the path, and followed it to the kitchen. Well, now, how long do you think all this took? It took over eleven hours before we were through in that kitchen. And then it was nearly twelve, midnight. So I was shown a good bed, and I tell you I appreciated it, too, as I had spent about 303 hours without any bed or anything to eat. And the next morning enjoyed some good country ham for breakfast. They all marveled at the greatness and accuracy of God.

So ever since then, more than ever, I have fought box socials, have suffered many a time by the stand I took, but have lived through all, and am as bold against them now as ever. I remember one time I had to walk sixty-two miles and carry a heavy grip, just because of the stand I took against box socials. I will say to our holiness preachers: Take your stand emphatically against them. Cry aloud, spare not, lift up thy voice against it; thunder it wherever you go. Let us rise up as one, pierce the serpent to its very center, until we have driven it from our midst. Well, the family soon sold out, and went to northern Michigan to the pine lumber belt. I saw the girl once at the Cincinnati Camp, and she still had a good experience.

I was once holding a meeting in Kentucky. I was invited to a home for the night, and about two o'clock I heard a terrible racket downstairs. I arose, went to the head of the stairs to ascertain what was going on. "Why, Brother Bevington, Lucy is dying with terrible cramps." Though I was a stranger to all of them, as that was my first night there, yet I went down, and found Grandma rushing in and out to the smoke house. Every one in the house was up doing all that they could to save the child's life. There she was writhing in pain. Three were trying to hold her, while two were trying to keep the hot cloth, and the contents of Grandma's smoke house on her.

The mother stopped long enough to wring her hands in agony, saying, "Brother Bevington, what can we do more than is being done? Husband is out in the woods after the horses to go for the doctor." "Well," I said, "sister, if you all let her go and take all of those remedies off her, it may be that Jesus will heal her." "Oh, Brother Bevington, she could not live five minutes without these applications!" So as they were doing their best, Grandma stopped, and said,

"Mister, did you ever see anyone healed?" I said, "Plenty of them." "Well," she said, "I have heard of such likes, but never saw one. No one never round here has done that way." And she looked so earnestly at me, as though she had done her best, and the child was suffering unbearable pains. "Well," I said, "if you will strip her of those remedies and let go of her, you all will see the power of God."

They all feared to venture on my suggestion, and wanted me to help hold her down, which I declined to do. The mother said, "Why, Brother Bevington, if we take our hands off her, she will plunge out of bed and kill herself, and we will be charged with murder." "Well," I said, "just do as you see fit." I left the room, but Grandma followed me upstairs, and said, "Don't leave us. Oh," she said, "I would love to see Jesus heal her. And are you sure He will if we let her go?" Well, I saw that they were so blind to the power of Jesus that I ventured further than I generally do, and said, "Yes, Grandma, He will, but can't get at her now as there isn't room for Him in that room."

So Grandma went into the room, and led me in, and said, "This man says that Jesus will heal her if we all get out of the way and take all rags and poultices off." At that the mother let go of the child, and wrung her hands, and said, "Oh, I can't assume all this responsibility. Oh, it is too much for me." And all this while there were four trying to hold the child down. I raised my hand, and the girl dropped down with eyes closed. The mother said, "She is dead." I said, "She is not dead but she is quiet." I said, "Now remove all those remedies." Grandma went at it, and had a pile on the floor as large as a half bushel. I then asked all doubters to leave the room. None left. I said, "Do you all believe that Jesus will heal this child?" One spoke up, and said, "Well, we none of us can say we do, but we will not be in your way in the least. We all would love to see Jesus manifest His healing power on this suffering child." So I took the oil, anointed her, prayed the prayer of faith, and in twenty minutes she was asleep.

I went back to bed and when the doctor reached there, he found her asleep, and said there was nothing the matter with her. He did not leave any medicines as he had been in the habit of doing. When the father came in, he rushed up to her, laid his hand on her, and said, "She is dead, Doctor." The doctor laughed. He had never seen anyone healed. It was new to him. The father had quite a time to believe that the child was healed. If it had been more gradual, he probably would have more readily received it. The doctor went home, and then they all went to bed but the father. He had not struggled as the others had, so he remained up to call them all in a few minutes, as he would have it that she could not be healed.

I went upstairs, walked the floor, bathed in tears of joy and in praise for what Jesus had done. I was called down to breakfast. I had pleaded that the child would get up of its own accord and go out to breakfast and eat a hearty meal; so when I entered the kitchen, there sat the child as well as ever. She jumped up and threw her arms around me, and just hugged me good and laughed and cried. I told her that she ought to hug Jesus as He was the one that healed her. "Well," she said, "I know He is, but you are the only one that has ever been around here with the faith that you have, for healing."

After breakfast, Grandma said, "Brother Bevington, come here." She took me out to the smoke house, such a sight — rafters loaded down with all sorts of remedies! Poor Grandma toiled days and weeks in the fall getting that great display of roots, herbs, leaves, barks — all for the keeping up of worn-out or disabled bodies. She said, "Good-bye", and she looked up, and said, "Now Jesus, if you can heal Lucy, you can and will heal all the rest of us." She said, "Brother Bevington, I want you to get them all down, for I will make a bonfire of them." I said, "Grandma, are you sure you can trust Jesus, as I won't be around here long?" She said, "Yes, Sir, I have seen what I have never seen before and I will believe and trust Jesus." I said, "Then you really want me to get them down?" "Yes, Sir." "Well, hadn't we better see your son, the father of Lucy?" "Well, you can see him if you want to, but I assure you that he will not object."

So I went out to the barn, and said, "Your mother wants me to haul down that drug store in the smoke house and make a bonfire of them. What do you think about it?" So he went up to the house to see if Lucy was still up, and he found her out in the swing, just laughing, and she said, "Oh, Papa, I never felt as I now feel. I know that Jesus healed me." So we went back to the barn, and he told me to do as Grandma said, so we had the pleasure of stripping those rafters and boxes and hooks of that great store; and Lucy, with a radiant face, lighted the fire. We all had a blessed time at the bonfire. I have seen them several times, but they say Grandma never gathered up any more remedies. Lucy was sound and well and went to school, which she had never been able to do. O Hallelujah, to our great Physician! Amen!

I was holding a meeting once, back of Willard, Kentucky, the former home of the famous Fleming boys. Their mother is still living there. I was invited home by the Ison family, strangers to me. We were in a jolt wagon, and the wife carried a large lamp so as to see the best road, as the roads were bad. The wife jumps out of the wagon with the baby. The lamp was handed her, chimney hot, and the baby got its little hand against chimney, and burned it badly. We put the mules out and went in. The little thing was screaming terribly, and the mother was walking the floor in great agony. The girls were trying to do something, but all to no avail. I said, "Sister (though I did not know how they would take it) did you people ever take cases like this to Jesus?" The mother was crying like her heart would break, as the child was screaming, but she said, "Do you believe that Jesus can heal the baby?" I said "Yes". Well she just handed me the baby, and sat down as calm as though nothing was wrong. I laid my hand on the burned hand, and in six minutes the child was asleep. To Jesus be all the glory.

I well remember how near I came to getting tripped up by Satan's schemes, as when I first thought of mentioning healing to the mother, it was suggested that I had better go a little slow as these were strangers to me, they would not take kindly to my suggestions. I did hesitate for a moment, but soon rallied from that position. As none of them were converted at that time, 'twas suggested that if I wanted to get hold of them, I had better go slow, as they did not take any stock in holiness and all that stuff. Satan took the pains to tell me that they were not saved. But I ran the chances, and in a few moments found out that they were both saved and were hungering for sanctification. So you see Satan uses stratagem. The baby slept well all night. Next morning, all the skin was peeled off the back of its hand; but the baby never cried any more. Praise God for such victories! The parents both got sanctified before I left, also two of their daughters got saved.

Now we all know that cause and effect are inseparable. Where there is an effect, we know that the cause is round somewhere. And one of the main causes for not allowing Jesus to heal us is the lack of entire sanctification, for when we fully die out, then we are so dead to this world and all its environments that we can trust God to do most anything.

For instance I held a meeting in Ohio, trudged along, had a slow hard fight, and so far as I could see just one family was brought in; but the heads were regenerated and sanctified. I went from there some twenty-two miles for another meeting, somewhat discouraged as to the results of the meeting just closed, as several had said it was about as near a failure as had ever been there.

Well, I went in as best I could at number two. The second night several fell at the altar. Well, right from the start it looked as though a great revival was just ahead of us. But after the first Sunday we began looking for seekers for the Holy Ghost. I preached the second work strong and incessant, but no one came. The seekers for regeneration were plenty. Well, I began weeping over the state, pleading with them, but there was not a seeker for the second work. The meeting closed in what seemed to the people a blaze of glory. Some fifty people had claimed to have prayed through. Well, we considered this meeting to be more of a failure than the other. In spite of all my preaching on the essentiality of sanctification and my fasting for them, not one sought it.

Well, I went away from there feeling pretty bad, and Saturday night put forth an extra effort, gave one of my best Bible readings on the second work of grace, but no one made any move. I said, "Brethren, regeneration is a most blessed and glorious work, but it does not complete God's ideal of a child of His." I said, "If you fail to go on into the second work, you will never stand." The closing sermon was a strong Bible reading on the second work. No one came. Well, this meeting was quite far-reaching in its sphere. Many came for miles, so it was considered a great meeting. Several asked the reason of the failure of the meeting over on the creek. Well, I said nothing, but felt that this was the greater failure of the two.

I packed up my tent, went forty-five miles from there, and kept going on, and have been going on ever since, Hallelujah!

But now back to the failure. I went to the Cincinnati Camp about nine months after this first meeting, and a Brother said, "Brother Bevington, I have a call to hold a meeting back on Noose Creek. I was told that you held a meeting there and it was a failure. How about it?" "Well," I said, "I do not call it a failure by any means, as the heads of a family got saved and sanctified." "Was that all?" "Yes, as far as I could see." "And we heard you held a rousing meeting over at the bend." "Well," I said, "that is what they called it," and I said no more.

He took his tent and turned the failure down. He went over on the bend where the rousing meeting was, pitched his tent and cut loose, expecting a rousing meeting, preaches eight days and not a soul at the altar. Well, he was somewhat discouraged, but sticks to it until Sunday night, but no one came. But Sunday, his last day, the man and wife from over at the pronounced failure, that were sanctified, asked him to bring his tent over to their neighborhood. The evangelist, not knowing that this was the place where I had the terrible failure, gladly accepted the call, glad to get most anywhere away from that place. The brother came after him Monday with a team. He begins his meeting Tuesday night, cuts loose on the second work, which they would not stand for over on the bend. So he feels impressed to open the altar, and eight fell at the altar for sanctification. This brother and wife had been holding cottage meetings during the lapse of time, and eleven had been regenerated, and three of them sanctified. So we need power, and faith is power, and it is hard to exercise faith with the "old man" in us.

Healing helps us in various ways. I was holding a meeting in Indiana, and there were two sisters, unmarried, lovely girls, good singers, good leaders and workers, beautiful characters; hence they had a good influence over those whom they met. The first service was Sunday morning. They were there and at their post. I saw that they were going to be a great help. Sunday night they did not come, and Monday night they did not come.

So I went over to see about it. "Well," they said, "Brother Bevington, we are here with mother, and we make our living on milk and butter, and the cows do not get up here in time for us to get to the meeting, and we actually haven't the time to hunt them up as they have a large range to run in." I said, "What time would it be necessary for the cows to be here in order that you could get to church?" "Oh they would have to be here much earlier than they come, so we just can't come." I said, "Now that isn't what I asked you. Please answer my question." "Well, Brother Bevington, I know, but they never come." "There it is again. Now please answer my question. What time would they have to be here?" "Oh, well, there is no use talking about that as they never come." "There it is again. Now please answer my question." "Oh, well, they would have to be here by 5:00 p. m." "All right, that is what I wanted to know. Now have they a bell?" "Yes, a large one." "Well, you listen for that bell at 4:45 p. m."

I went to my room, got down on my face and said, "Now, you know Lord we need these girls there, as they will save my voice, and add much to the good results of the meeting. So now please have that bell in hearing distance at 4:45." I kept digging and holding on as it was about two o'clock when I went on my face. At 4:30 one of the girls said, laughingly, "Well, our time is nearly up." The other said, "Oh, do you think those cows will be here at 4:45, or be in hearing?" Well he told us to listen, and there won't be any harm in listening and I am going out and open the gate." So after she had opened the gate she looked toward the woods, and, lo, to her surprise the bell was heard and she called to the sister. Out she came, and said, "Well, well, they are coming sure." I looked at the clock. It was just 4:45 exactly.

They both came to church early and told this experience, and it was a great boon to the meeting. Those cows came up at 4:45 every night during the meeting, and did more effective preaching than Bevington did, as it was noised all over and many came to see that fellow who could bring those cows up there at that unreasonable hour. I never had tried that before, and never have since; but if God should tell me as He did then, I should do so.

Now, I have more marvels of God's dealings — some I have never told from the pulpit; that is, these major-ones, though I have told them privately or to groups, and I suppose that those who have heard this one would consider the book incomplete without this — my straw stack experience. This one will complete the major experiences.

I was holding a meeting in Indiana. The weather was very cold, about thirty below zero, and there was plenty of snow. People came for miles in the old-fashioned sleds, with two horses, and bells could be heard for miles. Some came as far as thirty-five miles, as good sleighing rendered it easy on the horses that were not worked much at that time of the year. Many came to see the sights, and many of those who came from a distance got sanctified. Well, several had gotten down and been actually saved, four of those who came from a distance got sanctified.

Well, as the meeting progressed, these four said several times that I must come over into their neighborhood, to which I paid no attention as my hands were full there. But they kept urging me until finally I said, "Well, where do you live? How far from here?" "About twenty-five miles. We have a church over there, M. E., and you must come over." So as the time came to close this meeting, I said, "Well, have you the permission of your pastor for me to hold a meeting in said church?" "Oh, that is all right as the church is on father's place. He built it." "Well," I said, "it belongs to the M. E. Conference, and you would have to get permission." So I went up to my room and got on my face. I lay there for twenty-six hours, and then felt led to go over.

Next morning here came three of their leaders after me, but no call from their pastor. I sent them back, and he came over next day, and said, "I understand that some of our people have been attending your meeting over here and that they want you to come over there with us. I understand that you preach holiness." "Yes, as hot as I can." He said, "We are all John Wesley Methodists." "Well," I said, "I haven't been running into them of late. I don't find many John Wesley Methodists." He said, "Do you preach holiness to sinners?" I said, "I preach just as God gives me the message. Some places it is on holiness as a second work of grace, and then at others holiness is seldom mentioned."

"Well, we would be very glad to have you come over, as it would please some of our people; but we consider it very unwise to preach holiness to sinners. We would suggest that you preach regeneration to the sinners, as that is what they need; and then if you wanted to we could have some afternoon for holiness." I said, "Is this merely a suggestion or is it to take the form of a command or desire?" He said, "I think it is the only way we could permit you to come over." "Well", I said, "I can't come over on those terms at all." "How would it do to have one night in the week for holiness?" I said, "I could not agree at that, as it might be all holiness as a second work." And I said, "I could not come over unless I was to have complete charge and control, preach as long as God said so and just as He prescribed. I could not have any restrictions whatever. I might be led to call on you to pray and I might not."

"Well," he said, "isn't that bordering on fanaticism?" "You can term it whatever you wish. That is where I would have to stand should I come over." So he went back, and said: "Brethren, we can't have that fellow over here. Why, he is a genuine crank; he isn't going to let me have anything to do with the meeting, not even to pray, and may not allow me to be on my own platform. Oh, no, we can't have him here."

Well these four said, "If we can't have him in the church, we will fix up a tobacco stripping house, seat it, and put stoves in it. It will hold about as many as the church. We feel that man ought to come here, as souls prayed through every night over there; and you have been here three years and not a soul has been regenerated."

Well the pastor saw that this would never do, so he gave in and sent for me. I went over, and opened fire on his 300 members. The pastor had said that I ought not to preach holiness to sinners. I said that this doctrine of freedom from sin seems to please the sinner pretty well. He said that they had 350 members and all were saved, of course. Well, I thought that the four who had been over and gotten salvation and were then sanctified, were a pretty safe sample of the whole 350.

After the third sermon, the pastor said that the Ladies' Aid were planning for quite an extensive program for Christmas and that they could not locate a place for the work only at the church. He also said that they were quite sorry, as they would dearly love to have the meeting go on; but to please the Ladies' Aid we would have to close it. Well, though I had papers signed by him, that permitted me to remain in the church, yet I could not. Being permitted to preach the fourth night, I announced the action of the pastor, and the "aids." A man jumped up said, "We will go over to the schoolhouse." We, however, put it to a vote as to whether we should go into the schoolhouse; and it was said that every hand went up except that of the pastor and his wife. Even his son and daughter raised their hands. So we went over there the next night.

The next day this pastor hired five boys to cut up the seats, so as to stop the meeting. He gave them two dollars apiece, and they went at it in good shape. The board came in and said, "The boys are cutting up the seats badly," so we were requested to stop the meeting there; but the people had gotten another place. That night when I went to my lodging place, I found my grips out by the gate, and the house darkened. I took that for a pretty good hint and picked up my grips and started out, like Abraham, not knowing where to go. I could have gone, I suppose, to any of those four families, but did not know where they lived, and God did not want me to go there, as He had a better place for me. By my staying where I did He got more glory than if I had found any of these. Well, I kept trudging on in the snow, and it was very cold—so cold that men were cutting solid ice twenty-two inches thick out of a pond. I soon got tired, set the grips down, and said, "Lord, where am I going?" "What's that to thee? Follow thou me" was all I got in answer. I said, "Right", picked up the grips and started on.

The first thing I knew I was in a sort of lane. Great furrows had been cut out in the road as, in the fall, they had drawn corn out there and made deep ruts that were filled up with snow; hence I could not see them and got many falls, cutting my flesh, so that my face was bleeding in several places; also my hands were cold. I said again, "O God, where am I going?" and again came the answer, "What's that to thee?" So on I trudged, and soon saw a great hill seemingly in the road. As I was watching as best I could to avoid those ruts, I forgot the hill and soon ran into it; but it proved to be a straw stack. A voice said, "This is the place." I said, "All right," threw off my coat, and went to pulling straw, at which I got nicely warmed up.

I pulled straw until I was back in the stack some twelve feet, about three feet from the ground so as to be warm. Then I packed the straw all out, took in my grips, put on my coat, used one of the grips for a pillow, dropped down on my back, and said, "Well, praise God, I don't reckon Jesus ever had much better than this, and probably most of the time not nearly so good." At that the straw stack was lighted up so that I saw the most beautiful sight I ever saw. It looked just like crystallized straw, nearly as large as my little finger, lying in all positions, crossing each other and forming a beautiful net work. Well, I was frightened, as I feared that I had gotten a match lighted while pulling straw; my fears was soon banished, for I threw up my hands and there were the cold, damp straws.

Oh, beloved, I will never be able, this side of Heaven, to draw a worthy picture of that scene and also of the dazzlings going on down in the soul! I have often thought that was a foretaste of what Heaven is going to be. We are taught down here to view things according to laws. The appearance of those straws did not allow the working of natural laws, as each was apart from the others, and they did not appear to touch one another. I have thought many times that is the trouble with us: We must see things down here as under the lights of natural laws, while God often breaks through the natural order of things completely setting the natural aside; hence we fail to get the real import of His designs. That experience in that cold straw stack has been a great help to me many and many a time, enabling me to accept things that before I would have rejected on philosophical grounds. While God works through natural laws very much, yet I have found that He has special lessons for us which go far beyond the natural laws.

I have learned that ruts are dangerous channels to travel in; and God wants us so pliable that He can twist us up, or throw us here or yonder, and that we will recognize His hand though in other garbs or along other lines than those in which similar incidents have appeared. There is no doubt but that God would give us wonderful revelations if He could get us in condition to receive them; I am well assured that the deeper lessons which God wants us to have are all in line of the apparently ridiculous. They are not on the public highway. The casual traveler never sees them, for they are not on his route. 'Tis on the unreasonable, out-of-the-ordinary route that these lessons are to be learned—generally routes similar to my getting into this straw stack.

I learned invaluable lessons from that. As I told this to dear Rev. John Fleming one time, he burst out crying, and said, "Brother Bevington, I would have given a hundred dollars to see that straw stack when it was so luminously lit up." Had I appealed to reason as I came up against that stack, I would have taken the ground that to go in there when the thermometer was registering below twenty would be altogether out of reason. Everything would have stood against such proceeding. I would have produced about this sort of an argument: God has set forth His laws and demands of us obedience, relative to taking care of our bodies. So I can't accept this as the place where God wants me, as He has called me to preach, and He said that the laborer is worthy of his hire. And I am His child; and, Mr. Devil, I am not going to allow you to run me into such a place as this, on such extravagant lines, to bring on a tremendous cold and, probably, pneumonia which would more than likely cause a premature death. So I could quite logically have reasoned this all out; though had I done so, I would have lost one of the grandest lessons of my life. So we need to get where we will be willing to break all laws in order to get some of the private lessons the Lord has for us. Just those few words of acquiescence to His will, when I said, "Well, I suppose Jesus never had a better bed than this," gave me one of the grandest visions I have ever beheld. Yes, those few words spoke volumes which have enabled me to store up great quantities of knowledge of His will relative to me.

Well, now I will proceed with the marvels of God. He will open up great and unheard of things, if we will just allow Him to get us where these great and unheard of things are in operation, or where He can consistently operate them without knocking others of His lambs flat. So while this great manifestation of glory lasted only a short time, yet there were raptures of exceeding great joy which came in waves one after another so that I lay there wrapped in great splendor until, when I struck a match and looked at my watch, I was surprised to see that it was 4:30 a. m. Well, I turned over and went to sleep; and when I woke up and struck a match, I found that it was 5:30 p. m.

I crawled out, shook off the chaff, took my handkerchief for a towel after washing well in the snow, and started back to the house that had been offered us to continue the meeting in. I found twenty-five people there, with saws and horses. They had been drawing logs and sawing them into blocks twenty-two inches long for seats. Both rooms were nearly seated. I said to the man of the house, "I suppose these two rooms are about all you have." "Well," he said, "these will hold more than the schoolhouse." "Is there a room upstairs?" "Why, what do you want to go up there for? 'Tis a sort of unfinished attic." "Why, I want a place to pray," I answered. I spied a door on the ceiling, and said, "Can't I get up there?" He said, "Why, I suppose so; but there isn't any floor, and it will be cold." "Let me get up there". So he got a ladder, and up I went. I got close to the large chimney, across the joist, and burst into great sobs. I just lay there and wept, and could hear a noise downstairs, supposing that they were finishing up seating. I struck a match and found it was 9:30 p. m.

I then got up and went downstairs and found over a hundred people waiting for me. I had no message, but only a great burden that souls might be brought under such conviction as would enable them to see their real condition and fly to the Son of God for refuse. As there was some unoccupied space where I landed from the attic, I dropped down on my face. In about thirty minutes the preacher's son came, and said, Aren't you going to preach, as there are over a hundred people here waiting." I exhorted him and the rest to prayer. He said, "There is no one here that can do any good at prayer, as you have spoiled all of us; the only prayer that any of us ought to pray is the prayer of repentance." Well, I thought that he was about right. I got up, and said, "Brethren, this great battle must be fought out on our faces. I have no message to preach. You have had too much preaching. I have only a burden of prayer that each of you may be brought face to face with your real condition as God sees you, and fly for your lives to the Son of God who has made provision for your complete deliverance from sin."

At that I crawled out of the window near me, made a bee line for my hospitable quarters, and got on my face to plead, weep, moan, groan, and wrestle. When I struck a match, I found that it was 5:30 a. m. I soon went to sleep, and woke up at 4:30 p. m. Then I crawled out, took another wash in the snow (it was still twenty below zero) and I went to the house, where I found seventy-five people. More than twenty were down praying as if they meant business; some on their faces sobbing, others kneeling and praying, others with heads up, pleading and weeping, and others walking where they could find room.

But all that crowd pleading for mercy, mind you, were those saved people over at the church; and among the crowd were the son and daughter of the pastor. I raised the window and crawled in, as there was no room to get in at the door, and climbed up the ladder into the attic. I got on my face across those sleepers, close to the chimney as a rousing fire below was keeping the chimney warm.

By and by up came the man of the house and said, " 'Tis after eight, and they all want you to come down and preach." I said, "Tell them all to go to praying." "Well, I am afraid they will get tired of this way, and all leave, and not return, and all this work here will be lost." See, here was more logic to contend with, but I remained there. I heard them praying and singing. At 10:00 p. m., I went down and found about forty in real soul agony, especially the pastor's son and daughter, both of whom had been testifying to being saved for several years. I could see that God was working; hence, how foolish it would be for me to take the work out of His hands. So I just raised the window and slipped out and up to my private quarters, to plead with God for them. I got on my face and struggled, agonized, wrestled, wept, and held on believingly, really expecting God to work wonders. I struck a match and found it was 6:00 a. m.; then turned over and went to sleep, and woke up at 5:20 p. m. I went out, had another good wash in the snow, shook myself, and started for the meeting. I found about two hundred people there, most of them in great misery. One man and wife met me outside, and began to tell me about the trouble they were having with their bad neighbor. I said, "Go inside, get down on your faces and plead for mercy, throw open your hearts to God, get honest before Him, and let Him examine you." They did so. Another came to me, saying "What shall I do?" I said, "Get right with God". "Why, I am a good member here in the church." I said, "Get right with God. Repent. Get yourself properly fixed up, then matters can more easily be adjusted."

Two sisters were the next to unload the terrible meanness of their neighbors, saying, "We want you to pray for them, as they are a terror to the whole neighborhood." I said, "You two are the ones who need praying for. Never mind those neighbors; get right yourselves. Go through with God." "Why, Mr. Bevington, we are members in good standing in this church here." "Well, you are all the worse for that." "We want to get our children saved; my son and daughter-in-law and daughter and son-in-law." I said, "Go on in, get down on your faces and deal with God directly, not with Bevington." "Well, there is no room inside." "Make room, go into the kitchen." "Why, that is crammed full." I said "Go in, go in." So I left those self-righteous complainers, and went to my window, crawled in, and slipped upstairs, with but few seeing me.

Soon the man of the house came and said that about three hundred people were there. It was then about 9:30 p. m. I went down and found the man of the house, his son and daughter and wife were down with many others, pleading. The son came, crying, and said, "Oh, won't you preach? I am so miserable, I need help. Oh, please help. Tell me what to do. And my sister there is also weeping as if her heart were broken." I found no room only at the ladder, but stood there, and took the text, "Prepare to meet thy God;" and I am satisfied that never before nor since have I delivered such a message as was given there in forty minutes. Everyone was writhing in great agony; some walking and screaming. Only about sixty could kneel, but they were doing good work; and oh, how God did send out the lightning bolts in great torrents! Feeling that I had done all God wanted me to do there, I hoisted the window and made for my commodious apartment. I got on my face, and could do nothing but cry and groan and plead. I struck a match, to find that it was 4:00 a. m.; then I went to sleep, and slept like a baby until 6:30. After taking another cool bath, I started back to the house, and found about sixty there.

I stopped at the ladder, and soon the pastor came in. Of all the tongue lashing that a man ever got, he poured on me. He called me about all the names in the catalogue; but as I was somewhat accustomed to those vocal expressions, they did not disturb my equilibrium, and I was speechless through it all. He finally wound up by ordering every one of his members out of there, with the command never to return. Well, all went out but his son and the man and family of the house and another man and family — I think there were about sixteen left. Well, I felt like preaching, and so I did, on the judgment and wrath of God. The son and man and wife and the other man prayed through by 4:00 a. m. We had a blessed time, and that son did some wonderful preaching.

The pastor, the night before, had taken his daughter by the dress collar and dragged her out, threatening to punish her severely if she ever returned. The son was a little bit too big for that kind of treatment, so he had to go off without the son. Well, I slipped out, went to my hotel, wept until noon, then went to sleep, wakened up at 8:00 p. m., and went out for another good dry bath in my large toilet room. I went down and found that only twenty-two were there, but all were down pleading for mercy, except those that had gotten through, and they were seeking sanctification. The pastor's daughter was there. I felt led to remain there all night with them, so I remained until 3:00 a. m., and then went upstairs. Soon the woman of the house came up, and said, "What shall I do? I think I will throw all those blocks out, and clean the whole thing out, as I am convinced now that I am all right. The pastor says I am, as I have been a member here for years. You are just making fools out of all of us, my husband and son and daughter." I said, "Woman, get down those steps as quickly as you can, and go to screaming for mercy. You may be in hell in twenty minutes." Down she went, and I followed; and I tell you she changed her tune, and in forty minutes she struck fire, and did some fine preaching there until after daylight. I slipped off back to my headquarters.

Now this brings me up to the ninth morning. I had not had a mouthful to eat, and had lain on straw and sleepers. I might mention that among the many names given to me by the pastor on that notable night was that of a hypnotist. Well, that word was not used where I went to school so I was somewhat interested to ascertain what I had filled as hypnotist, filled in the annals of incidents, so I wrote the word down as I stood there by the ladder, intending to investigate a hypnotist's standing and profession. Well, upon consulting the best of authority, I failed to find his whereabouts, so I let that part of the tirade drop from the anathemas that plunged from that pastor's storehouse.

Well, when I returned, the man of the house met me outside, and said, "Brother

Bevington, where are you stopping?" I said, "None of your business." "Now, see here, it is my business, and I am going to make it so. I went today to Reynolds' where I supposed you were stopping, and they said that you were not there. I went to all the places that there would be any likelihood of your being, and none of them knew where you are stopping. Now, Sir, tell me." I said, "None of your business; go on in there and pray through and get the Holy Ghost." "No, Sir, I'm not going in until you tell me." So I just pointed in the direction of the straw stack. "Wife, this man has been sleeping, or staying, in that straw stack," and he capered around there about all he dared to as a seeker of the Holy Ghost. "Well," he said, "where have you been getting your meals?" I just pointed to the skies. Then he yelled, "This man hasn't had a mouthful to eat these two weeks." Of course he overrated by three days.

He said, "Come in and get something to eat," but I declined as it was about 9:00 p. m. I went in and about a hundred were there. I see that I have made a mistake. This was the eighth morning instead of the ninth. Well, that morning, at three o'clock, the daughter got through, and she said, "Now, Brother Bevington I disobeyed my father for the first time in my life. I just had to come here, as I feared I would lose my soul." She said, "Now you pray that I may be willing and able to endure the punishment," as she knew something of the temper of her father. I said, "All right, I will go up into the attic and plead your case. You be loyal to what you have received." So up I went.

She and her brother had about a mile to walk. He was seeking sanctification, but as he had a whole lot to undo, it was a somewhat tedious matter. We plead that the experiences of the two would so melt up the father that he would be compelled to surrender, and at 5:30 a. m., I felt the burden all gone. Light broke in, and I raised up off the sleepers, praising God for the daughter's victory.

So I went to the straw stack, this being the ninth morning; and it was that night that I was located by the man of the house, and I was listening to his quizzing as to where I slept, when here came the pastor, bareheaded, with the daughter and son in a cutter, and the sleigh bells ringing. He was being sifted, as the son and daughter went into the room where he was sleeping (he supposed she was upstairs in bed).

She called him, and said, "Father, I had to disobey you last night. I just had to go up there or go to hell, and now, Father, I am ready and prepared for my punishment." The son was standing at her side, with head bowed, pleading for the salvation of his father, and that this should be the means to that end. "Well, go on to bed. Let me alone," he said. "No, Father, I want my punishment. I disobeyed you. I am ready." At that he gave a yell, bounded out of bed, fell on his knees, and went to crying for mercy. The son and daughter dropped on their faces; and in ten minutes the mother climbed out, and said, "Oh, children, pray for me, too, as I need just what I believe you both have." So they wrestled all day until about three o'clock when the mother prayed through. The father did not get through.

He asked us back to the church that night, but as both rooms were full (as many had heard of the pastor's actions and came back) we held the meeting there that night, and I preached from "If any man be in Christ Jesus, he is a new creature," and so on. God gave me a blessed message. The mother prayed through at 4:00 a. m., for sanctification; but the father did not get through, and as soon as it was daylight, he hitched up and went to every one of those men and women whom he called out of there, and asked forgiveness. It took him three days to make the circuit, but he did it. He said that at the first house he went to, he asked forgiveness and invited the people out to the meetings, and started out; but a voice said, "And is that all?" Well, he looked around; and as he saw not a person near, and not being used to the voice of God, was puzzled. By the time he reached the gate, he heard the same voice with the same words. He said that he had to go back and fall on his knees before them and ask forgiveness. H e gladly knelt and asked forgiveness of all of the three hundred.

Well, we went up to the church and spent three weeks there; and as my straw stack experience had capacitated me for a good meal, I had it at the parsonage, but after that ate only one meal a day, during the three weeks.

If I felt clear to tell you, it would no doubt be refreshing for me to relate many of the incidents which occurred during those three weeks; but will cut the account short by saying that I preached only two sermons, and they were on the last day of the meeting. I lay on my face on the platform day and night. The pastor's wife, son, and daughter prayed through and got sanctified. There were several incidents in his seeking that were of interest, as it took five days and nights to kill him out. He just rolled on the floor, perspired freely, made restitutions, and put up in a five days' struggle; but he got through and was a good witness for several years. I saw him at the Cincinnati Camp three successive years, and on the platform he delivered good messages of full salvation. Yes, if all that was said and done were recorded it would make an interesting volume for all to read. They said that over three hundred people fell at the altar, and that someone was getting through most all the time, day and night. Wonderful was the preaching of many who prayed through. Restitutions were made in many instances.

Now I see I have left out a whole lot of this five weeks campaign, but I guess this will suffice. But I want you to remember that all this time that I was in the stack it was twenty below zero, and that while trudging up there the first night, I cut my face and hands severely by falling on the frozen ruts; but that neither from them nor from sleeping in the stack I ever caught cold, nor was incapacitated in the least from struggling for souls, and all the sleep I got in the five weeks was in the daytime.

I was holding a meeting up the river from Cincinnati, and was making a sled for Brother Ben Otten then on his place. I did a lot of boring with brace and bit in hard seasoned oak; and as I threw my weight on the brace in boring, a sudden, severe pain took me just above the heart and rendered me helpless for about an hour. I got some strength and went to the house still suffering and soon went back to boring. But after dinner I could scarcely breathe, for the sharp, severe pains. I prayed over it some, but kept on working until I had finished the sled. That night I slept but little. I was busy puttering round, as on a farm there is always so much to do; but after dinner I could not straighten up, and told the folks what I had done, and my present condition.

They were a little alarmed, as they saw that the trouble was quite close to my heart. Well, I started to go out behind a shock of fodder, but failed to get there. About an hour afterwards, as it was getting so much worse, I said, "Well, I must do something." I went back to the shock, and said, "Now, Mr. Devil, this has gone just about far enough." I fell on my face and began to plead the promises in earnest, and held up the Bible, claiming 1 John 5:14. I held onto that for awhile, but the pain kept increasing. I got so that I could not breathe without intense suffering. I finally got desperate, and said, "Lord, I am not going to leave this spot until I am delivered." So I began to reckon it done, and counted it done. I saw that my faith was getting clearer, hence stronger, and began to praise God, and saw that I was getting deliverance. I raised my hand again saying, "Oh, Hallelujah, it is done, it is done, it is done!" and as I said the last word the third time, it was done. I jumped up, running and shouting, and Brother Ben and his wife stood and wept for joy because Jesus had so delivered me. Oh, praise the Lord! Let all the people praise him!

I was holding a meeting in Ohio. I preached four nights in a prominent church, and on the fifth night I ate no super, and went somewhat early. But I found the door locked, so sat down on the steps and went to reading the precious Word. I got interested, and did not notice the time until a man stepped up, and said, "Is the door locked?" I said, "Yes." He looked at me rather serious for about five minutes, and said, "Did you not know that they locked you out?" I said, "No, have they?" "Yes, they have." "Do you live near here?" "Yes, you were at my house last Friday, but I was not at home. You prayed for my wife, and she has been well ever since." I said, "Are you a saved man?" "No, Sir," and off he went.

I said, "Lord, locked out, eh? Well, how about that message Thou didst give me this morning? Where am I going to deliver it?" So Satan whispers, "You can deliver that tomorrow night, as they will let you back into the church." Now, note the danger here, as this sounded right good and reasonable, and would have been accepted by many. It was then after 9:00 p. m.; but I had felt so deeply impressed with a certain subject that I could not very well let go, so I said, "Lord, it seems that I must deliver that message, somewhere." But there being no one in sight to preach to, I saw no prospects whatever. But that message kept revolving and enlarging, gathering material at each revolution, in spite of the absence of visible prospects. As I sat there, I saw a large oak tree that threw its branches out over the road. While I was admiring its beauty, a voice said, "This is the place."

Well, I looked around, but there was no one in sight. However, I strolled up to the tree, got down on my face, and soon heard something. Thinking that it was hogs eating acorns, I stayed on my face, seemed to be held to the spot, could not move. And that message was still developing, but I could not preach to hogs eating acorns. I soon began weeping and struggling as I saw the terrible condition of the people, and prayed, cried, and wrestled until I heard moaning and groaning and crying and praying. I looked up, and there were seventy-two people under that tree, about one-third of them praying, and they were praying on the very message that had been burning on my heart. They all had the message; I never had to deliver it. Well, I just remained on my face, praying that God would burn the message in on them all. The pastor's daughter was among them, and was desperately in earnest, weeping and praying.

Well, at 1:30 a. m., I got up and closed up on my message—the part they had not reached as yet. After the firing had ceased and the smoke cleared away, there were found to be thirteen who had been badly wounded in the skirmish, so much so that they seemed unable to get up and away. At 4:15 a. m., though none had gotten through, there lay about fifty people—men and women, boys and girls. At 5:30 the pastor's daughter got gloriously through. She just ran all over the space occupied by the people, shouting and laughing and crying. By 6:20 over a hundred people were under that tree, and I was still on my face, weeping and groaning. Many were knocked over by the power of God, and someone said that over sixty were praying at once.

While this daughter was preaching, the pastor, being over at another point, missed this good feast. I was told that his wife came down, and remember how I dreaded her appearance; but I just pleaded for protection as I lay on my face. But she had no spirit of interference, but just began helping the rest, as also did the daughter. The benediction was pronounced at 4:30 p. m., the pastor himself announcing that there would be meeting at the church that night, though he had ordered the church locked against me. So it always pays to mind God.

7

Children's Chapter

TO THE DEAR CHILDREN, Greeting:
This book would be incomplete if there were no children's chapter; so here it is: I will just have a good time with my little friends, as the dear children have always been my friends, and have been such a comfort to me when I needed comfort. I feel that Jesus would be pleased to have me tell of several incidents in which He has blessed the children. Many of the incidents I am telling have been told in children's meetings and Sunday schools. I have told them also by home firesides, as many of the long winter evenings, when I was not otherwise employed, have been spent amusing the children.

I feel impressed to tell of little Katie and Edward. I knew them when I was in the mission work in Cincinnati.

I found a wretched home, where both the father and mother drank hard. They drank up all the money they could get, and lived in filth. They had a little girl, Katie, then seven years old. We got clothes for her and got her in Sunday school and in the day school. We looked after them closely. As little Katie had never been in school, we started her in the kindergarten. She would learn the little songs, and the blessings that were taught at their little tables at their lunch time in the kindergarten. It was a very sweet crowd to look upon. We would slip in many a time just to see them in their little red chairs. So little Katie would take the little things that they were taught to make home with her. She would repeat the songs, and especially the blessings at the table. She would say their little blessings at the table at home. This was amusing to the parents.

Her father has told what a time Katie would have in getting him and her mother and the older sister and a brother all quiet while she would ask the blessings. Oftentimes they would be drunk, and she would have an awful time in getting them to fold their hands. They thought it quite cute in her, and so would allow her to ask the blessing. But by and by it got hold of them, and soon both were found down at the altar, crying for mercy. Well, God had a great time in getting them saved from their awful habits of so long standing, but He finally got them both saved. I soon got them a job out at Ivorydale at the Proctor and Gamble Soap Factory, where the famous Ivory Soap is made. Soon two years slipped by.

One time as I was visiting the poor, I found a family that had not a thing in the house to eat and there were four little children. I started up to Muth's Bakery where I could get bread (baked the day before) two loaves for a nickel. I had just twenty cents, and was going to get a soup bone and some potatoes and two loaves of bread. Well, as I was walking up toward the bakery, a voice said, "Go out to Katie's." I well remembered Katie, but just then was going after something for those four hungry children. It would take the twenty cents to go out to Ivorydale and back, so of course I thought that I couldn't go, and kept on going toward Muth's Bakery. But that voice kept on ringing in my ears, "Go out to Katie's." Well, I stopped and went through my pockets to see if I could find any more money; but I had not a cent more, and kept going on after the eatables. Then the voice said, "Will you, or will you not, go out to Katie's?" I stopped, seemingly paralyzed, and was trembling (something I seldom did) and said, "Lord, I will go."

I looked up and here came an Ivorydale car. I got on and went out. I stepped upon the porch and knocked on the door. I then heard a sob, and a faint voice said, "Come in." When I stepped in, there sat Katie back in the corner caring for the baby. She said, "Oh, Mamma, here is Brother Bevington." Well, I saw that Katie had been crying, as her eyes were all red. I stepped up to her, laid my hand on her head, and said, "What is the trouble with my Katie?" She had grown so much in those two years. At that the mother came in, gave me a hearty hand shake, and said, "Brother Bevington, I am so glad you minded God and came out. I have been praying these twenty-four hours for God to send you out. Sit down there, and I will tell you why Katie has been crying so much.

You see that house?" (pointing to it). "Yes." "And that path going from ours to that fence?" "Yes." "Well, those people are quite well off; have lots of money. They have a boy, Edward, about Katie's age, a nice boy. He has plenty of money to spend, so he bought a croquet set, and it was in the orchard under the trees in the shade. When out of school, Katie takes the baby over there and she and Edward play croquet. Well, night before last, as they were playing, Edward's mamma called him to go to the grocery, so Katie waited for him. Soon he returned and they resumed play, but soon his mother called again, and said, 'I am sorry but I forgot something. I guess you will have to go again.' So off he went (as every boy should when mamma calls) but was gone longer than usual, so Katie came over to assist me in getting supper. Well, soon Edward came back, gathered up the set, and counted the balls and found one missing. He counted them over again. Yes, one was gone."

Now listen, children, as to how Satan will be right on hand to get children into trouble. He said to Edward, "Now Katie stole the ball, as she was the only one that was out there." "Yes," said Edward to himself, "she surely did, and I am going to tell her, too." So he ran into the house, and said, "I ain't going to have Katie Brown come over here any more!" " "Why, Edward, what is wrong with Katie?" "Why, she stole one of my balls." "Now you know better than that," said his mother. "No, I know she did." So he ran over to Brown's, and said, "I ain't going to have Katie come over any more." "Why?" "Well, she stole one of my balls." "Oh, no!" "Yes, she did, no one else was there, and one is gone." Well, Katie was in the dining room caring for the baby and she came to the door and said, "Why, I never did." "Yes you did," said Edward, and he went out and nailed up that hole in the fence. Well, that was a hard blow on dear Katie. Although her parents had been drunkards, now that they had not drank any for over two years, she was being looked upon as a nice girl. Now, to have this said to her was just about all she could stand, so she cried and sobbed all night. So the mother told the father. Well, he said, "We know she never did."

Then Katie did not want to go to school; but they coaxed her to go. At recess none of the children would play with her nor allow her to play with them, as Edward was the leader in the school as he would buy things for the other children, so they all looked up to him. He had told them that Katie had stolen his ball, that she was a thief, and that they must not play with her. Well, poor Katie just sobbed and cried when she came home at noon. She told how the children had treated her, and said, "Oh, Mamma, don't make me go to school!" Then her mother said, "Oh, Katie, I think you ought to go to school. Mamma doesn't want you to miss a day. I will go to praying for God to send our Brother Bevington out, and he will help us get the matter straight." Well, Katie went; but they treated her worse. They all called her a thief and, as they came home at night, all of them went on the opposite side of the street. The worst thing was that they said that her father was nothing but an old drunkard anyway and wasn't fit to live with decent folks. She just could not stand that, and hurried home crying as if her heart would break, and said, "Oh, Mamma, please don't make me go to school tomorrow. Oh, Mamma, I just can't endure it. Let me stay at home."

When the father came, he said, "Well, let her stay at home, and we will pray for God to send out Brother Bevington." And so they prayed. The mother prayed all night. Now, children, I want you to see how God will answer prayer. After this all-night prayer, you see God was asking me to go out to Katie's; something that seemed foolish to me, as I had started for eatables for that poor family. But God had to answer that mother's prayer; so He went to work on me that morning. All the time that her mother related all this to me, Katie sat in the corner, sobbing. So I went over and laid my hand on her head. She wiped the tears away, and got a damp cloth and wiped her face. I said, "Now Katie, I am sure you never took that ball." "No, I never took it; but we can't prove it, and it will kill me unless we move away from here." I tell you she was crying as if her heart would break. I said, "Katie, you belong to Jesus, don't you?" Between sobs, she said, "Yes." "Yes," said her mother, "Katie is a real Christian girl. All in the school say she is and she has learned to read out here. She reads the Bible and prays every night and morning. Yes, I am sure Katie is a little Christian, and she loves Jesus. She has gotten over twenty-five scholars in the Sunday school. She is a faithful little soldier for Jesus."

I said, "Katie, don't you remember the time that Jesus healed you down town?" "Yes, I do." "Well, don't you believe that He will answer prayer today?" "Yes, I know He does, but how could He show Ed. where that ball is?" "Well," I said, "let's get down on our knees, and let Jesus talk and work for us. " I called on the mother to pray and she prayed, "Yes, dear Jesus, I know that you can do things. I know that you healed Katie, and have done other things. I know you have and can do these things." Well, she kept praying that way for some time. Finally I said, "Sister Brown, you are not hitting the mark at all." Children, I want you to remember that we must pray definitely. To know and to say that Jesus has done such and such things isn't enough. We have to go farther than that. So I called on Katie. She was still sobbing, and she had quite a time getting out a few words; but she did better than the mother; she got to the place where she said, "I believe you will show Ed. where it is." Well, that was getting pretty close to the mark, but not close enough yet. You see, children, if I wanted to drive a nail into a board, it would not affect the driving of the nail any unless I hit it. I might just glaze it, but that would not do. I might hit close up to it, all around it; but if I didn't hit the nail square on the head, I would never get it in. So it is in our praying. We have to hit the matter square by saying, "I know Thou art doing it right now." You see that is real faith, and will bring the answer.

Now children, I want to tell you something. I want to show you how Satan will work. It was about 3:00 p. m., when I went to praying, they were having recess at the school, and Edward was there at school. Now the suggestion would naturally arise, How could we expect Ed. to be finding that ball when he was at school, some five blocks away from where the ball was missed? So when I began praying, Satan said, "It is foolish for you to say that God is showing Ed. that ball now. for he is at school five blocks from here." You see here comes the test. I knew I would have to claim that Jesus was showing him right then where the ball was; so I kept praying up to the point, and the Holy Spirit kept leading me on, and in two or three minutes I had reached the point. I said, "Yes, dear Jesus, Thou are showing him right now." "Hold on," said Satan, "He can't be doing that." Then I shouted it out as loud as I could, "He is doing it right now." I said that three times, and at the third time the glory fell, and Katie jumped up, threw her arms around me, a-laughing and crying, "Oh, Brother Bevington, I do believe it; oh, I do believe it! Oh, I am so happy." I rose up and looked in her face, and all the tears, all the furrows, were gone; all was bright, and she looked so beautiful as she smiled cheerfully.

While I was on my knees, I heard a "rattle-te-bang" and off went that board, and here came Edward in with the ball; his hands covered with blood and his face scratched. He knelt down in front of Katie. He said afterward that that was the first time that he was ever on his knees. But he just wept there like a good fellow, and asked her to forgive him, as he had found the ball. Well, we had a great time rejoicing over it, and I said, "Now, Edward, we want you to tell us how you found the ball and why you are not at school."

Now listen, children, here is something I want you to remember, God knew that morning that I would go out there, and that I would claim Edward's finding the ball about 3:00 p. m., while that was the time Edward was usually in school, which would have been impossible. So that morning Jesus made Edward unusually studious. He studied hard and all his lessons seemed to come so easily that by recess in the afternoon he had all the lessons. He went to the teacher and said, "I have all my lessons, would you like to hear them?" "Why, yes, I will." So she heard him, and said, "Well, you have them all; so now if you want to you may go home." So he started down the street, running, so glad to get out of school. Now I would like to draw you a diagram of where the schoolhouse was from his home, but guess I will have to abandon that thought.

Well, the schoolhouse was on a street running east and west. His house was on a street running north and south. His was the third house from the corner of the street that the school house was on, only the schoolhouse was five blocks west of this street he lived on. Now Edward's father had six acres there, and on it was a large orchard. His lot ran back to the street west of the one he lived on, and part of it extended out to the street that the schoolhouse was on or the one Ed. had been coming down on from school. When the father was at home more, they used a path running from their house, across back to the street west of theirs and up to the corner of the street the schoolhouse was on. So Ed. would go through a gate at the corner and go across to his house, thus save going down to the east street a-turning south to his house.

Well, his father got into politics, and neglected this lot of berries until they had grown up all over and covered this path so that Edward had not gone through there for several years. Now I wonder how many, from this explanation, could draw a diagram of how to get from Ed's house to the schoolhouse by the streets. I told this once in a schoolhouse where I was holding a meeting, and a boy ten years old gave me a correct diagram of it the next day, on paper. So make it out and send it to me, and I will be thankful, and if I have any money I will buy you a present of some kind. Then it will enable me to get acquainted. I want your age and address, both boys and girls. Direct either to Ashland, Kentucky, or Kingswood, Kentucky, and I will get it if I am this side of Heaven.

Now I will tell how he found this ball. He was running down this street east and west, and when he got about halfway down from the corner of his father's lot west of him, he said that a voice said to him, "Go back, and go through the orchard." Well, he stopped and looked around, and there was not a person in sight. "Why, what could that mean?" he thought. So he started on down for the lower corner where he would turn south for his home, and this same voice said, 'Go back, and go through the orchard." "Why," he said, "what can this mean? I can't go through the orchard now, with all those briars in there, covering the path," and still kept going on. In a minute he was stopped still; he could not move, and the same voice said, "Will you, or will you not, go through the orchard?" So he turned back and went up to the corner, got down, looked down that path, and said, "Why, I can't go through there, what does this mean? Am I going crazy?" He starts back down the street for home, and again was stopped still; he could not move a foot, and had to go back and get down on his hands and knees and crawl through those briars, scolding almost all the way, and when he was about two-thirds of the way through, his hand struck something that moved. He brushed the leaves away, and there was the ball.

Now I want you to see how God answered prayer, and see how He had to work miracles in order to do so. What a time He had with me in the first place to get me to come out there, and how He made Edward study and how He helped him in his lessons, as that was the first time he had ever done that. Then see what a time He had in getting him to go back and through those briars, scratching his hands and face. But you see God had to answer this mother's prayer by sending me out; and then answer my prayer by making that boy do the ridiculous. So now, remember this, God will answer prayer. I want you to realize that we have to shut our eyes to what we might see, and just blindly trust God. Had I failed to mind God, that opportunity would have been lost, and poor Katie would have been branded a thief, and probably her life would have been wrecked. I had to come to the place where I counted it done, even though Edward was in school. You see God had it all planned out.

Children, God wants to perform miracles, but we often have to do what seems ridiculous in order that He may. Well after this all took place, the mother said, "You stay until after supper." I was glad to do that, as it would give me a chance to visit with them a little, and also find out how that ball got up there in the orchard. That interested me much. So I felt that the best way was to go out with the children and have a game of croquet, praying that God would reveal just how the ball got out there.

While we were playing here came a pup about half grown, grabbed a ball, and ran up that path in the briars. I said, "Oh, Edward, that is the way that ball got up there." So you see, all things are possible to them that believe and obey God. Amen and Amen! You see, children, I might have consulted my watch and said, "Well Edward is in school now so we will postpone this until later. Then you see God's plan would have been frustrated, and we never would have found out; so you can readily see how God can and will work through us if we are fully His and fully yielded up to Him.

Well, I like to preach to children as they are such good listeners, so I will tell you of a dear little boy. I was holding a meeting not far from Lexington, Kentucky, while I was in the mission work in Cincinnati, and this boy, then nine years old, got blessedly saved. He would testify and pray in public, and he was a sweet little singer. His name was Harry, if I remember rightly. This was in the spring. In the fall he sent me money to come back and hold another meeting, as he said he wanted to get sanctified. He gathered walnuts that fall and hulled them, and had his hands all stained when I got there. He sold the walnuts, and sent the money to me. Well, I went.

He was present with his singing and prayers until the fourth night when I missed him. I came home and found him in the dining room. He had the table covered with papers that he had been figuring on. I said, "Harry, I know you must get your lessons; but I missed you." I went on upstairs (we roomed together) and that dear boy did not come up to bed. He figured all night on that sum. His teacher said, "Harry, I can show you where the trouble is, but I would like for you to discover it, as that will be a great help to you."

So next night again he was not at the church. I came back from the meeting and there he sat, eyes all red, studying and figuring. I said, "Harry, I don't like to have you miss the meetings. I need you." I went upstairs, and soon the father came up and said, "Brother Bevington, what are we going to do with Harry? He has an example there that he will injure himself on." I said, "Let's go down." We said, "Harry, you belong to Jesus don't you?" He looked up with those watery eyes and said, "Yes, I do." "Will you pray?" "Yes." "And don't you believe that Jesus answers prayers?" "Yes, I know He does." "Well, can't you believe that He will show you where the mistake is?" Well, that puzzled him. He knew that God had healed his little sister in the spring, and other evidences stood out before him; but to think that God would come down and show him how to do that example was too much for him.

I said, "Let's pray." I called on the father. Well, he was about like Katie's mamma. He prayed all around the nail, but never hit it. So I stopped him and called on Harry. Well, Harry came closer, but was not hitting it at all; so I had to stop him. I took it up, and in ten minutes was hitting the nail square on the head and driving it through. I brought my hand down emphatically, saying, "Thou art showing him where the mistake has been, right now." I said it three times, and as I said it the third time, he jumped up and said, "Brother Bevington, I've got it." He sat down, and worked it out on a piece of paper the size of my hand. Before he had used up three ten-cent tabs. Yes, the Spirit in answer to prayer showed him. So, children, Jesus will help you if you will trust Him.

While I was in mission work in Cincinnati, there was a kindergarten, then under the charge of Rev. Gilson. A man who had a veneering plant just below us passed there quite often, and saw the little jewels there, and took quite a liking to them. Soon he began inquiring as to what we were doing with them. Well, I invited him in once to see them in their room. He had a little tot of three years, a dear sweet little one, with curly hair, and she was often with her papa.

One time I was walking up Sixth Street, and saw some small red, white, and blue, splint baskets. I stopped and looked at them, and said, "Oh, how nice those would be for our kindergarten children." I went in and asked the price of them by the dozen. He told me. Then I went and saw Mr. Gamble, the soap man, and told him about them. I wanted them to draw in those children, as I knew every child would want one. So he gave me the money to get five dozen, with the understanding that they were not to be sold nor given only to those attending the kindergarten. So I took them down, and gave one to each child.

Soon this man with his little curly-headed girl came along, just as the tots were going along with their tiny pretty baskets. "Oh, papa," said the little girl, "I want one of those pretty baskets." So he saw me in a day or two, and told me what the child wanted. He said, "I presume you have seen my little girl." "Yes," I said, "I have noticed her frequently; a very bright sweet little child. "Well, now she says she just will have to have one." I said, "Mr. Gamble gave us the money to buy them with the understanding that they were only for the kindergarten tots." "Well, I will give you a dollar for one," he said. "Oh, Mister, I daren't sell them," I answered, and then said no more, but earnestly prayed that God would bring the child in with us. We had learned that they were Catholics, and a very fine family.

So, children, I just kept praying, and the next morning, here she came with her big sister for one of those pretty baskets, and they both coaxed very hard. It seemed that the little tot got about everything she asked for. The man told his wife about them, and the tot went to mamma, coaxing her to let her come to the kindergarten, so she could get a basket. I prayed that the Lord would not let him see where I got them, as they were wealthy people, and scarcely ever went up this street where I got them. So the papa was willing that the tot should go, but mamma said, "Oh, no, not by any means shall my child go to such a filthy place as that none but the offscouring go there." "Well," he said, "I never saw much dirt there. It always looks clean and nice." "Well, I have heard about the place, I have heard that it is a disgrace to Cincinnati, as all the bums and drunkards and bad women go there."

Well, the man thought he would investigate for himself; so that night in he walked, and sat down about midway in the hall. Well, of course, I went down, and gave him a hearty handshake. He remained all through the meeting, and heard some brilliant testimonies, something they didn't have in his church. I saw that he was quite well pleased with it all, so invited him back. He went home, and next morning said, "Wife, I would like for you to go down to that mission. It is not as we have heard. They are plainly but well dressed, and they are surely a happy people." "What, me go down there? Never!" This older daughter of fourteen summers had noticed the children going in and out of the mission, so one day she stopped and inquired as to what they were doing. She was informed by one of the teachers, and was invited in. She remained all through the session, went home, told her mamma where she had been, and said, "It is a fine place. Oh, how they work with the little tots, and they are nice and clean." Well, the mother was not favorably impressed with the idea of their daughter being mixed up with that crowd, for as it was vacation, she was a frequent caller there and learned their songs and would play them for them. She would bring her lunch and eat with the little tots.

I saw that God was answering prayer, and that we were destined to have that little child, and even then saw the whole family in there by faith. Well, the daughter gets the mother to come down, as the little child just coaxed and cried for one of those baskets. So the mother came down to investigate, which resulted in her readily giving her consent to let the child come. She was a bright child, well brought up, and her sweet refined ways were a great blessing to those who were not so well brought up. She learned those songs and the blessings asked at the table. We would compose a blessing each month for them. She would learn these and, like the other little girls, she just would have the blessing asked at the table. Well, it amused the parents, and the older brother and sister as she would go around, and say, "Now, papa, you must fold your hands." She would go all around and each one would have to fold hands, and then the blessing was asked. Often the brother would unfold his hands, and down she would get from the high chair, "Now you fold u hans, taus I'se doin' ter ast de blessing." This was kept up, and we were praying for God to use these songs and the blessings.

In less than a year that daughter was down at the altar and prayed through; she just went wild over the new-found joy. Her brother was there, too. He just wept all the time she was rejoicing; then she led him up to the altar. Well, we were so late the father came; and, as he entered, the daughter ran to meet him, threw her arms round him, saying, "Oh, Papa! Oh, I have something I never heard." She was such a sweet child anyway that she just looked like an angel, so innocent and pure. Then he was melted up, as he saw his only son there. So, children, we want you to see how God can work through a little child. He has said in His Word: "A little child shall lead them." Lots of us big folks can't do that, but it is given for the child.

So the father went back, leaving the son at the altar and the daughter there. He wanted to satisfy the mother that the children were safe. Well, the mother was thunderstruck; she raged quite a bit. But in two hours the son and daughter went home. The son was about sixteen, and just fell on his mamma's lap, threw his arms around her, and wept for joy. Well, there was something about the two that their mother had never seen nor felt; and the next thing was that the mother was weeping, and both the son and the daughter were on her lap, hugging her and showering her with kisses. It just broke her all up. So the next night the whole family came, and all were at the altar. They did not get through, but the following week they did, and then they went to their church and all gave in their testimony at prayer meeting, much against the custom. They were finally given their letters. They all got sanctified, and it all came about because of that little basket in the hands of that little child.

You see Moses had a rod in his hands, a piece of wood, and see what he did with that rod: He covered all Egypt with swarms of flies and vermin, turned the waters into blood, walled up the Red Sea so that the people could walk through, and so on. So God in this case used the little basket in the hands of a child. Remember, children, that you can do much for Jesus.

I went once into a home in Cincinnati for dinner, and noticed the mother was anxiously running to the window. I said, "Sister, is there something you want?" "Yes," she said, I am looking for Bessie to come. I want her to run to the grocery. She is late today from school." I said, "Let me do the errand for you." "Well, I want a loaf of bread." "All right; where do you get it?" "Round the corner, first grocery." So I took the nickel, got the bread and started back. The clerk said, "Wait, here is a penny." So I took the penny, laid the bread and penny down on the sister's plate. Soon she lifted up her bread and saw the penny. She said, "Brother Bevington do you know how that penny got there?" I said, "I dropped it there." "What for?" "Why, the clerk gave it to me."

Well, children, I wish I could draw a picture of that mother's face, as I told her this. I saw that there was something going on down in her heart and soul, it showed on her face. I said nothing, but wondered what made all those rapid changes in her countenance. So Bessie came. We had our dinner, and after Bessie had gone to school, the sister said, "Brother Bevington, I am in great sorrow." I said, "I see that something crossed your path from the time you found out where that penny came from. What is it?" "Well," she said, "Bessie gets two loaves of bread daily, and she never has given me any change, as you have. I will go down now and see the grocer."

Soon she returned crying as if her heart would break, and said, "Oh, Brother Bevington, what am I to do? Bessie has been keeping these pennies now for three months, since they cut bread down to four cents. Oh, what does it mean?"

She just sat down and cried. I did up the dishes for her, and tried to make excuses for Bessie; told her maybe Bessie was saving them up to surprise her with a present later on. "Oh, I wish it were so, but oh, Brother Bevington, my heart is about broken. I am fearful, I am fearful!" How she did cry! Well, she said nothing till her husband came home from his work and then she revealed the case to him. She said, "What shall we do?" I had left before that.

Well, I was gone about two months; then came back to the city. I was anxious to know about that penny affair, so went up, and the mother told me that they waited until after supper, and then asked Bessie. Well, Bessie just broke down and cried. She got up from the table, went to her mamma, and threw her arms around her, and wept, saying, "Oh, I am so sorry." When she got through crying, she told them how it came about.

Now children, remember Satan is watching all the time to trip you up, to get you to do something wrong; so you must be careful. Bessie said that when she started out with the first loaf after the cut in the price, the grocer called her back and gave her the penny. She intended to give the penny to her mamma. But as she was going out of the door, a schoolmate met her, and said, "Oh, Bessie, did you get a penny?" "Yes." "Well, now, you know you lost your slate pencil and your mamma will think you very careless in so doing; so if I were you, I would get a pencil, and then your mamma won't know you lost yours. Tomorrow you can give her the penny."

Well, that looked all right to Bessie, so they went to the store, got the pencil, but Bessie felt quite badly about it, and before she reached home, said, "I don't feel just right about this. I will go back and get my penny, returning the pencil, and tell mamma all about it." But another voice said, "Oh, no, just go on; you can begin tomorrow as the cut was just made today. One day won't matter." So this naughty voice prevailed. She went in, fully determined to give her mother the next penny that evening; but as Satan had gotten her to do wrong once, he was right there to see that she kept it up, as it would not do to let her go now that he had gotten her started. So that evening she got another penny. When she started home, the good voice said, "Now give mamma this penny." But the bad voice was there, and said, "You know they are having taffy on the stick now at the candy store for a penny, and you have always been such a good girl and papa don't give you pennies, and you haven't had any candy now for three weeks; so you go over and get one. Tomorrow you can begin giving mamma the penny, and she will never know but what the cut has just begun."

So Bessie stopped, looked in at the window, and thought, "Oh, that taffy on the stick is so nice. Oh, I just want one so bad." But she bit her lip. That good voice said, "No, you give mamma that penny." And she said, "I will," and started for home. But that bad voice stopped her, and Satan made her mouth oh, so hungry for that candy! She turned around, and said, "I will begin tomorrow," and again yielded to Satan's bad voice. That night at her prayer she had quite a time in stammering it out, but Satan was there and made her bold; so she got through after a struggle. Well, next day, it was not much trouble for Satan to get her to get some more candy; and each day he had some new thing for her until she could say her, "Now I lay me", without any trouble. You see children, Satan was hardening her conscience, and silencing that alarm bell in her bosom, so that she could steal her mamma's pennies, and say her prayers without much trouble.

But listen, God saw that her mother must know of what was going on, so He sent me around there to have the thing exposed. He managed to keep Bessie late from school, so I could go after the bread. Children remember that the Bible says, "Be sure your sin will find you out." Bessie thought she had all this covered up, and was planning what to do with her pennies, two a day.

Well, Bessie came to the altar, confessed it all out and got forgiveness from God, and her parents never whipped her for it; they let God punish her, and He let it all come out. So she never did anything like that afterward. You see, children, Satan was making great headway with Bessie; he would first have her steal pennies, then nickels, then dimes, and so on; until, if she went on, she would even kill a man for his money, or sell her virtue to get it.

So avoid bad beginnings. Satan has many a snare to trap the dear children, and when he can once get them started to speak or act wrongly, then he has many ways of leading them to worse deeds. Oh, how that mother did weep and pray that God would take care of Bessie, keep her pure and honest. God had to answer that precious mother's prayer by sending me around. God used me in uncovering Bessie's sin. So children, mind your parents.

Well, the next time I saw Bessie, ten months later, she came running, jumped into my arms, and just hugged and kissed me. She said, "Oh, Brother Bevington, God sent you around here to get me out of that tangle. That would have made a very bad girl out of me. You came just in time to save me." She was glad that I had uncovered Satan's well covered plan to ruin her. Bessie grew up to be a fine mother and is watching her precious jewels that God has given her to be a blessing in this dark world.

When I was in Cleveland, Ohio, in the mission work, one day I was going down a very filthy street, among the very poorest of people. I heard a sweet melodious voice, and stopped to listen. I was charmed by that marvelous voice coming from that quarter. Everyone on that street was very wicked; so I dreaded to inquire as to that voice and prayed: "Oh, God, send someone out so I can find that voice." It seemed to be back, well out of reach. Well, as I was standing there, a door opened, and a poor, dirty woman said, "Come in." I said, "I don't wish to come in, but I would like to know where that sweet voice is that I heard a moment again." "She said, I reckon it was Old Pete." "No," I said, "it was a young voice." "Well that's what everybody calls her, 'Old Pete'." "Where is she?" "Oh, back there in the dirt." "Could I see her?" "I reckon." "Well how can I get to her?" "Over that fence," she said, and then disappeared.

So I climbed the high fence, and back there in the dirt sat this girl, jibbering to herself. I said, "Good morning, Sis." She looked up, and said, "Say, Mister, give me a chaw terbacker." "I don't use it," I said. "Well, gimme a nickel, and I will get old Sal to buy me some." I said, "What is your name, Old Pete? Where do you live?" "There with old Sal," she said, pointing to a shack. "Is she your mother?" "Nop." "Where is your mother?" "Ain't got any." "Where is your father?" "Ain't got any; never had any father nor mother — just old Sal." "Could I see her?" "I reckon. Hay! old Sal, com'ere, man wants you." So here came a poor, dirty, ragged woman; I couldn't tell whether she was a black or white woman. She said, "Come in." "No, I don't want to come in," I said. Then asked, "Is this your child" "No, not mine. I am just raising her." Oh, I thought, what raising! I said, "How long have you had her?" "Two years." "How old is she?" "Don't know." "Well, would you like to give her to me?" "Well, yes, but she is no count girl; can't walk nor stand on her feet." I said to the girl, "Are you the one that was singing Annie Laurie a while ago?" "Yep." "Well, sing it again." "I will if you will give me a nickel ter get terbacker with." "No, I won't give you a nickel, but sing again for me." So she did, and of all the beautiful, clear, sweet voices I ever heard, I thought hers with the sweetest.

I said to the woman, "If you will give me her clothes, I will take her." "Laws' sake, she ain't got any only what's on her back! " I picked that child up and oh, what odor came from her poor filthy body! I said, "When did you have a bath?" "A what?" I said, "A bath." "What's that?" Poor child, eleven years old and never had a bath and lived in filth. I carried her across the creek to a home that had been at one time about like the one this child was found in. The woman took her in. I got clothing for her, and she was cleaned up. I went back the next day and hardly knew her. She had beautiful eyes as that was about all I could see of her the day before.

Well, I began to teach her our songs. I would carry her up to the mission, and out to the street meetings, and it was wonderful how she would learn those songs and sing them. We would keep her well dressed, and how she would enjoy nice clothes! She was a marvelous child, Well, to cut it short, I kept her two years. All this time she was learning songs and singing them on the streets; drawing great crowds by her sweet childlike voice. One day, or rather one evening, a man stopped to listen to her. He waited till the service was over, then came up and said, "Is that your child?" I said, "No." "Well, she has the sweetest voice I ever heard. Are you giving her music lessons?" I said, "No, I would like to, but am in the mission work here and haven't had the money to do it." So he went with me to where I carried the child, then up to my mission. I saw that he was interested in the child.

Next morning he came in, and said, "I am a traveling man; make big money, and if I will give you the money, will you give her music lessons, the best you can get?" I said, "I surely will." He gave me forty dollars wand said that he would be back in two months. I secured the very best musical talent that I could find, and had to take the child to the home twice a week. She would practice on the mission organ. I made her a high chair with a back to it, so that she could sit and play. The man came back in two months and was delighted in the progress the child was making. He brought her a fine high chair, much better than the one I had made, and left me fifty dollars for some clothing and her music lessons. We got her three nice suits complete and shoes. She had tiny feet about the size of an eight-months' old baby's, and could not stand up. She never had, but she was now developing rapidly into a beautiful girl, and such a sweet cheerful singer. The traveling man came back in two more months and was well pleased with her progress. He went out, and soon came back with a fine four-wheeled carriage with levers so that she could guide it, and it had a very nice cover. He paid eighty-eight dollars cash for it. Well, she could go anywhere with it. And oh, she nearly went wild when this friend put her in it, and said, "Now this is yours, yes, yours!" "Oh, is it really mine! Mine to keep always?" "Yes, yours." She asked me to take her out and to put her in his arms, which I did, and she just hugged him and showered kisses upon him.

Well, as usual I would give out tracts. So one day the girl said, "Papa (I had taught her to call me papa) can't I give out those tracts from my buggy?" "Why certainly," I said, "would you like to?" "Oh, yes; I can go on the streets and give them out." So she did, and God would bless her in doing it. Now I had been trying to tell her what salvation was, what Jesus died for, and how she ought to give Jesus her heart; but it seemed that she was so carried away with the great change that had taken place in her life that I just could not get her to see that she ought to be regenerated. I would pray, "Oh, God, what am I going to do? How can I impress her?" I would talk to her, read the Scripture to her, and tell her that if she should die, she would go to an awful hell. Well, that all seemed idle to her, like a dream. I could not get her interested. She seemed to think that the transformation that had already taken place was sufficient.

So, now children, see how God answered prayer. As she would be giving out tracts, she would find time to study them. I had been teaching her to read all these weeks and months, and she could spell out any word. She had the tract entitled "Anna's and Nannie's First Prayer." Well, she would be working on that in her leisure moments while on the street, and would get me to read it to her. So that one and other tracts brought her face to face with the question of salvation. She saw where she was and what she must be. So one night as I gave the altar call, she was in her buggy, and she said, "Papa, I want Jesus, too." So she wheeled up to the altar, and there in her buggy, about 10:00 p. m., gave her heart to Jesus and was blessedly saved there. Oh, how she would sing after that! She would clap her hands so much while singing.

Her main helper would come back every two months and get her clothes and pay for her music lessons, so we kept her at music four years. She was then about seventeen, as nearly as we could find out her age. She was then an accomplished musician.

The man came and said, "Mr. Bevington, if you will give me that girl, I will take her to Indianapolis, Indiana, where they make limbs, they would nearly make such as she perfectly whole." I said, "Would you want her for all time as your daughter?" The question brought tears to my eyes, and he saw it. "Well," he said, "you love her. I will put her there, and then give her back to you, a perfect, walking lady." Well, I very much disliked the thought of giving her up, but knew it was the best for her. I was then in Louisville in the mission work, having left Cleveland some time.

So he took her to Indianapolis, and kept her there over two years. He brought her to me at Cincinnati, a lovely young lady well developed. She could walk as well as I could. She had artificial limbs, but could use them, and she had been studying all this time. Then I took her to Mr. Gamble. He sent her to school two years and then she went to the Fiji Islands, as a missionary under the M. E. Board. She was there several years and established a great faith home and school, and then went from there to Heaven. So see dear children, what God can and will do if we will trust Him.

I might have said, "Oh that poor, miserable, dirty, ignorant, uncouth girl can never do anything for Jesus," but see how God opened the way for her to be an accomplished, pure, brilliant, young lady and then sent her away over to those poor dear heathen, where hundreds were brought to Jesus. Oh, praise the Lord for her life and that God could use such as I in bringing her out.

Dear children, if God could take such as she was when I found her and bring her out to where He did, just think what He might do with you children if you would let Him. Dear children, you must realize that God can help you and will help you; but He wants you to trust Him, to give your heart to Him, as He says, "Give me thine heart." You must be born again, regenerated, made a new creature in Christ Jesus. So see to it that you do not put it off too long. Jesus said, "Suffer the little children to come unto me—for of such is the kingdom of heaven."

I want to meet every boy and girl who reads these pages, in Heaven. I am going there, and surely do thank God that He gave me a praying mother. I well remember when I was about seven, that after prayer my mother said, "This boy (laying her hand on my head) is going to preach the Gospel." While as a young man I never entered into deep sin, I was so reckless—loved the world, dancing, theaters, and so on—and most anyone seeing me those days would have said, "Well, that fellow's mother missed it when she said he was going to be a preacher." I forgot my mother's benediction until after I had been preaching some time, and then a cousin reminded me of it. God had that prayer of mother's to answer, and praise His dear name, He did; and He will make preachers out of you boys and girls, if you will let Him.

When I was in the mission work in Cleveland, I met a crippled girl about fourteen years of age. She was small, and had never walked. She had a brother who had his back broken when he was twelve, he was then sixteen. He could sit up. They were very poor I got them clothes, wheeled them to and from the mission in a wheelbarrow. They were bright, ambitious children, could read and write. The girl said, after I had given a missionary talk, "Oh! I wish I could make some money for those dear children over there." She had never heard of them before and she was greatly worked up about them. I got to thinking. I went home and made a few lighters out of papers, and took them down to a factory to see if I could sell them. I told the foreman about those two children and how they needed help. While I was talking the manger came, overheard what I said. and asked the foreman, "Would these be cheaper than matches?" He said, "Yes." Well, now much could we afford to give for them?" The foreman said, "Not over thirty cents a hundred "

Well that seemed small, but I went back, got a lot of paper, and took it to these children, and showed them how to make the lighters. They soon became experts at it, and would make a hundred a day. This brought them thirty cents, a big pile of money to them; and as poor as the parents were, they said they could give half to the heathen. So they did. I would take the lighters to the factory and get the cash for them. This man had a cousin in another part of the city, who also used gas stoves. So he got him to take several thousand. Those children got so they could make 200 a day, that was 400 that both made. Well, now, at thirty cents per hundred, how much would that be a day?

Those children bought their clothes, and went to night school. I would wheel them there and their father would come after them. And they got saved and could sing. The girl took lessons and learned to play, just from the money earned by making those paper lighters. So children where there is a will there is a way. Why they kept up giving half to the foreign field and two years after I left there, they both were engaged in the office of this factory. Both of them had learned stenography, and they lived good Christian lives.

Four years after, while I was at the Cincinnati Camp, there came to me a young man and a young lady, on crutches. They were fine looking people, and they smiled and said, "I guess you don't know us." Well, I didn't. So they told me. And, oh, how proud I was of them. They have been faithful to their God, and He has prospered them. They were living in their own home, and paying for it out of their wages they made in this factory. And the father and mother still kept them in paper lighters.

Now one more short story. I was holding a meeting down below Rising Sun, Indiana, and was in a home where there was a little tot. She couldn't talk plain, but could say her, "Now I lay me," every night and morning. So one night she failed to say it. So Mamma said, "Gracie, aren't you going to say your prayer?" "Nope." "Well, why?" "'Tause I'se baksid." I never had heard anything like that from such a little tot, and I was so amused that I had to go outdoors. Mamma shook her head at me, as she went where the tot was. She said, "Well, Gracie, how did you come to backslide?" " 'Tause I dot mad at Jim; said a bad word." "Well," Mamma said, "you must get back to Jesus again." So the dear little thing just prayed and cried. Then she rose and said, " 'Tis all right, I'se all right." I tell you that was a good lesson to me. You couldn't get her to say saved, sanctified up-to-date, while she was doing wrong. If all children were that honest, it would be a rebuke to many an older person.

Well, now dear children, we have had quite a time. I have enjoyed this chat with you all. So in closing this chapter, I want to invite you all to Jesus, whom I have been well acquainted with now these thirty-three years, since I was sanctified, and in whom I have all confidence. I feel sure that if you will give Him your hearts, He will care for you as He has for me. I want to meet every one who reads this chapter, up in Heaven where Jesus and the angels are, where we can forever be with the Lord. God bless you, one and all, and the papas and mammas of all.

With love and best wishes, I close.

Your friend and well wisher,
G. C. Bevington
Ashland, Kentucky, or Kingswood, Kentucky.

8

Instances of Healing

UNANSWERED PRAYERS AVAIL NOTHING. 'Tis the prayers that get through that will count for us and for those for whom they are offered. So, mothers, don't be careless or indifferent in your praying. God wants real, earnest, effectual, prevailing prayers. Many prayers are heard and answered, as we often hear Him say to the recording angel: "Get your file and record that prayer, it has a good sound, clear ring to it; so we will have to put it on file ready for adjustment." God does the giving, and we do the taking; so what we do not take we do not get. God cannot give us what we will not take.

> *God has His choice things for the few*
> *Who dare to stand the test;*
> *God has His second choice for those*
> *Who will not have His best.*

In which crowd are you?

> *Faith drops out where our doubts step in,*
> *And faith stops just where doubts begin.*

> *Faith, mighty faith, the promise sees,*
> *And looks to that alone;*
> *Laughs at impossibilities,*
> *And cries, "It shall be done!"*

Yes, it shall be done! Amen! If you are now ailing, now suffering, look up; count the healing done, and it shall be done. Hallelujah! "According to your faith;" not according to how long you have had the trouble, or how it has baffled all efforts; no, but "according to your faith." So look up, count it done now. If healing depended on our "shalls" or "is", it would be quite different; but listen, 'tis a "shall," uttered by our omnipotent, omniscient, omnipresent God. Hallelujah! We have a right to trust Him to the limit, and count it done. God wants men and women with iron in their blood, and fire in their bones, and a pick and a shovel and a subsoil plow to turn something up. Amen and Amen! We sometimes get to the place where we can't pray the prayer of faith; as we may be too weak or suffering too intensely, which lessens our faculties, and renders us incapacitated for prayer.

I was one of the first students in God's Bible School, Cincinnati; and about a month before the first term closed, I was taken down with acute neuralgia. It was very painful and kept getting worse. I went to bed at 9:30 p. m., as I was working down town for my board and going up to the school afternoons for recitations, Bible review, and other lessons. That was before I had stepped out entirely on healing, but I was not taking any remedies.

So after about a week of suffering I woke up one night at midnight, and I think I never was in such misery as then. Well, I tried to pray; but I was in too much misery and began to cry out to God to make someone else pray for me. I said, "O God, wake someone up who will pray for me." I plead that for about ten minutes, when I began to get better, and in thirty minutes the suffering was all gone, and I was sound asleep. I was sure God had answered.

In about ten days I received a letter from California, stating that at such a morning about 1:00 a. m., the writer was awakened, and a voice said, "Get up and pray for Bevington." Well, she did not know where I was, but knew that my last address was Cincinnati, Ohio. She said, "Oh, I am so sleepy," and tried to go back to sleep; but that voice kept calling her. She spoke to her husband; but he said, "Oh, you are just dreaming that; Bevington can do his own praying; you ate too much supper last night, go to sleep, don't bother about Bevington; he will pull through all right."

Well, she tried to go to sleep, but could not for that voice ringing in her ears. Her husband said, "Well, I guess you had better get up; it doesn't matter where he is, you get up." She did so, and the moment her knees struck the floor she was engulfed with great misery in her head. She told her husband to get up, and go to praying. He, being a blessedly saved man, got up, and 'twas the same with him; he was taken with severe shooting pains in his head. So they clasped hands across the bed, he on one side, she on the other; and in seven minutes their pains stopped, and so did mine. They knew that they had reached the throne in my behalf. So you see God had to wake someone up away over in California. That was the first time I ever did that and have never done it since.

I don't know when I may; but the lesson is, that we must mind God regardless of how things look.

When God told Samuel to anoint David, a stripling sheep herder, to be a king, Samuel know that Saul had not been dethroned but was yet their actual king, and that to anoint another would be equal to treason; yet in face of all this and the danger of being killed, he minded God. Now you may ask, was it necessary or best for me to rub my temples for relief occasionally and then to be praying for someone else to rub them when I knew it would be impossible to get anyone?" Well, was it necessary for Samuel to make a sacrifice offering in order to save his life? Samuel had said, "Why, Lord, if I go down there and anoint David king, Saul will kill me, as he is the lawful, legal king, and is now on the throne." Now, you tell me why God allowed him to make a feast, and so on. God has to appeal to the human at times, in order to create or stimulate our faith and often to overthrow our own plans.

While at Ashland Heights, I was called one evening to come over to Fairview to preach; and as I went by Brother Wamsley's in Pollard, I stopped to get them to go along. Brother Wamsley was on his porch. He came out, and I said, "Are you and your wife going over?" "Well, I guess not; wife has been suffering for three days with neuralgia, and dare not go out, and I don't want to leave her, as she is suffering now really beyond her strength." I said, "Tell her to come out." "Why, Brother Bevington, she dare not expose herself to the air; she would not live ten minutes." "Tell her to come out." Well, he stood there astonished at my ridiculous request, but I repeated, "Tell her to come out." "Why, she would not dare to venture out a moment." "Tell her to come out." I just stood there repeating this wild request, and praying, until they got tired of hearing it, and out she came, with her head all tied up. I bowed my head, pleaded the promises, standing there on the street where others, who were unsaved, were looking on. I raised my hand, claimed her healing, stood still counting the work done, and in fifteen minutes I heard a whoop, and off came the bandages, and she had a shouting spell right there.

I started on to Fairview, praying the Lord to send them over. About halfway over, I said, "Boys, she is coming; she will be there soon after we get there." They said, "Oh, I reckon not, as she has been in a critical condition, and 'twould be dangerous for her to attempt it." I said, "She is coming." We had just begun singing when in she came, shouting and swinging her sunbonnet. She just set the whole house on fire, and at the altar service she was all aglow with the power of God on her, and prayed a poor, discouraged backslider through. To Jesus be all the glory!

A sister in South Ashland was, as the doctor said, on her deathbed with consumption. I was invited over, and went with a sister. I had read a chapter and got on my knees, pleaded earnestly, got the victory. I claimed her healing, jumped up, grabbed my hat and rushed out, saying, "She will be out of there in ten minutes." I had not gotten out of their yard until she was out of that bed, praising God for complete healing. She went to the Pilgrim Holiness Church of which Rev. John Fleming was pastor and testified to her healing. Brother John witnessed her healing.

He will testify to being healed more than once, as will his dear faithful wife. The first year after he moved to Ashland, from Willard, his saintly wife was on her bed very sick. He sent me word, and I prayed for her that night. I got blessed during prayer, and claimed her healing; but the next afternoon he drove up on the hill after me, saying that his wife was very much worse. I jumped into his buggy and went with him to her room. There she lay, speechless, and very much resembling a lifeless form. I fell on my face in the corner, to ascertain whether God wanted to heal her or not. I lay there over an hour; then being satisfied that He wanted to heal her, I rose on my knees, laid my hand on her cold brow. Soon she opened her eyes, and smiled, and the glory fell. Brother John shouted, "Brother Bevington, she is healed." I jumped up, walked the floor about five minutes, then went out and got into the buggy, and drove down town rejoicing over her healing, though all the visible evidence she had given was th e opening of her eyes and smiling. But the glory flooded me all the way down town. I did my errand, came back under the power of God, and found her up praising God. So Satan was foiled there. Hallelujah to Jesus' dear name!

I had a number of cases of healing while at South Ashland, but can't remember the details. I remember while at Willard, in 1917, a case was reported of a very sick woman. She had been in bed six weeks, looked quite helpless, and was a backslider. The children needed care, and the house was pretty well littered up. As I approached I felt intense darkness; but I said, "Can I afford to let this woman die unsaved?" I went to prayer and had a struggle, as everything seemed so dark; but I kept praying and dynamiting and blasting until, finally, after two hours, in tunnels and caves, I began to see streaks of light. I will never forget how that encouraged me. I don't remember when I was so grateful as there in that dark home; as everything seemed against me except, I think, five children that appealed to me, and I took them as my reasons for pleading for her healing.

As I went to praising God quite softly, the clouds began to lift, and my faith seemed to be climbing the rugged peaks, from one to another. Though rather quiet, I claimed her healing, and got up, and met the brother who had sent me there. He said, "Well, what did you do?" I said, "I believe she will be out of that bed soon." I went up to the home of Frank Fleming, a brother to the Fleming preachers, John and Bona. This was nearly a mile from where the sick woman lived, and I heard nothing from her during the night, or early in the morning. So I refused breakfast, and held on with good encouragement, and kept pushing right up the hill for two hours after I got up. Then I said, "Lord 'tis done! 'Tis done! 'Tis done!" At the third utterance, Sister Fleming came to the door, and said, "Oh, Brother Bevington, just listen; that woman is out yelling like an Indian." I had claimed her victory, and was rejoicing, sweeping through the clouds, mounting the more delectable heights, praising God for her healing. Well, she just leaped the fences, ran from one house to another, shouting and praising God for healing and reclaiming her.

To the Brothers and Sisters in the Lord, Scattered Abroad:
I want to take the advantage of this opportunity to testify to all to the glory of Him who said, "I am the Lord that healeth thee." I am praising the Lord today for healing me of a severe case of gallstones. I feel like saying sometimes, This one thing I know, that whereas I was sick, I am now well. Praise the Lord! Since the flu swept the country, I had been a victim of gallstones which developed after I had the flu. I had always been a believer in Divine healing, but I never could get faith strong enough for the healing of my own body. I remembered that the Bible says: "If two of you shall agree on earth as touching anything that they shall ask, it shall be done;" so I wrote to Brother G. C. Bevington, who was at Kingswood, Kentucky, at that time. He joined with me in prayer in behalf of my body; and on January 2, 1921, the Lord wonderfully and instantly healed me. Ever since, I have been trusting Him for constant good health; and He gives it, praise His name! Of course the devil tries to tell me that I am not healed and that I still have the gallstones; but I know that I was healed. So I get the victory over the old devil, and go on praising the Lord. Amen!

Knowing that there are so many people destitute of faith for the healing of their own bodies, I want to say that it is not an easy thing to give up all remedies and trust the Lord; for the devil would like to keep us sick, and would even like to kill us. So it takes a lot of encouragement and trusting and prayer and light on how to trust the Lord for complete victory over the devil. I have often wondered if I would have been healed, if it had not been for the wonderful letters of encouragement and light I received from Brother Bevington while he was praying for me. He has such a matured experience, and such a grip on God; and he has undaunted faith, especially on Divine healing.

—R. W. Wolfe, Fort Gay, W. Va.

I went over to Ironton, Ohio, taught a class in Sunday school and met an old acquaintance, whom I had not seen for several years. He had been healed in the country. I was called to his home to pray for his wife's healing. I soon said, "Sister, are you sure that you are a sanctified woman?" She had claimed that experience. She broke out crying, and said, "No, brother, I am not and never have been. I thought I was once, and have testified to it here in the church, as I was told to claim it and testify to it."

Now here is danger. I never ask people to testify to sanctification until they are sure they are sanctified. I encourage them to take it by faith if they are satisfied that their consecration is complete. Then they may say that they have taken sanctification by faith, and believe that they are sanctified, and stand on that. Never say that you are sanctified until you know it. This sister was doing what holiness preachers told her to do, as they are supposed to know. But when she got down face to face with God in that prayer circle, God revealed to her that she was never sanctified. Well, I just turned my whole outfit in another direction from that which she was aiming at, and poured out my desires that she might have a real revelation, a real heart searching. She rose up, saying, "Oh, brother, I want the real thing this time! " So I loaded up heavier, and bombarded the citadel of hell pretty strong for about two hours, when suddenly she was laid out as white as could be. I just kept up the firing until she made an unconditional surrender, which she did in about an hour; and, I tell you, she took the house sure. Then she settled down, saying, "Oh, glory, I know 'tis done now!"

When the bombarding ceased and the smoke cleared away, I heard someone groaning. I looked behind me, and there lay a son about sixteen, crying for salvation. So I turned my guns on him, and in ninety minutes he was shouting. He grabbed me and carried me all over the room. We had a great praise service. Then I said, "Now, sister, how about that sickness that you called me here to pray for?" "Oh," she said, "I had forgotten all about that. I guess that is gone with the 'old man'." And sure enough it was. So we need to be ready for most anything these days. I just carry a full kit with me all the time, so as to be ready for any emergency.

Here is an incident which occurred in Ashland Heights. I was going down the hill from the church, and slipped and sprained my ankle. Well, it was quite painful; but I went on, walked down town and back. My foot pained some on my return, but I did not bother the Lord with it; as I considered it most too small a matter to bring to Him. However, next morning, it was quite painful and so swollen that I could not get my shoe on. The joint was stiff, and I could not move the foot. I had planned to put out tracts that day, and saw that something had to be done, and that right away.

When I had done my dishes and put them all away, I got the Word and opened it and saw where the lame man was healed instantly. Well, as I plunged down that trail, I was scooping up power at every word, so that by the time I had reached the place where it says, "Immediately his ankle bone received strength," I dropped the Bible, and shouted, "Yes, and here is the same!" I jumped up, leaping and shouting, and was perfectly healed right then and there. I tell you I well remember that morning. How the glory did fall! Ah, God will heal.

I see here a record of getting a letter about Bertha Bolander, a former student of God's Bible School. 'Twas a special letter from the husband, stating that his wife was in the hospital with no hopes of recovery. So I took the letter and the Bible, and spent nineteen hours pleading for her. I saw her rise up and raise her hand, as plainly as I ever saw anything, though she was two hundred miles from me. Well, you might again ask, "Why did it take that long; inasmuch as she was suffering so and needed immediate help?"

Well, as usual it took me some time to get still, as many other cases were clamoring for a hearing. Satan is always around to remind us of the many important cases that we ought to attend to. He knows that will divert us from the main line, switch us off, and blockade the whole thing. So it took hours to find out whether the Lord wanted to heal her. It took only two hours to see her raised up after seventeen hours were spent in getting the mind of Jesus.

Many devices of Satan were used to head me off. I would get drowsy, sleepy, and unconcerned, all of which were only to get me discouraged, and to drop the case. But I felt that the case was worthy of my best efforts; and I well remember that while I was pleading, I brought pretty good reasons for her speedy recovery. But I would be met by about as reasonable logic as I was presenting, from a natural standpoint. Particular stress was put on the point that we must not close our eyes to the natural; that as God is the founder of natural laws, we must give heed to them. All of these arguments present a pretty broad and solid front, somewhat difficult to break through at times, especially if others are clamoring for attention. But I would and did continue the fight for her life. I saw her lying just like a corpse, but I did not give up at that. Satan said, "She is now dead. There is no use putting in any more time on her case. You have been very faithful and done your best, putting in seventeen hour of your valuable time."

Well, you see all this was tinged with logic, if it was somewhat flattery; but I still fought all this logic and rose from my face, demanding immediate attention. I held up the Bible, saying, "Lord, Thou dost hear; Thou art interested in Thy children. Keep Satan off. Is she dead? I am now listening to Thee."

Soon the scene changed, the clouds vanished, and no more logical presentations were given. I said, "Lord, I can't believe she is dead." Now listen; this is what was given me. "The afflictions of the righteous are many, but the Lord delivereth from them all." I grabbed my Bible, and began praising God and soon had the evidence that she was not only alive but healed. Oh, Hallelujah! How the glory did fall! In a few days I received notice of her sudden recovery.

Sister G. L. Medler's healing at Kingswood, Kentucky, May, 1921.

I want to tell that God has wonderfully relieved me of my severe suffering. Divine healing is wonderful. First, it shows God's wonderful love for us. I have been Divinely healed many times, though this time seems more wonderful because the suffering had been of so long duration. When a girl in my teens, I was taken with a very severe case of rheumatism; and I do not know that I was ever free entirely from suffering from that time until now. Praise the Lord, He has removed the suffering! Many physicians did their best to relieve me, though the disease only tightened its already fastened fangs. As time went on, I think there was none of my flesh or sinew but had through and through, many, many times, this sawing, cutting, gnawing pain.

No joint or nerve had escaped this continual suffering. When I slept, my hands swelled, the joints becoming stiff and useless. When the worse suffering settled in my hands, they would be out of shape, so they hardly looked like human hands. Then the severe suffering would move to some other part of the body, and the joints would loosen, and my hands would return to a semblance of hands, though not normal, as the joints would be enlarged and knots formed.

I do not claim to be healed from the effects of rheumatism, though I am relieved from the awful suffering. I do thank the Lord for it. It was His love and His power that relieved me. I cannot describe what a sufferer I was for forty years. One doctor refused to do anything for me as he said it was an incurable case. He said I was past help, and never would use either of my hands again.

About twenty-three years since, I suffered all winter with rheumatism in my head, and many other times also. About seven years since, one doctor said, "I will send you another kind of medicine; if it does not help you, there is not anything that will." I took that medicine exactly as directed, regarding diet and everything, but grew worse every day.

Over a year ago rheumatism settled in my head again, and especially in the brain. I cannot explain the suffering. My neighbors offered to come and pray for me, though I said, "I have no faith for my healing; I have suffered so long and so severely. This is a hopeless case."

This spring, Dr. Shoemaker, a sanctified physician, our only doctor here, advised me to ask Brother Bevington to pray for my healing. At first I was not much interested, as there had been so many attempts, and none effectual, that I had given up all hopes. But after some time of continual suffering, the Lord began to talk to me about asking Brother Bevington. So I began to take heed, and hearing of others who were being healed through his prayers, I began to get interested.

The third week in April I decided I would ask Brother Bevington to pray for my healing, though I had not decided just when and how I would put this decision into action. The Lord knew that it was time then for action; so it was settled on Sunday, April 24. When I attempted to get up, I fell back on the bed, I did not give up and lie down, I fell. When I decided to wake Mr. Medler and tell him that he would have to get up and get his own breakfast, the Lord said, "You get up." I said, "I did not suppose I could get up." The Lord never tells anyone to do anything impossible, so I saw that I could in His name.

When it was time to get ready for Sunday school, the Lord said, "You get ready and go." I was more surprised at that command than the other, though again I believed that the Lord knew, and I obeyed. When about two-thirds of the way there, I felt that I could go no farther, though I kept saying, "Well, the Lord told me to go, so He will help me the rest of the way." When I arrived, I was very, very sick. Then the Lord said, "Get Brother Bevington to pray for you." I was so blinded that I could not see to write a note to him, so Mr. Medler wrote and told Mr. Bevington that I was at the college, and very sick, and asked him to pray for my relief. That was all I would have asked, as it was as far as I could see — just relief, as I had no faith in healing.

After I went in and took my seat, there seemed to be a black, weighty something about ten feet square with the center of it pressing on the top of my head. Our pastor told me that was the devil trying to keep Brother Bevington from getting a prayer through for me.

After a while, that was removed; and the blind, dizzy, deathly sick feeling left me, though the severe pain did not cease until the next afternoon. When we got home, he told how Brother Bevington got down and talked to the Lord about my case, and how he felt the mighty presence of God. He said that Brother Bevington prayed: "Now, Lord, I believe she is your child; and if she is, we have a right to claim healing for her; yes, complete healing." Then my faith, for the first time, took hold, and I said, "Yes, Lord, I am Thy child." And I said, "I shall be healed on the ground that I am Thy child." That noon I went to bed, as I thought, for the rest of the day, but after I took a nap, the Lord said, "Get up and go to class meeting." I did so, and in my testimony I said, "I have suffered very much the last few days, and especially today, though the Lord is going to heal me, Brother Bevington is praying for me; and he said that if I am the Lord's, I can be healed. I know that I am God's child, and I am going to be healed. Praise His name!"

It was nearly five weeks before I reported to Brother Bevington complete relief from rheumatism, and I suffered during that time. I had tonsilitis; and our pastor, Sister Brown, came and prayed with me, and I was instantly healed of that and the severe cold I had also. The devil tried hard to keep me from getting the victory. The Lord did not remove the rheumatism suffering all at once, but the Lord's way is the right way always, and the best for us. Praise His holy name forever and forever! I praise His for victory for the soul and body. Through the precious blood I am saved, sanctified and completely healed. Hallelujah.

—Mrs. G. L. Medler, Kingswood, Ky.

While I was at my home at Ashland Heights, Brother White came over for water and had his boy of four summers with him. His head was covered with eczema. I enquired the cause, and being informed, said, "Well, I guess our Doctor can cure that. Brother White, don't you know that Jesus can heal that head?" "Well, I reckon He can, as He can do all things." I said, "Come in, let's anoint him for healing." "Well, Brother, I am afraid I haven't the faith." "Well, come in." So in they came, and I anointed him, and prayed the prayer of faith. Next evening, they came back and the little fellow was healed. Oh, how blessed to be yoked up with such a power to relieve suffering, and that, too, without money and without price. Hallelujah.

Now, this reminds me that this well was the only one that was near there, so numbers of people came to get water. I would give them tracts and talk salvation with them. "Well," a neighbor said, "Brother Bevington there is a spring down the hill; and you had better send these people down there, as your well will soon go dry. Too many are drawing from it, and it always goes dry in the summer." Well, the water soon got roily; but still the people came; and it was suggested that I put a sign out asking them not to get any more water until it rained. Well, I thought that was all right, and went so far as to write up the sign. I got the tacks and the hammer, and started out to put the sign up; but when I got part way out to the gate, a voice said, "Where are you going?"

Well, I was startled and looked around, really expecting to see someone behind me; but there was not a person in sight. I just stood there, and again the voice said, "Yes, where are you going?" I tell you that settled it. I tore up the sign, dropped on my knees, asked God to forgive me for venturing that far into the realms of Doubting Castle, and began praising Him for rebuking me. Just as I got off my knees, here came three women with large buckets, so I got a small bucket and gave it to them to draw with, as the large bucket would get but little, and I availed myself of the opportunity of going in to get some more tracts and talking salvation. One of them had never been there, and I felt that God sent the message home to her, as she had four precious children to train. Being let alone they would not need any training for hell as they had the thing in them that would land them there without any human help. Well, they had a time getting their three buckets full, but I just kept sweet. I said, "Lord, send them on. I

8: INSTANCES OF HEALING   165

would rather pack water from the spring ninety rods away than to miss an opportunity of warning those lost mothers."

The day passed. I went out in the evening with a two-quart bucket, let it down and got it half full of roily water. I said, "Well, Amen, I can go to the spring," so I started off with two buckets. I had two hills to climb, and was impressed to leave one bucket, and did so. I started to the spring, and, lo, the voice said, "Bevington, where are you going?" Well, I knew the voice; hence never looked around, but instantly turned and went back into the house, and had somewhat of a struggle in getting where I could easily praise the Lord for rebuking me, as I had to have water. I was then thirsty. I prayed my way through the darkness, got up, and then the neighbor came in with a quart of nice cool water that she had gotten some distance from home.

Well, I began to see that God wanted to send water into the well though there was no rain nor signs of rain, and the well had always gone dry at that season and remained dry for three, four, or often five months, they said. I got down and began praising God for stopping me and for sending in the sister with the water. I had been in the habit of taking a good drink just before retiring; and there was where Satan had confused me, as he had kept saying, "What are you going to do for that cool drink that always helps you so?" I had to tell him it was none of his business what I was going to do about it; so I had a struggle for three hours over it, but got the victory.

I retired, claiming two feet of water in the morning, which had not been since we lived there, and I told the neighbor that we would have at least two feet of water in the morning. She was a dear woman, a member of a church, but know nothing about God answering prayer. She looked at me, puzzled, and said, "Brother Bevington, what makes you think that? I have never known of there being two feet of water in that well. When there comes a freshet it leaks out." The well was seventy-two feet deep. "Well," I said, "we will have it." She said, "I see no signs of rain." I said, "I do." Well, that puzzled her more than ever as the firmament was decked with brilliant stars. I went to bed, praising God for two feet of water in the morning, so that I could have plenty for the neighbors.

I had a two-quart bucket that I drew out with the windlass and, without thinking, in the morning I started out with this two-quart bucket. But there it was again. I had to be rebuked again. It seemed that the bucket spoke up as did Baalam's ass, and I dropped it, as if it were a hot poker, and stopped, and said, "O God, forgive me! Oh, forgive me!" and felt the touch. I went to the well, let down the large bucket, gave it the usual time to sink, started to draw it up, and felt by the pull that it was full. I shouted, "Oh, glory! " Out came this neighbor. I said, "We have our two feet this morning." She came over by the time I had the bucket up and out, and there it was full and as clear as a crystal. I just stood there weeping for joy. She ran into the house, got a cup, took a drink, and said, "Well, that is a marvel. Your God surely has answered your prayer." She broke down, and we both stood there by that well, weeping. She said, "Brother Bevington, that is something new to me; but do you really think there are two feet?" I said, "Yes." "Well, please measure it." "No," I said, "I would not do that, as it would be displeasing to God." "Well, may I?" "Certainly." So she measured it, and found there were two feet and nine inches of water, and that amount was kept up all summer and fall.

Now I have left out what, to me, was the cream of it. Satan bothered me, tormented me all he could all night. He woke me up to notify me that it had not rained during the night. "Well," I said, "I am not looking for rain; I am after water, rain or no rain." While I was dressing, he just poured in his logic and came near drowning me; but I rallied. I got dressed, dropped on my knees, as prayer is generally the best weapon I can use; but I seemed to make a slow progress for the heights. I jumped up, and said, "Mr. Devil, I have two feet of water out there!" But that seemed to have no effect on him, whatever. I said, "I will see what our calendar says." I struck a light, and referred to the daily Scripture on the calendar. Now listen, what was there: Isa. 33:16, "Bread shall be given him; his water shall be sure." Oh, how I did rejoice. Think of it, that after all that struggling, God had that very passage there on the canvas for me, for my special use. I tell you I have never been without a Scripture calendar since. Oh, God answers!

I see here recorded, in 1920, several cases of the flu. One family had two doctors all night. As they were sinking fast, they sent for me. I went, and anointed them; soon they showed signs of life, so I held on. The woman opened her eyes, and smiled, and said, "I am healed." In a few hours she was out of bed, and gaining strength. The next morning she got breakfast for the family, and there was no more flu in that home.

I was called to a sister who was very low. Her husband had just gotten out of bed after a long siege of it, and she was well worn out from caring for him. He was still very weak. Two children were in another bed with the same disease. I felt awful darkness — it was, oh, so dark. I sat there wondering what could be done, and was almost persuaded to leave. Oh, such a pressure! There was nothing congenial, no encouragement. The sister was unconscious. She had not lived any too close to the Lord, as she had many hindrances in the home, unsaved girl, and an unsaved husband. Well, as I sat there, I said, "Oh, God, what can be done?" I seemed to get no answer, no light. But there I was; I had been sent for by the daughter. There was a possibility, and should I ignore that? I had not been where there was such a heavy pressure, in a long time; but I was held by the power of God. There she lay, giving no sign of life. The medicine sent out its fumes, and had a stupefying effect on me. But I rallied, and said, "Well, God is able." At that the man raised his head from an apparent stupor, and nodded assent.

Satan was there surely, and warned me about remaining there in that atmosphere, as there had been severe cases for four weeks, and the rooms had not been fumigated. Well, all this was logic and rather hard to meet, and I was having such a hard time in breathing that I could scarcely get my breath. But could I leave one of my sisters, who was needed in that home, and who was evidently at the point of death? Could I leave her? Would God get any glory out of my leaving? Then came more logic. "But you surely can't stand it long in here with this flu odor so thick, and you were up all night last night. If you undertake to pray through, you will smother in here, hence fail; it would be better never to have come. Then you must remember that it was the unsaved girl who sent for you, and did it through simply human desires to have mamma get well. God has nothing to do with your coming here." Well, I tell you all these were staggering, and it was getting very difficult for me to breathe.

But I compared the sister's usefulness to mine. I said, "Mine is of little importance; but there are three babies and two in their teens, all needing her." I stepped out onto the porch, got a whiff of fresh air, and called for a drink. But I had to get it myself, as there was no one to wait on me nor others. I fell on my knees, but never undertook such stifling environments. I could scarcely get a word out, but I pushed through, cried to God mightily from my heart if not with my voice. I said, "O God, Thou wilt hear! O God, Thou wilt hear!" I got that out audibly, and that encouraged me; so I proceeded up the hill, grabbed a root here and there, and saw that I was coming out.

That gave me courage, and I tell you I did some earnest scrambling. As the foot holds and hand grabs were more frequent, I could see that I was making better progress, and was actually climbing the steps. I began to breathe freer. Soon I realized that I was nearing the peak. I could see glimmers of light up the hill, and believed I was soon going to have an over-the-top experience. This encouraged me to work the harder. Soon the sister threw the covers, and bounded out of that bed, shouting, "I am healed." And so she was. So it pays to venture.

One thing that made it harder for me was that I had been informed she had sent for several saints to meet me there. But they did not come, which gave Satan a good opportunity to throw a wet blanket over the proceedings; as he will plan and execute all sorts of maneuvers. He said, "Now, you see those saints were wiser than you, as they knew the danger and wisely stayed away." Then another thing, I had asked the daughter if her mother had ever been anointed, and she had said, "Yes." I was impressed to anoint her, but her having been anointed seemed sufficient, and I must avoid all indication of self. So I had a struggle at that point. I well remember that I did not get light until I laid all reasoning aside, just closed my eyes, got still, and pulled the curtains down. Then I had strength to meet the Goliaths. Hallelujah!

I anointed her as I was told to at first, as often we have to do the ridiculous. We must learn to mind God whether conditions are favorable or not. I went from this home into the home of an other woman who was confined to her bed with the flu. I anointed her, and in forty minutes she was sitting up, a healed woman. Next night she walked three-quarters of a mile to our street meeting, and gave a thrilling testimony to God's healing power. This testimony proved a great blessing in that meeting, as did her life after that.

There was a heavy sleet and ice; and as I was going down a grade to a neighbor's I slipped and fell pretty hard and struck my side on a root of a tree, which knocked me senseless for several moments. When I rallied, I saw that my side was hurt, and had some trouble in getting up; but I finally did, and kept going all day. At noon I felt quite a pain; and during the afternoon it kept getting worse, so that every move brought severe pains. At night I mentioned the matter to Jesus, and retired; but every move more emphatically reminded me of the fall, and to turn over in bed became an impossibility. However, after each move I got the victory and dropped off to sleep, only to suffer again at my next move. The pain kept getting worse, thus each time taking much longer to get the victory.

At 4:00 a. m., I felt that I must turn over, but found I could not; so I said, "Well, it is about time I was doing something." Then I started to pray out loud; but that brought a paroxysm of pain, so I pleaded inaudibly for a few moments. Yet I felt no relief. I said, "I will pray by the help of God: I will pray. In the name of Jesus I will pray." I began to pray out loud, and it did not hurt me. I soon stopped praying and went to praising God, and at five o'clock leaped out of bed entirely healed. Oh, isn't that better than suffering so long and paying out so much money that might be used for better purposes? Then, it is so much better to honor God than not.

I heard a holiness preacher say that he first tried Jesus, and then when He failed, he went after the doctor. I said, "I guess you always have the privilege of going after the doctor." I am so glad I am not occupying that position. I have found no case in which He has failed in these thirty-three years. I am not speculating, I am expecting; hence I get. Glory to Jesus!

The next note of interest is dated April 27, 1920. I took my departure for Kingswood, Kentucky. I mention this merely to show how God looks after us. It was raining when I woke up at Ashland, and I was to take an early train. I said, "Now Father, I have two grips to carry to the depot, so, please, slack up the rain until I get there anyway." When I got about ready to go, it was still raining. Satan, as usual, was there to remind me that I had prayed for it not to rain while I was going to the depot. "Well," I said, "I haven't started yet."

I got my traps, and went down to say good-bye to the people. "O Brother Bevington, it is raining too hard for you to start out." I said, "It will stop." So when I got outdoors, it stopped. Praise God! It rained while I was on the train. I had two transfers, but had prayed to have it dry while I had to be out; and God answered. The weather was quite cool, and in the evening it rained all the way from Louisville to Irvington. I had to transfer there, and get my suit case, but it did not rain there. I got on the car to go to Harned, the end of my railroad journey, from where I had five miles to go in a jolt wagon. As soon as I left Irvington it began raining, and Satan said, "Now you will have a long, cold, wet drive in this rain." I stuck to it that it would not rain, though up to within twenty minutes of our arrival at Harned it was raining. It was then dark, and this was my first trip to Kingswood; but as I got off the train, I said, "Oh, praise God, no rain!" We had a beautiful ride by moonlight all the way to the home of dear Brother and Sister Shelton, whom I had met at Rockdale, Kentucky.

Now that I have given several instances of healing of human bodies, I feel like inserting one instance of the healing of stock, as God is interested in our minutest details.

I was back of Chillicothe, Ohio, one spring, holding a meeting; and the brother with whom I was stopping came in, and said, "Wife, I don't know just what to do as Bolly (the mare) was too lame to get to the barn, much less to take a load of truck to Chillicothe." "Well," she said, "go down to your brother's and get his." He went down, but came back without the horse. She said, "Go up to my brother's." He went up there, but came back without a horse. As they were talking in regard to what could be done, as the people were depending on his load in town that day, I said, "What is the matter with your horse?" "Come down to the barn." I laid my Bible down and went out to the barn.

The horse's limb was swollen twice its normal size, and she could not raise it. She had eaten nothing all night and that morning. The brother and I went up to the house, and I said, "Brethren, don't you believe Jesus heals?" The sister said, "Oh, of course I know that He heals human beings. When you were here last fall, He healed our girl through your prayer. But Brother Bevington, did you ever hear of His healing animals?" I said, "That isn't answering my question. You will admit that He healed the girl last fall." "Oh, yes, most assuredly, and we all three have testified to that here in our church; and most everybody believes that Jesus did heal her, but—." "Now," I said, "we don't want any of those 'buts' here in this case. Jesus didn't use them." "Well, what shall I say?" I said, "If nothing but these 'buts' has a voice, you just keep still." Well she just laughed heartily, and said, "You seem to believe that He will heal Bolly." "Why shouldn't He?" "Oh, Brother Bevington, I would be so glad if He would; not simply that Bolly might be healed so we could use her; but it would stir this whole neighborhood, and be a great help in this meeting." "Well," I said, "what are we going to do about it?" "What are we going to do?" she said. "It is up to you," I answered. The husband had been a silent listener. This was entirely new to him. I said, "Can't Jesus heal Bolly?"

Silence reigned for about twenty minutes. The girl had come in, and also was a listener to what had been said. Finally, she said, "Well Jesus healed me, and Bolly is worth more than I, so why wouldn't He heal her?" Well, I just let them reason and think for about an hour. Finally I said, "You folks are not getting anywhere. Can Jesus or can He not heal this morning?" Another spell of silence gripped them for about ten minutes, which was broken by the wife's saying, "Brother Bevington, if you will believe, I will." I said, "Do you mean that?" "Yes, I do." I said, "Come on." Then I said, "Now, brother, if you can't believe, you stay here at the house." He began to cry and we all stood there. Soon he said, "I will not stay here. I will believe." We all went down to the barn, and I said, "Now, lead her out here." "Oh, Brother Bevington, we can't. She can't lift her foot over that sill." So I went in. I said, "I will lay my hand on her limb. Each of you do the same, putting your hands below mine." So they did. "Now as we pray, we will move our hands down as the Lord leads." I began to get warmed up on the subject, and was impressed that we move our hands down some, perhaps an inch. Well, we kept that up for about forty or fifty minutes; and as our hands went down, the swelling went out, so that by the time our hands reached the hoof, the swelling was all gone. Well, the man just wept like a child. He had never seen anything like that. He took the mare out, hitched her up and took the load to town; and there was not a limp, either on the way there or back. I forgot to say that as soon as we reached the hoof the mare whinnied. Then we opened our eyes, the swelling was gone. The man said, "She is now hungry." He gave her thirteen ears of corn, which she soon had demolished. He stood speechless and crying, while the wife and I were rejoicing.

So, as the woman had said, that was a great boon to our meeting, as the mare had been limping all winter, and many knew of her swollen limb. Many came to the meeting who never were there before, and quite a number got salvation. So all we need is faith, and all faith needs is a stimulant. Now that I have touched on the healing of that animal, I feel like telling of an answer to prayer in the grain kingdom.

I went from this meeting, about sixty miles to hold another. We had good crowds and good order; but that isn't all that is needed to satisfy God. Well, I just prayed, fasted, wept, and preached my best; but no break came. I had preached six nights before opening the altar, and Sunday night was the seventh night. I went to my room, threw myself across the bed, and cried out mightily. When I looked at my watch, it was 3:30 a. m. I had some encouragement, but could not get permission to close the meeting. I got up and went out, and said, "Tell everybody there will be a meeting tonight." I went back to my room and to prayer. Soon a man came along, and called, "Hey!" The man of the house went out.

The caller was the wife's brother, and he said, "Jim, if I were you, I would plow up that cornfield and sow it in buckwheat, as the grubs are taking it clean." "Well, I reckon I had better; I was out Saturday and saw that it was being taken." The man drove on, and while they were eating breakfast (I was not eating any that morning) his brother came along. "Hey, Jim!" He went out. "Jim, if I were you I would plow that cornfield for buckwheat." "Well, Will was along just awhile ago and told me the same thing." The brother said, "You ought to have plowed that up in the winter, and that would have killed all the grubs." "Yes, I know that; but all winter either one or the other of my horses has been too lame to do it, and I just couldn't get it done as I had no means to hire a team. I believe I did my best." Well, the brother went off. I had heard all this conversation.

Both the man and his wife were blessedly saved. I went out, and said, "Well, brethren, I presume you did your best to get that field plowed this winter, but circumstances prevented." "Yes," they both answered. Then I told them about Bolly, and the girl who was healed over at the crossroads. They began to look at each other. They had never heard of any person being healed, much less animals, and grub worms killed. Well, I began to read them Scriptures on healing and the goodness of God, and I said, "I am sure that God's goodness isn't confined simply to the human body, but He is interested in everything that pertains to us as His children."

I said, "I believe that Jesus can kill those grubs." "Why, Brother Bevington, did you ever hear of such a thing?" "No, I don't know as I ever did; but you are His children and have just started up here, being married less than a year, and have not the means; and I believe you did your best. Now can't you join me in a faith raid on those grubs?" I forgot to mention that he plowed about two acres in January, but was taken down sick. I said, "What would you think of turning that field over to God and letting Him kill those worms, and then you replant?" Well, this was entirely out of the ordinary to them; hence was not sanctioned very readily. Well, I waited until the next morning, and then brought up the subject again. I said, "Now it isn't necessary for you to lose all that seed and work."

The seed of course was gone, but the work was not lost. I took my Bible and read in Amos and in other places where God interposed in regard to crops, so that by 10:00 a. m. there were evidences of faith in their hearts. The next morning I brought up the matter again in prayer, reminding God of some things He had done, putting stress on the fact that He was none the less able today.

After prayer, I came down heavier on them, as I felt that they were worthy, but ignorant of God's power to help. The wife said, "Well, I know that God can do these things, but— ." "Whoa, hold on there! No 'buts' in this case," I said. She laughed. In about ninety minutes we three could be seen wending our way out into that grub patch of six acres. We were all very quiet; not a word was said from the time we left the house until we reached the field. When we got there I said, "Now, what are we going to do about this?" The man looked at his wife. She was looking down. The corn was up about two or three inches.

The brother said, "Brother Bevington, do you think that God could kill these worms, or that He would?" I said, "Please tell me why He would not." Well, that staggered him. His wife said, "Brother Bevington, we never heard of God doing these things until you came; but He surely can." And he said, "What do you say about it, Brother Bevington?" I said, "God can and will do it if we can agree that all things are possible." He said, "Are you clear on it that He wants to?" I said, "Yes, I am." "Well," he said, "what shall we do? We will follow you." I said, "Come on." So we went out into the center of the patch, and I said, "Now, are we agreed that He will?" He bowed his head. I pleaded for unity, and soon felt a real oneness. I began to pray; and as I advanced, we were soon in a state of real quietness, no noise. We spoke just above a whisper, but felt the power and presence of Jesus. Soon the sister began saying, "Oh, glory! Oh, glory!" so softly and sweetly; and the brother began saying, "Amen, amen." They kept it up some time, while I was going right up without a break, and soon reached the peak, claiming every bug killed. I got up, and she stepped aside, scooped up a handful of dirt, and said, "Oh, Brother Bevington, here are ten dead grub worms."

Well, we all stood there and wept; not a word was uttered. Oh, that was a blessed time. He soon began to laugh, saying, "That is surely a wonder." He stooped down and scooped up a handful and counted seven dead grubs. "Well," he said, "it is surely done as you said in your prayer." So we went back to the house praising God. In about twenty minutes her brother came back from the shop, and he said, "Plow that field, as it is ruined. I went over and scooped up a handful of dirt and counted eight worms in it." I waited for someone to speak; but as all were silent, I said, "Sir, those worms were all dead." He looked at me as though he pitied me. He was a good meeting house man, and did not believe much in anything that did not come through his meeting house.

I said, "Sir, I will give you a penny for every live worm you find out there in the lot of corn." He said, "All right. That will be money made easy. Get your wallet out." He took a peck measure and went out, and the sister went upstairs where she could see him. He went over the whole field, and went home through the woods, and never came back for the contents of my wallet. Well, the man soaked some corn, replanted the field, and had a fine crop.

Now this was the first and last such venture as that. I have never felt like venturing again on that line; but it simply shows that God is for us, as is recorded in the Word, in the book of Amos. It refers to the same thing; that is, He gave crops to one and destroyed those of another. We saw this couple at the Cincinnati Camp the next year, and the brother testified to all this in a large open air meeting. God got glory out of it, as it stirred many to go down deeper. Let's praise God for His interest in us as His children.

Well, yesterday as I got quiet before God, I was reminded of many cases of healing and other answers to prayer that are not recorded in this book. But I feel that I have recorded enough to push most anyone out on the Bible promises on healing but you must not think that Bevington is confined to healing alone in his prayers. I get letters asking me to pray for backsliders, the unsanctified, the unsaved, and in regard to matters that hinder progress. Some that we pray for get through, but not all. No, not all that I start in to pray for, for healing, get healed. God usually shows me whether He wants to heal them or not, and often it takes days to find out. I have been reminded of several cases of healing where the people failed to testify to their healing, and God allowed the disease to come back. I will record one instance.

In Chillicothe, a great society girl was down with lung trouble. I was requested to call on her, and did so. She finally said that if God would heal her, she would give Him her heart and serve Him wholly. Well, I went to prayer, and God raised her up. She did not get to the meeting, but wrote to me after I left, that she had prayed through, and was going to serve God. In about nine months I was back there again, holding another meeting. I asked about this girl, and was told that she was back in society, and just mocked at salvation.

Well, about nine months after that she wrote to me to pray for her again. I answered and told her that she had lied to God, and that I could do nothing for her until she got right with Him. They said that she died raving and cursing God. Oh, we can't trifle with God! That girl gave dancing lessons and was the belle of the town. So it is with people that will not keep vows they have made to God. And she never testified to her healing. I put a lot of stress on telling it, repeating it. Keep on telling it, and it will become a blessing to you and others, as the Lord always has someone that He wants to hear just such news. Can you do it? Will you do it? Tell it so loud as to knock out every prop from under you, and thus enable you to swing clear out into the celestial spheres. Amen, Hallelujah! Still saved, still sanctified; yes, and still healed. Glory to God! I am nearly seventy-four and love Jesus this morning more than I ever did, simply because the capacity is enlarged. We ought to be crying out for greater capacity, larger vessels, increased ability.

Well, we now come to some of the cases at Kingswood, Kentucky. I had over eighty cases of healing there during the two winters spent there. I can't mention all of them, but one case appeals to me as most suitable for this volume. A young lady had been ailing for weeks. She had fever, and kept getting worse; but did not want to take remedies, though the kind doctor was near and renders good service when called upon. But he prefers having people call for

Jesus; he delights in seeing them healed without remedies, as he himself was once healed by Jesus. Well, this girl kept getting worse, so Sister Thomas came over and said that she wanted me to come and anoint her and pray for her healing. I did so, and prayed for some time. I got good encouragement; but Sister Thomas was called out, thus leaving the girl and me alone, so I went to my room.

The next morning Sister Thomas came, saying, "She is sinking fast, and something will have to be done at once." She said, "What do you think about the case, as several are finding fault with us for not having a doctor?" I said, "Well, I believe that if you could arrange to remain here with us, God would heal her." Well, she went out to get a girl to take her place. Then she and I went to prayer, one of us on each side of the bed. I lay there pleading, but the girl seemed to be sinking. Those waiting on her came in and found fault with our being there without a doctor. Sister Thomas was called out again. I went back to my room, dropped on the bed, and had a good time for four hours praying for her. I saw her sitting up eating. Next morning Sister Thomas came over, and said, "I think I can stay in there now." "Why, isn't she better?" "Oh, no, she is worse." "Why, I saw her sitting up yesterday as I lay on my face." "Well she did sit up yesterday afternoon, and ate a hearty meal; but she has had a relapse, and there is talk of having us arrested for not having a doctor. I told them if the girl wanted a doctor she would have one; but she still insisted on Jesus healing her."

Well, I went over again, and found that she was no better. As I entered the room, had I been influenced by what I saw, I surely would have backed out; but I closed my eyes to her looks, as she lay there apparently lifeless, noticing no one. I took my former position, and held it for twenty-four hours. Then I felt a heavy load, which seemed as if it would crush my life out. I seemed to be smothering. Realizing it was all from Satan, I jumped and went to fighting the powers of darkness; and I tell you I had some to fight, and I could feel that Sister Thomas was doing her best. We fought the powers of hell for about fifty minutes, until the pressure was gone, and the clouds were lifted to some extent. I began praising God for victory, and I actually heard snappings like the breaking of bands or cords. That encouraged me, and I said, "Sister Thomas, she is a healed girl." At that, the girl raised her hand, and said, "It is done," and burst out laughing. By that time Sister Thomas was up, laughing and praising God.

I slipped out and went to my room to retire; but before doing so, I said, "Now she is healed, Lord, so make her get out and go over to the dining room."

It was then about 3:00 a. m. I wrestled some time that she might go over and give a rousing testimony to her healing. Suggestions came in fast as to the unlikelihood of such a venture as that, as she hadn't strength to walk over to the dining room. But I fought them all, and held on until I went to sleep. Having been up so much, I slept well and was awakened by several boys rushing up the stairs, yelling, "Brother Bevington, get up quick! That girl is over in the dining room, running and shouting." Well, that ended the fevers and lung trouble with her. Praise God!

There are perhaps thirty or forty in Kingswood who would stand as monuments of God's power to heal. The healing of even a headache or a toothache ought to be heralded from pole to pole.

Sister Yarborough told me that God healed her three times in answer to my prayers, and Sister Stikeleather will testify to being healed, also her children. Sister Brown was healed of nervousness, and many others that we will not take the time to record here. God doesn't have advertisements in the papers as to His healings, but He has His sign hung out in the corridors of everyone that will give room for it. We must go after Him as He isn't running around hunting up jobs. On Sunday, April 24, 1921, Brother Medler came and told me that his wife was at the chapel, suffering terribly, and wanted prayer for relief. He said that she had been sick for years. So I went to prayer, and claimed the victory for her; but heard no more from her until Wednesday night, when she handed me two dollars, saying that she was wonderfully delivered. Brother Medler is our sanctified grocery-man. He and his wife are very precious people, and it does me good to take these precious saints to Jesus to be delivered of their ailments.

On May 27, Brother Shelton was taken down with nervous prostration. He seemed worse on Saturday, and I was notified of his condition. I prayed for him, but, as usual, the doctor was somewhat in my way. It is quite hard for us to get around these doctors. Some are so large we just can't get around them. On Sunday, as usual here of late, I remained in prayer; and about six o'clock Brother Bond called, and said, "He is worse." He had sat up with the brother that night, and said that he had suffered terribly with his back and head, was very nervous and out of his mind most of the time. About eight Brother Smith called, and said, "He is sinking fast, out of his mind all the time, and exercising his body far beyond his strength." I lay on my face, pleading as best I could, and I saw a vision of him laid out on a board, and his wife and children bereft of their main stay. Well, I could hardly accept that, but it was so hard for me to get around the doctor. So while I was pleading and weeping, about 9:00 a. m., I seemed to be

8: INSTANCES OF HEALING   177

stricken with a sense of my own unworthiness; and from that I was much occupied in viewing my mistakes, blunders, ignorance, and the many times that I had ignored God through a lack of faith, and how little I had accomplished for Him. Then over against that came the ever-merciful God. His love and patience; the forbearance of God in that He just overlooked my blunders, lack of faith and so on. While all of these must have grieved the great heart of God, yet He just loved me and blessed me, looked after me, put up with me.

As I took this retrospect, it seemed that about all I could see was the greatness of God and the nothingness of Bevington. Then I found that I was losing sight of the doctor and getting a new vision of Jesus; and my faith was mounting up, so that by 10:30 a. m. I had struck rock bottom. I was claiming the victory for Brother Shelton. As I had not heard anything from him, Satan was right there to notify me of his terrible condition; but I held on until about 3:00 p. m. When I was at the children's meeting, someone said, "Brother Bevington, have you heard of the remarkable change for the better in Brother Shelton? I said, "Yes, I was there when it took place." I found out that it was at the same time that I prayed through for him. He was up Monday, and went a-hunting. Oh, let's go in for greater things, as faith sees the invisible, believes the incredible, and claims the impossible.

Sister Thomas' mother, living some distance away, was going blind, or was blind, and asked Sister Thomas to see me. I went to prayer; and after waiting on the Lord some eleven hours, I saw a woman reading a paper. I got up and told Sister Thomas just what time her mother received her sight, and so on. In a few days the mother wrote that at a certain time she received her sight, saw a paper near her, and went to reading it, just as I saw her. Oh, praise God!

In December, I was getting up wood for the winter, and no doubt I overtaxed my body, so that the second morning I woke up about two o'clock with a severe pain in my side. The pain kept growing in intensity; and was approaching my heart. I could scarcely breathe. I tried to get out of bed to get my hands on the Bible, but could not do so. I fell back nearly whipped, but after lying there a few moments, I said, "This will never do, as Thou art the God that heals, and I am not going down to Egypt for help." I began to plead the promises, right in the face of apparent defeat.

I dared not look at conditions, but fought the powers of hell for one hour, though in great misery. I raised my head in the name of Jesus, and this did not hurt me. At that I jumped out of bed and grabbed my Bible. I came near falling, as a severe dart struck my heart; but I grabbed a chair, and soon rallied. With closed eyes, and my hands on the Bible, I said, "Lord, Thou didst say it." I repeated this seven times; and at the last word of the seventh time, the pain all left me, and I went back to bed entirely healed. Hallelujah! Oh, isn't that better than suffering and going down to Egypt?

Yes, these are days demanding a stiff backbone, one that will stand a tussle with the enemy of our souls and bodies. The best stiffener that I know of is just to do as I did, make a charge on the enemy and stand your ground until you win.

I well remember that while at the Cincinnati Camp, as I was waiting to get into the dining room, a large crowd gathered at the door. Brother Williams, an M. E. holiness preacher, came up, and said, "Brother Bevington, I am suffering with a severe headache, and have been all day. Please pray for me." Well, I hesitated, as there were so many around, but I was impressed to lay my hands on his head. To do that there seemed somewhat assuming; but he pleaded for me to pray for him, so I felt that I must. I laid my hands on him, and stood there pleading the promises and looking for relief. In twelve minutes the headache was all gone. The promise is, just according to your faith, not according to the condition or surroundings, just your faith.

I feel a tinge of sadness as I am nearing the end of these blessed hours in rewriting this volume. It reminds me of the many dear friends here at Kingswood who have stood by me so nobly while I have been writing this.

They all have a big interest in this volume. Writing this is much like spending several weeks in a precious home and then taking the departure. I see here that Brother Ira Shelton asks if I mentioned his being healed of appendicitis. I said, "I guess not. I guess I have forgotten it." So he sat down and told me of it in detail.

"In November, 1919, I had an attack of appendicitis. I was so sick that our family physician said that if I were no better by morning, I would have to have an operation. But I got better, and was not bothered with it until the spring of 1920. I was then working in the clearing, when I began to have severe pains. As I was very busy, I kept working, thinking I would get better. In the evening, Rev. H. P. Thomas sent Brother Bevington, who was then staying in our home, and wife and me to come up to pray over some matters pertaining to the school. While we were at prayer, the suffering became intense; and I was wondering what an operation would cost and how long it would disqualify me for work. I was in such misery that I could not remain on my knees. I made my condition known, and Brother Bevington said, 'Well, can't Jesus heal you?' Brother Thomas said, 'Yes.' They anointed me, and while Brother Bevington and Brother Thomas laid their hands on me, the pain all left and has never come back. As Brother Bevington has told of cases of healing, I will say that it pays to take Jesus as our Healer."

I want to add, for the glory of God, the account of the healing of Sister Yarborough's baby. She sent me word to pray for her baby. Well, I went to prayer, but next day, June 5, 1921, word came back that the baby was worse. She said, "If God don't heal the baby at once, it will leave us." I said, "Sister, it may be that God is wanting a baby up there. Will you loan Him yours? " The true-hearted mother gave vent to tears but she said, "I will if He wants it."

Well, after the children's meeting I went to my room, and after about eighty minutes I was convinced that He was not necessarily needing the baby just then and was willing to let it remain on this planet awhile longer, to beautify it. Then the next thing to do was to make application for the removal of this troublesome sickness, so I laid the axe at the root of the tree by making a bee line for my family Physician. He soon responded to the call, and in another fifty minutes I had the evidence that the baby was healed. Last night Sister Yarborough sent one of the boys over to tell me that it was entirely healed. Oh, praise the Lord!

Well, I suppose you are wondering if I will ever quit. You know that often it is hard for a holiness preacher to find the stopping place, and so it seems with this. I feel that I would be leaving out an interesting event should I fail to record the home-going of dear Sister Goddard, Sister Shelton's mother, who took her departure from this troublesome world to be in a better one on Wednesday, January 19, 1921, at 11:50 a. m. She had been sick but a short time.

On January 15, Saturday, I went down; and after others had prayed for her, I prayed and got blessed and, without much consideration, I claimed her healing. But on Sunday, as I spent all forenoon in prayer relative to her case, I did not make any headway, though I did my best. She seemed to be getting worse. As Monday was my wash day, I did not get down until evening. I prayed silently, but could not make the headway I wanted. I began searching myself to see what was lacking. I went home, did my ironing, and went back in the evening again, only to be held in the dark as to her healing. On my way home I told Brother Thomas that I feared she was going Home, and that we would not have her long with us. I retired, but did not sleep till towards morning. I dreaded the thought of her leaving us, as we all needed her, we all thought, oh, so much.

Wednesday morning, I returned, and slipped into a corner. She lay silently on the bed, noticing no one; and several were in the room, ministering to her needs. A holy hush pervaded the room, oh, such a sweet and holy quietness! I made no headway in praying for her healing, and was soon hurried off on another line. All I could do was to petition for her an abundance entrance. I remained in that corner ninety minutes. As I lay on my face, pleading for an abundant entrance, I saw a large, beautiful mansion which looked as if it were glass—so transparent, so lovely to behold. I had never seen such a radiant building—such glittering walls, such dazzling floors, such brilliant rooms; and it was so beautiful outside, too. I saw beings dressed in spotless white garments extending to the floor, and, oh, such faces, such hands, such crowns, and everyone was busy, not one standing still or sitting. They were carrying wreaths of lily-white flowers of such brilliance as I had never seen. They were hurrying in and out as though putting on the last touches. Each one had wings and, oh, so beautiful, but all their wings were folded.

All were, oh, so busy getting ready for the soon home-coming of someone. So I just concluded that they were Sister Goddard's ushers. I suppose that orders had been given, and mention of her soon coming had been made. I got up, and said to myself, "She will not be here long." Sister Shelton said to me, "What did you get?" I said, "Mother will soon be leaving you." I went home and told some of the students that sister Goddard would soon leave us. It was 11:00 a. m., when I got to my room, so at 11:40 the last touch had been put on. All was ready for her home-coming, and the summons was sent for her to vacate the old rickety tenement that she had occupied for many years, and come up and occupy the brilliant, massive mansion for which she had been sending up material for a number of years.

Sister Shelton was taken sick, and was getting worse. They sent me word of her condition, so I rallied my forces, and bombarded hell for her healing. After four hours of heavy firing I routed the enemy, and took possession. Word came that at a certain time she jumped out of bed, perfectly healed. Yes, I had a stiff fight right there, but I held on until victory came. I soon had the pleasure of seeing Sister Shelton safe at home, and a well woman. Hallelujah to Jesus!

I have had a most blessed time while writing this. It has boosted me up the heavenly highway several miles. I am more than ever determined to press salvation and healing. Look up, weary one; Jesus is the same today as when He walked the Judean hills and healed the many there. He wants to heal you, to get a chance to heal you; but you will see that it takes a bold, determined fight to get our rights.

8: INSTANCES OF HEALING 181

May the dear Lord make this volume a blessing to many. I would be delighted to hear from anyone who reads this book. My address while down here will be Ashland, Ky., or Kingswood, Ky. Wherever I am, mail will be forwarded to me.

Send this volume out; pray for the widening influence of the contents, and meet me in Heaven, as I am going there. I am ticketed through for there now! Hallelujah! Amen and amen!

If you enjoyed *Remarkable Incidents and Modern Miracles Through Faith and Prayer* by G. C. Bevington, you will want these related classics!

Touching Incidents and Remarkable Answers to Prayer/Shaw (#3654)

In the genre of Bevington's *Modern Miracles*. Story after story of answered prayer, God's provision and miracles, as well as touching stories to tug on the heartstrings. SB Shaw knew GC Bevington. Chapters include stories of amazing miracles and answers to prayer, reports of murderers hindered in the midst of their crimes, young martyrs; much, much more.

Remarkable Conversions & Striking Illustrations/HC Morrison (#1023)

Dr. Morrison was a great preacher, revivalist, illustrator and past president of Asbury Theological Seminary. These true stories will never die. Chapters include "The Man with Snakes in his Boots and Monkeys on his Bedpost," "My Arrest and Rescue," "Unloading a Cow," "Plowing Deep," more.

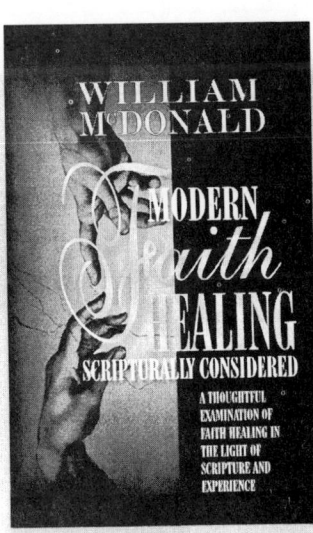

Modern Faith Healing Scripturally Considered/ McDonald (#3980)

Is there a scriptural basis for healing? Of course! But what about a precious saint who was not healed? William McDonald (one of the founders of the National Holiness Association) stresses that those who seek an ever-deepening walk with the Son of Man must be willing to submit to his lordship, fully and completely. This book answers the "hard questions."

Members of Schmul's Wesleyan Book Club buy these outstanding books at
40% off the retail price!
It's like having a discount Christian bookstore in your mailbox! In addition, buy any book in our warehouse, already on our extensive list of published titles, at 40% off!

Act now!
**Join Schmul's Wesleyan Book Club
by calling us toll-free**
800-S$_7$P$_7$B$_2$O$_6$O$_6$K$_5$S$_7$

Put a discount Christian bookstore right in your own mailbox.

You may also order direct from the publisher by writing:
**Schmul Publishing Company
PO Box 716
Salem, OH 44460**